AT HOME ON THE RANGE:
GEORGE R. MCINTOSH, WESTERN EVERYMAN

By Robin Priebe Branstator

First published by Dog Ear Publishing
4010 W. 86th Street, Ste H
Indianapolis, IN 46268
www.dogearpublishing.net

ISBN: 978-145750-370-2

This book is printed on acid-free paper.

Printed in the United States of America

To my mother

TABLE OF CONTENTS

PROLOGUE

One day in 1991 a small, frail old man, ill and near death, asked to be taken back to the farm where he had grown up. Located on the acres his grandfather had homesteaded almost one hundred twenty-five years before, the farm had a particular hold on this elderly bachelor who had lived there for most of his ninety-one years and he yearned to look at it one last time. He sat silently, an unlit pipe clamped between his teeth, and gazed at fields much diminished since he was a boy. The lake named for his grandfather was now dominated by a cluster of modern homes. Soothing his anger about these alterations was the knowledge that he had made the correct decision in disposing of the land that remained to him. The acres meant everything to Neil "Shorty" Lohr (1900-1991) who mused there that day, just as they had to his grandfather, George Robin McIntosh (1837-1924).

Today the land is hemmed in by a busy highway on the north and the housing development to the southeast. A paved hiking trail brings urban walkers to the edge of the farm and around McIntosh Lake. Most of the surrounding acres are now subdivided, encroached upon, and diverted from their original purposes. But this was the then unsettled land that so captivated George McIntosh in the 1860s that he had to have it for the farm he craved. Today, thanks to his grandson's careful planning, the site has been turned into the Agricultural Heritage Center (AHC) at the Lohr-McIntosh Farm in Longmont, Colorado. There volunteers tell visitors about the local history of agriculture and outline

Neil "Shorty" Lohr, George McIntosh's grandson, looking out over the land that was part of George's original homestead, 1984. Photo by Cindy McIntosh.

George's biography. But few people know the complete story of the man who was George R. McIntosh.

Virginia Woolf once wrote, "There is the girl behind the counter – I would as soon have her true history as the hundred and fiftieth life of Napoleon or seventieth study of Keats."[1] George McIntosh is like that unknown girl, but he is the farmer behind the plow, representing a virtually anonymous segment of the vast agricultural grid that bound the United States together in the nineteenth century. Unless they rose to prominence in other areas, these men and women whose labor and creativity made it possible to feed a vast nation have been largely ignored or forgotten entirely. Like Woolf's "girl behind the counter" George McIntosh, too, has a story that deserves to be told.

It was Alexis de Tocqueville (1805-1859) who observed in his *Democracy in America* (1835) that, "Once the trace of the influence of individuals on the nation has been lost, we are often left with the sight of the world moving without anyone moving it."[2] Although he had no political, philosophical or literary gifts, George *was* someone who could shift the world just a bit, a man with a gift for farming and ranching whose agricultural acumen helped turn the interests of the United States westward. He and his ancestors represent the countless pioneers who overcame enormous obstacles to make the West, from Ohio to California, a feasible extension of the original thirteen states. His is not the overblown western mythology of gunfighters and saloons, cattle barons and range wars, but the tale of a solid citizen who had a vision of farming in northeastern Colorado. The path to that farm was circuitous – George mined for gold and freighted before he finally found the right land in Boulder County. But once he *had* found it he used innate talent, grit and a certain amount of luck to become a noteworthy man in his corner of the world.

CHAPTER ONE

The Reluctant Emigrant

Most people assume their places in the world with some expectation of success, but not all will achieve their goals. The question is, who will thrive and who will not? This is, on one level, what Banquo asks of the three witches in act 1, scene 3, lines 58-60 of William Shakespeare's "Macbeth": "If you can look into the seeds of time, and say which grain will grow and which will not, speak then to me…" The play does more than provide lines that serve to open George Robin McIntosh's saga; its protagonist leads us to George's roots in ancient Scotland and thus to some of the answers about his ability to thrive rather than wilt in the face of difficult circumstances. It turns out that George came from a line of resilient Scottish men who chafed over the centuries against authority and the status quo, even after arriving on American shores. [3] Sometimes their actions improved their situations; sometimes they resulted in expulsion from or shunning by the more orderly communities they affronted. These rebellious, proud, chance-taking ancestors left their marks on George's personality and it is with one of them that his story begins.

The Mackintoshes (the spelling of the last name changed at some point in the late eighteenth century) came from the Inverness-shire area of northwest Scotland, a region of rugged, low-lying mountains, valleys, and lakes. The capital city of Inverness has several claims to fame, not least of which is that the real Macbeth (c. 1005-1057), king of Scotland from 1040 to his assassination in 1057, is said to have lived in the castle that stands just half a mile northeast of the town. Almost seven hundred years later on a forlorn moor six miles east of Inverness Scotland's Bonnie Prince Charlie challenged England's George III's right to rule and almost a thousand Scottish troops died there at the hands of the Duke of Cumberland and his troops. [4] More modern renown comes to the area from Inverness's situation on either side of the twenty-four-mile long Loch Ness.

The Mackintosh clan can be traced back to at least the twelfth century in the Inverness region. [5] The original name, *Mac an Toisich*, means "son of the chief/thane". [6] The families lived primarily around the Firth of Moray, a fish-rich North Sea inlet. This powerful clan, of which George's great-great-great grandfather John Mackintosh (c. 1630-1691) was a member, deserved their threatening motto of "Touch not the cat bot [without] a glove". They never hesitated to leap into fights against other clans and, as was common with most of these groups linked by kinship, the Mackintoshes also suffered intra-family strife that involved both intrigue and brutal physical contests. As George Pomeroy Anderson has noted, "The Mackintosh…who did not fight was not a true Mackintosh." [7] Shakespeare's version of Macbeth's story vividly portrays the kinds of complex and changing allegiances that plagued not only the Mackintosh clan, but also the history of the Scottish Highlands. It was one of these periods of shifting loyalties that provided the unlikely opportunity for George McIntosh to become a seed that would take hold with vigor in a land of which his Scottish forebears had no knowledge.

By the 1630s the fighting Mackintoshes drew nearer to the time when their battles would take place far beyond the Highlands. The trouble that would embroil them began in 1637 when the Presbyterian Scots locked horns with King Charles I (1600-1649), a member of the Scottish Stuart family. Charles was determined to impose English Anglicanism on those of his northern subjects who had accepted Reformation teachings, most of whom belonged to the Presbyterian Church. The Presbyterians not only practiced their religion differently than the Anglicans, but they also greatly resented any interference on the part of the state in those practices because, "…Presbyterianism stood in Scottish history for freedom, and for the rights of the middle classes against the crown and aristocracy…" [8] Charles pleased many of his English subjects little better when he decided to govern without the benefit of Parliament — rebellious voices began to mutter.

Revolution, the first but not the last of such upheavals to pull a McIntosh into its clutches, stirred. But the appearance of Oliver Cromwell (1599-1658) on the scene briefly delayed decisive action. Cromwell, who had begun public life as a Puritan member of the English Parliament, neatly eliminated the hindrance to Scottish religious preference by having King Charles beheaded on January 30, 1649. However, instead of acclaiming Cromwell's action, the Scots were appalled by this act of regicide that did away with a royal Stuart. [9] Their Parliament declared that Charles' nineteen-year old son, who had been in France at the time of his father's execution, was now king.

The young royal had to defend his throne against Cromwell's brazen assumption of leadership in England. As the head of the powerful English army, Cromwell had the well-oiled means to prevent Charles from being crowned King of England, too. In order to secure his title, the inexperienced young man desperately needed Scottish recognition of his right to the crown. But the Scots were wary of another Charles who jeopardized their deeply held religious beliefs by continuing his father's goal of forcing the Presbyterian church to follow Anglican exercises. Before legitimizing his claim to the throne, they compelled Charles to sign two covenants guaranteeing their religious rights, the elimination of Catholicism in Scotland, and the promise of peace between Scotland and England. [10] With the covenants agreed upon and Scottish backing of Charles assured, war between the Royalists (to whom the Mackintoshes were loyal) and Cromwell's army was almost inevitable.

By 1650 Cromwell had bolstered his power by becoming commander-in-chief of "all the forces of the Commonwealth" and Lord Protector of England.[11] When Charles and a force of 22,000 largely Scottish soldiers marched that year south to Dunbar, twenty-five miles east of Edinburgh, Cromwell met them with his expertly drilled army of 17,000 men. It was an event that would change John Mackintosh's life forever.

The Scots were far from being a professional militia. Instead, in the words of a late-twentieth-century historian, they were "a host of ill-trained religious zealots." [12] The unequally matched armies clashed on September 3, 1650 at the Battle of Dunbar, leaving Cromwell's men victorious and four thousand Scottish casualties lying on the field. [13] An equal number escaped, but the 10,000 Scottish soldiers taken prisoner faced penalties such as servitude in English salt mines or transportation to the colonies in America.[14]

Just over nine months later, after the young king's Scottish coronation, another pivotal battle took place on exactly the same day that the Dunbar conflict had erupted the year before. This time the violent struggle occurred at Worcester in England where the king was temporarily in residence. Charles favored this location in which to make a stand, having heard that he had Welsh sympathizers nearby. Worcester's other advantage was its renowned ironworks industry (a situation that John Mackintosh might have thought wryly of five months later) that could produce the arms essential to his ill-equipped army. [15]

Young John, about twenty-one years old and just a little younger than the king he had vowed to defend, joined that army and marched the 300 weary miles from Scotland with thousands of other Scottish men. Not all who began the trek finished it. A number of men thought better of the mission and deserted, fleeing northward. Although most would not abandon the king, the Royalist Scots were hardly eager warriors, especially when they recalled how easily Cromwell had crushed their kinsmen at Dunbar. Dysentery ravaged the remaining bone-tired soldiers. Both armies suffered from the wet weather that drenched their garments or, in the case of the Scots, their own skins, as most of them lacked adequate clothing and footwear. When they finally arrived at Worcester, the rag-tag army occupied the city, much to the dismay of its residents who feared looting by the wild-looking men from the north.

So despite John Mackintosh's youth, he was in far from top-notch condition when Cromwell's 30,000 troops ranged around the Royalist-occupied city. John was likely part of a regiment of Mackintoshes whose skills in an organized battle would have been negligible, dependent more on instinct and unrestrained recklessness than on honed finesse in meeting the enemy. [16] The paucity of Royalist ammunition almost mandated "hand-to-hand combat as the only practical alternative to being shot down at a distance." [17] But ferocious blows struck at close quarters could not win the day. Once again another bruising rout destroyed Royalist hopes for re-establishing Charles on the throne of England.

The Scots suffered huge losses. Charles fled to France, [18] leaving 9,000 Scottish men to become prisoners of war. Among them was John Mackintosh. He would never see the Highlands again. He must have thought his fate dire, but, as it turns out, he was one of the luckier ones. Some of his compatriots became mercenary soldiers purchased by Continental factions [19] while others slaved in the salt or coal mines or languished in dank, disease-ridden English jails or prison ships. [20] John's future held much more promise, but at first he could see nothing but darkness ahead of him.

The English treated the captured men roughly, depriving them of most of the rags they wore and forcing them to walk barefooted to confinement. Their plight (and the view of their starved bodies) evoked sympathy from some onlookers who tossed bread to the ranks of feeble men staggering by. Already weakened by wounds and exhaustion and without adequate nutrition, many died in prison. [21] Those who escaped or were released to return to Scotland were not necessarily more fortunate than their imprisoned compatriots. The English had seized Scottish family estates, reducing many of those repatriated to a life of poverty. Many turned to begging or robbing from others to sustain themselves. Had John's path led him home he might very well have become a brigand. But a more honorable and productive way of life lay in his future.

English committees culled the prisoners in various ways and decided what was to be done with them. They began to authorize transport of some of the captives to the New World "plantations", the name given to a settlement until it had been "officially granted town status" [22] So John Mackintosh was deported as an indentured servant to the young colony of Massachusetts. What turned out ultimately to be a new chance for him required him once again to withstand great physical discomfort and danger when, along with approximately 300 other prisoners, he was sent to America aboard a ship called the "John and Sara", captained by John Greene.[23]

His name appears on the ship's passenger list where it is recorded as *John Mackenthow*, the transcription from the Gaelic only vaguely suggesting the actual surname. He was not the only Mackintosh prisoner aboard. Both Daniell Mackendocke and William Mackentoss, whose names also suffered from arbitrary spelling, were shipped out along with him. We do not know their relationships to one another, but the surname binds them somehow. [24] They set sail from London in November or December of 1651. [25]

The long winter sailing (most ships destined for the New World embarked during months featuring better weather, but then most passengers paid for the crossing and could be a little choosier about when they left) exposed the "John and Sara" and her passengers to terribly rough seas. Stagnant air pungent with the odors of unwashed and ill men, livestock, and decomposing food must have made the below-decks prison almost unbearable even in an era when people were none too fastidious about unavoidable smells. The crowded conditions led to frayed nerves. Seasickness and the spread of diseases like scurvy, typhus and smallpox [26] assaulted the Scotch as the ship plied the cold, turbulent sea.

The "John and Sara" arrived in Massachusetts on about February 24, 1652. Not all of the prisoners survived the crossing. Twenty-eight men died during the voyage and a few more of those who disembarked would succumb on their long, cold walks from the landing point at Boston to various other Massachusetts communities. William Mackentoss went to Braintree while John was consigned to the ironworks at Saugus. [27] The men who had survived the trek from Scotland, battle, imprisonment and finally, the transatlantic crossing were delivered by the English into the hands of various overseers. The prisoners who stumbled off the ship were physically unfit for the work they faced. But they had outlived many of their fellows and had been inured to hardship. That toughness stood John Mackintosh in good stead and many future members of the family, including George, would inherit genes that allowed them to overcome physical liabilities that held others back.

The Saugus Ironworks, active from 1646-1668, was the brainchild of John Winthrop Jr. who went to England in 1641 to form a group of shareholders in a New England ironworks enterprise called The Company of Undertakers of Iron Work in New England. [28] In 1623 he returned to the Massachusetts colony with about a score of experienced English ironworkers who would manufacture the implements and tools so desperately needed by the colonists. [29] The site he chose for this infant business was along the Saugus River, not far from Massachusetts Bay and the Atlantic. Boston, a town that would figure prominently in the life of George McIntosh's grandfather, lay ten miles to the south. The swamps in the area contained masses of good bog ore, essential for the manufacture of iron. [30] Surrounding the meadows and bogs were many varieties of evergreen and deciduous trees, dominated by huge stands of oak that could be transformed into the charcoal that fueled fires to forge iron.

When John stepped ashore, the Saugus Ironworks had been in business for six years. The year before his arrival the English had sold sixty prisoners from the Battle of Dunbar to the company, so the settlement was accustomed to the presence of Scotch men. Accustomed, but not necessarily welcoming. John and the men who arrived before him represented a new element in the small, tightly knit Saugus community that almost immediately perceived the newcomers neg-atively because they seemed to benefit from special treatment. As indentured servants John and the others stood out, not just because of their national iden-tity and their Gaelic words, but also by virtue of their status as single men who were not true colonists committed to the fledgling settlement's survival. Most of the first emigrants to New England had come "as families and were wealthy enough to pay for their passage." [31] Because the transported soldiers initially lacked skills the other colonists now possessed, the inhabitants of Saugus did not see them as threats to their occupations, but they most definitely feared that the Scots would drain scarce resources.

To John Gifford, the colony's agent for the ironworks, fell the responsibil-ity of restoring the prisoners to health and maintaining them for their terms of servitude. He expended significant sums on their clothing, tobacco, and liquor.[32] Some found shelter with the families of ironworkers, but others slept three to a bed in the accommodation known as the "Scotch House", a dwelling built specifically for them. [33] Poor Gifford was chided from England by one of the officials of the ironworks for incurring large expenses to outfit the new laborers, "We wrott you that we desired the Scotts should be dieted by some ther in the County those that would have [supplied the] best and cheapest and not to have it done by you at such a high Rate the company not being willing to allow above the 3s 6 per week and you being 5s." [34]

It seems that Cromwell would not have agreed with the official's harsh pol-icy. Just before his death the Reverend John Cotton (1585-1652) countered the English board's objections to the expense of maintaining the prisoners. Cotton, the grandfather of Cotton Mather (1663-1728), was a Puritan esteemed by Oliver Cromwell and by his fellow colonists (he had arrived in the Massachu-setts Bay Colony in 1633), although the colonists revised their high opinion of him in the coming years as he grew increasingly intolerant. [35] He was at pains to assure Cromwell that John and the other prisoners shipped to the colony received solicitous care, writing that, "...we have been desirous as we could to make their yoke easy. Such as were sick of the scurvy or other diseases have not wanted physic or chyrurgy. They have not been sold for slaves to perpetuall servitude, but for 6 or 7 or 8 years, as we do our own." [36]

But, although treated fairly well, the men could no longer call their lives their own. They were chattel whose "owners" determined their every move. It must have been a galling time for the fiercely independent and proud prisoners, especially for a man like John Mackintosh who came from such a notable old clan. He asserted some private status of his own by signing his ancient surname of "Toish" on a deposition he made on January 25, 1654, perhaps to remind himself that he was indeed descended from Scottish chiefs. As soon as he regained his liberty he shed Mackenthow and reclaimed Mackintosh as his surname. [37]

Gifford managed to get the men in sufficiently good shape for them to labor on the ironworks' farm and at other tasks essential to making iron. In 1652 and 1653 many of the men were set to work chopping down oak trees to be converted to charcoal for fueling the iron-making furnaces. Both the farming and wood chopping jobs were unfamiliar to most of the captives. They had to learn the techniques required, as well as the English language in order to understand directions. It was backbreaking work. Five cords of wood (a pile of cut wood stacked eight feet long, four feet high, and four feet wide) produced the approximately one hundred-forty bushels (four thousand-five hundred quarts) of charcoal needed to smelt one ton of iron. In 1652 the Scots "cut and corded more than four thousand cords of wood." [38] So it seems that, although the initial outlay spent on the prisoners dismayed the owners and stockholders in the company, the indentured men more than redeemed themselves by their labor.

John Macintosh undoubtedly felt at first like a voiceless pariah in this community so far removed from everything he knew and where the resident Puritans lauded Cromwell's victories at Dunbar and Worcester. [39] During the process of the prisoners' assimilation all were subject to the gazes of their curious neighbors who, at least until sometime in 1652 when the practice was outlawed, enjoyed the "show" provided by the men employed at their various jobs.[40] In the time elapsing between their arrival on American shores and their freedom from bondage (John obtained his release at some point in 1659), these men "mingl[ed] with their farmer neighbors in the hundred contexts of a frontier settlement [and could not have] failed to influence the shape of the whole community as they themselves were changed." [41] They altered the community by impressing upon a fairly insular group that there might be room for "others".

In 1641 Massachusetts had enacted a law decreeing that people who had fulfilled seven years of servitude should "not be sent away empty", a sentiment deriving from *Deuteronomy* 15:12-13. [42] So the men were let go after their seven years of labor to make their ways in the world of New England as best they could, carrying a few essentials such as clothes, some grain, and tools to allow them to begin their new lives, mostly as farmers. Unless John made a point of describing himself as a former prisoner of war, he would not have been distinguished from other hired laborers and so would not have borne that stigma after he left Saugus. [43]

Freedom gave John the chance to become his own man. His decision to leave Saugus followed the practices of early New England families who adhered to migratory patterns established in Old England. And it was not just poor people in search of better economic opportunities who moved frequently, but people from all walks of life: "They were newcomers to a strange and evolving land, and new to the whole enterprise of colonization. When the soil proved rocky or inadequate, when a commercial enterprise failed, or when a church changed to the distress of its members, geographic removal offered the sure way to preempt conflict." [44] "Geographic removal" in a variety of forms and for a variety of reasons would mark future generations of Mackintoshes for centuries.

Still a young, healthy and most important, free person, John must have been eager to set out on his own in this new country. His search for farmland led him south approximately twenty miles to the community of Dedham, Massachusetts Colony which had been founded just about twenty-three years before. For a man possessing little except the clothes on his back Dedham offered prizes that, while not exactly glittering, certainly glimmered with promise. The Massachusetts Bay Colony had granted Dedham about 200 square miles of uneven, rocky terrain for a plantation. Thirty families, including that of John's future wife, occupied the small village, located in the northeastern corner of the tract. The inhabitants had to conquer not only the stones and hummocks that afflicted the land they hoped to tame, but also its dense forests, the wolves that lived in those forests, and extensive swamps. But the families had managed to create small farms out of the unpromising land and became an extremely close-knit community. Like the residents of Saugus, they were not especially eager to allow unfamiliar young men to enter their world.

The original Dedham residents closed ranks early and wrote a document known as the "Dedham Covenant" that outlined the town's concept of a well-ordered society. Male residents were required to sign the agreement that included a vow to "practice Christian love in their daily lives." [45] The sincere, idealistic attempts of this small band of Englishmen to form a perfect society failed in the long run, thwarted by human nature and the tendency of the next generations, like one of John's sons, to rebel against the strict regulations and conformity decreed by the Covenant.

But when John Mackintosh arrived in Dedham in about 1659, the Covenant was still very much in force and the men who had formulated it were still vigorous influences in the community. They would not have automatically welcomed him into this society made exclusive not by virtue of rank but by the mandates set forward for citizenship and the almost complete Puritan compo- sition of the population. John must have presented himself as an acceptable res- ident who would not be a burden on them because, as in many American colonial towns, there were strict guidelines for the behavior of citizens—and non-citizens—as is evident in this snippet from the Dedham town records in the year in which John arrived: "Libertie is given to Small Crosts to sojourne at James Thorps so long as he demeane himselfe as he ought." [46] Although there is no record of him signing the Covenant, John must have known how to "demeane himselfe" for the community to admit him into their ranks.

Dedham residents had made some decisions regarding land ownership toward the end of 1656 when John was still working for the ironworks, deci- sions that would have ramifications for their future citizen from Scotland. Its seventy-nine male inhabitants became "proprietors" of Dedham's "public lands". From then on "only these men, their heirs, or approved newcomers who purchased some of their proprietary rights would be entitled to join in the periodic division of land." [47] When he arrived in Dedham, John badly needed acreage on which to establish his own farm. He achieved this goal partially through his choice of a mate.

John's marriage to Rebecca Metcalfe (1637-1667) in April 1659 when he was still new to the settlement was one sign of his acceptance. Rebecca's father was Michael Metcalfe (1586-1664) who had been a "master weaver" in Tatter- ford, Norwich, England. As one of the town's early members (he was admitted to Dedham in 1637) [48] and its seventy-year old schoolmaster in 1656, Michael was a father-in-law with some standing. The Puritan Metcalf had butted heads with Anglican church leaders in Norwich, compelled, so the story goes, to escape their wrathful threats against his life by sailing to America with his wife and family in 1637. Unless the 1637 date is incorrect (records do err), it seems that this was his second voyage to the New World. According to his own words, he had embarked upon an initial trip on September 17, 1636, arriving in New England at Christmastime, a very long journey by the standards of the day. He must have seen potential in the area before he decided to return to England for his family. [49] Rebecca was the youngest of Michael and Sarah Elwyn Metcalfe's (1593-1644) children, an infant during the crossing. Perhaps she was enthralled by comparing accounts of John's voyage with what she had heard about the perilous flight of her own family. She would have been in a position to understand that, just because a man had been imprisoned, he was not necessarily a bad person. It is difficult to know at this remove what brought the two young people together and why John might have impressed Michael as a suitable mate for his child, but so it was.

John and Rebecca probably lived with her parents while John worked in the expectation of acquiring a lot of his own. The couple had to wait two years. Town records show that in 1661 "John Mackintoch" was granted a "parcel of land for a house lott...not exceeding 3 acres..." [50] Setting a pattern that George McIntosh would follow, John added to his land holdings as the years passed. In July 1664 he purchased another three-acre parcel of land just to the east of the lot where his house stood, a parcel described as "shruffey [scruffy] and rockey upland lyeing upon the south side of his present house Lott and the swampe. between the same and the brooke that runne in the swamp." [51] John must have had some trouble in coming up with the funds to buy this land because in 1670 he appeared before the town selectmen to pay twelve shillings remaining on the debt. [52] But even as a slightly needy property owner John became a genuine citizen. No longer the voiceless, young indentured servant, his status as a landholder now gave him voting rights and a say in the community in which he had settled.

When John and Rebecca set up house, they joined a group of small-hold farmers (an estimated eighty-five percent of Dedham's population farmed) [53] who grew a limited range of crops: "peas, barley, wheat, rye, oats, hay" and some fruit. [54] These yeomen were hard workers, but their restricted agrarian vision and apparent satisfaction with subsistence farming reflected the English village tradition common to most of them [55] and their efforts produced consistently limited results.

John's home was as unassuming as his farm. Tax records suggest that his house was neither the poorest nor the grandest dwelling in town. Even holders of more land and wealth than he would ever amass often lived in relatively modest homes. Most Dedham houses followed the English village pattern: they ranged in size from one room with a half-attic for sleeping to eight rooms. They had dirt floors and contained not much more than basic furniture and clothing. [56] Perhaps Rebecca brought some Metcalfe family silver or pewter objects to the marriage. Such treasures would have been among the few bright spots in an otherwise dim interior because windows were few and often papered over, allowing little light to penetrate.

For a while the Dedham community thrived as it was originally shaped. Insular, content with the centuries-old ways and in many respects stifling to its citizens, Dedham held little allure for succeeding generations, many of whom left to found new towns such as Medfield (incorporated in 1651), Norfolk (1673) and Wrentham (1673). It was the latter town where George McIntosh's great-grandfather Moses would live for a short time until he was compelled to leave. Despite Dedham's outward homogeneity, as in any social community there were occasional disputes, settled during John's life there by the town selectmen. John was involved in at least two of these wrangles, one a public offense and the other a mysterious domestic dispute that was only the first of such commotions to upset McIntosh households right down to George's.

On September 3, 1663, approximately four years after his arrival in Dedham, the councilors took John to task for cutting precious timber from the town's "common" land in order to build his barn. [57] After four years of residing in Dedham he can hardly have misunderstood the rules regarding wood growing on the common land. He certainly neglected to ask the necessary permission before he began to cut. John appeared before Dedham's selectmen, men he knew, and "confessed his offence…and aledged his ignorance of any Towne order forbidding such his takeing timber…" [58] Admitting his ignorance of the law seems to have pacified the men and they did not fine him. John, who was no shrinking violet, took advantage of the pardon, requesting leave to cut a little *more* timber for his barn as well as some "fencing timber"! One can imagine the selectmen grinning behind their composed countenances at the Scot's seeming (or scheming) guilelessness as they granted his request. [59]

By 1664 the Mackintosh family tree had begun to sprout American branches. John's namesake was born on May 15 of that year. William, likely named for John's fellow prisoner and probable kinsman, William Mackentoss, appeared the following year. Rebecca died two years later at the age of thirty, leaving her two young sons motherless. It would have been highly unusual for John not to have found another mate. From the practical point of view alone he needed someone to care for those boys while he was in the fields. In 1668 he married a widow named either Jane or Joan Holmes. [60]

It was on the domestic front that John again encountered some difficulty with the town. The selectmen would be compelled once more to intervene. There may have been some friction between sixteen-year old John and his step-mother because on November 21, 1680 the selectmen confronted John about matters within his family:

> Upon information that there is some inconvenancy [sic] and disorder in the family of John Mackintosh, the select men sent for hime" and he not giving them such satisfaction as they desired" they deputed Ensign Fuller and Set Wight to goe [sic] to his house and take Particular notice of the State of his family, and make return to them that so they might act accordingly. [61]

A bit of John's personality showed through in this exchange when he appeared reluctant to have the town's officials interfere in his private business. The men refused to accept his evasive response and somewhat later thought "it meet to dispose of one of his sons, almost undoubtedly John, to service with…Timothy Dwight." [62] Even allowing for traditional posthumous hyper-bole, it seems that Timothy Dwight (c.1629-1717) was a good man. Nearly the same age as his ward's father, he was the son of one of Dedham's founders and already a selectman. People described him after his death as "a gentleman, truly serious and godly, one of an excellent spirit, peaceable, generous, charitable, and a great promoter of the true interest of the church and town." [63] Placing a child or young adult into the service of another household was generally viewed as a positive educational opportunity, even if that child occupied a lower social rung than Dwight's own children. But the senior John's history must have made it a bitter pill to swallow to have his elder son occupying any state of servitude, however kindly meant and however much it relieved household tension.

Despite John's sporadic bumps in the road to conforming as a citizen of Dedham (he was not the only citizen who sometimes ran afoul of the town's stringent rules), he had found his home for the remainder of his life. He died in 1691 in his early sixties, predeceased by his son John who died in 1690 and about whom an enigmatic cloud swirls. Dedham's otherwise exact and detailed records do not note John Jr.'s demise, leading to speculation that the authorities did not know the exact date of his death because he no longer lived in the community.[64] In an era when most sons remained on the family farm, especially when there were just two of them to share the property, his possible disappearance from Dedham is all the more strange. This apparent estrangement from family and community reinforces the notion that he was the son removed from the home. Despite the disruption, the Mackintosh family continued with second son William about whom we know little except that he married Experience Holbrook (1673-1714) in 1692 or 1693 [65] and died on September 9, 1724. Their children were Rebeccah (1696?-?), William (1700-?), John (1704-?), and Moses (1708-?), the latter of whom was George McIntosh's great-grandfather.

Handicapped by being neither English nor a Puritan, John had made the most of his involuntary transport to a strange new land. He provided the family with its foothold in the New World and, significantly for his great-great-great grandson George, established the traditions of standing up for one's beliefs, of making a go of farming, and of improving his lot in life. What John could not provide was sufficient land for endless subdividing among William and William's children. [66] In his *Letters from An American Farmer* of 1782 J. Hector St. John de Crevecoeur asked an important question that applied to the future of the Mackintoshes:

> What should we American farmers be without the distinct possession of that soil? It feeds us, it clothes us, from it was draw even a great exuberancy, our best meat, our richest drink, the very honey of our bee comes from this privileged spot...[our farm] has established all our rights; on it is founded our rank, our freedom, our power as citizens, our importance as inhabitants of such a district. [67]

It was unfortunate for the MacIntoshes that, for a generation or so, absence of "possession of the soil" led to a downward economic trajectory. Without a farm, George's great-grandfather Moses was hard-pressed to clothe and feed his family and he certainly lost status as a citizen. But this nadir was redeemed in a glorious burst, at least in a historical sense, by the revolutionary activities of his son, Ebenezer, George's grandfather.

CHAPTER TWO

The Rabble Rouser

Moses Mackintosh faced life with the deck stacked against him. Orphaned at the age of seventeen when his father died (Moses had lost his mother eleven years before), as the youngest son he had few prospects. On November 19, 1725 he became the ward of Joseph Wight (1681-1742) of Dedham. Wight, a selectman and deacon of the First Church of Dedham was an upright and religious man who no doubt tried to give his charge direction, but Moses may have been something of a ne'er do well. [68] By the age of seventeen he should have been well into the process of learning a trade, but he seems never to have acquired a marketable skill. He did not remain long in Wight's household, but moved on to Boston to seek his fortune.

Luck was not with him. He began looking for work when Boston had reached a difficult economic crossroads as it moved from being a largely agrarian (especially in its southern part) to a mercantile society. As James A. Henretta notes in an article about the town's economic development and its effect on families, "The fundamental link between one generation and another, the ability of the father to train his offspring for their life's work, was endangered by a process of change which rendered obsolete many of the skills and assumptions of the older, land-oriented generation and opened the prospect of success in new fields and new places. [69] This kind of future eluded Moses. He turned to the refuge of many a young man feeling his way in the world and became a soldier.

He was stationed at Castle William, the fortress that guarded Boston Harbor, from about April 1730 until his discharge almost exactly two years later upon which he moved to Dorchester, Massachusetts. On August 5, 1734 he married Lydia Jones, the daughter of his friends, Ebenezer and Lydia Jones. Moses and Lydia had two children: a girl named for her mother, born on July 17, 1735 and Ebenezer, George McIntosh's grandfather, who entered the world on June 20, 1737 (a century before George's birth) in Boston where the family had moved. The boy was named for his maternal grandfather, Ebenezer Jones. [70]

From the moment of their marriage money problems plagued Moses and Lydia and at some point Lydia moved back to Dorchester, probably to stay with her parents while Moses resumed soldiering in 1742. She died in 1743 when Ebenezer was six years old. About the fate of his older sister we hear no more, but Ebenezer had to grow up even more quickly than his hapless father had. Moses' duties left him little time for the boy. And, although by 1753 Moses had risen through the ranks to be a "second gunner", one rung above sergeant, public records several times portray him as an irresponsible character who was unable to manage his own life, let alone his son's. [71]

First, he was "warned out" of Boston in the very year he advanced in rank. The warning out implied that he was indigent or in danger of becoming indigent and legally freed the town from the obligation to offer him charity. Moses would have been free to remain in Boston with his small family, to find work and pay taxes, but he could not claim public assistance. He took the path of least resistance, returning to his hometown of Dedham where on March 30, 1754 he married his second wife, Mary Everit. [72] Whether or not the couple offered to take Ebenezer with them, the spirited seventeen-year old remained in Boston to make his way alone.

It is perhaps unfair to judge Moses too harshly for his inability to support his offspring. The decades of the 1740s and 1750s in New England were difficult ones economically. All kinds of people suffered from money woes during the French and Indian War (1756-1763) when markets were often cut off and supplies dwindled. Warnings out increased steeply. [73] Also, Boston's rigidly stratified society disdained the undistinguished man simply because of his Scottish origins. And yet, while others eventually discovered means to support themselves, Moses never found secure economic footing and he bounced back and forth with Mary among the colony's towns. He gave up his army position and the couple moved to Wrentham, Massachusetts where the town fathers there warned them out in 1761, so the unfortunate pair traveled back to Boston. There Moses obtained employment when the selectmen named him one of Boston's "Fence Viewers" in 1764, 1766 and 1767. [74] The position involved inspecting fences demarcating property boundaries and noting if they had been changed in any way. But fence viewing either did not pay enough to support the couple or they mismanaged the income or Moses did not do the job properly because once again he was warned out of Boston in 1770 when he was sixty-two:

> November 14, 1770, Moses McEntosh Last from the Castel. [H]e has lived in Several towns in the Country or Provance [sic] But has been warned in his Majestys [sic] Name out of them all. He says he was warned out of Boston abote [sic] 17 years ago By 2 men in Boston. But he says he was born in Dedham. Warned in his Majestys [sic] Name to Depart the town of Boston in 14 Days. [75] (Punctuation added for clarity).

Eight years later his fortunes finally took a turn for the better when he returned to Castle William at the advanced age of seventy to once again become a soldier. [76]

Ebenezer's decision to remain in Boston as his father and stepmother went from town to town and job to job twisting on Fortune's wheel ultimately put him in the right place at the right time to become a hero to much of the town's populace. But before that moment arrived, he lived a distinctly humble existence. As a young, slightly built teenager (the usual age at which a boy became an apprentice was sometime between the years of twelve and fourteen), [77] Ebenezer had begun to learn the trade of cordwaining, or shoemaking, in Dorchester before he left for Boston. Ebenezer probably learned the trade from his mother's brother, Ichabod Jones (1694-?), an experienced cobbler, because he would not have been able to pay apprenticeship fees for learning any trade, let alone more skilled work such as silversmithing which required many years of training in artistic craftsmanship. Because making shoes offered little prospect for accumulating wealth, its apprenticeship entry fees were low, but Ebenezer could not have afforded any amount. His slender physique made work that required upper body strength, such as ship building, impossible, but it was ideal for sitting at a low cobbler's bench. Even after he acquired skill at the trade, he worked mostly as a door-to-door cobbler. His itinerancy eventually became an advantage, affording him the opportunity to overhear politically stimulating conversations in the homes where he labored just before the American Revolution. [78]

An apprentice commonly boarded in his master's home, so Ebenezer would have lived with his uncle until he was qualified to work independently. As important as providing a roof over Ebenezer's head was his master's responsibility for ensuring that the boy learn how to read and write. [79] Although never a man of privilege with many books of his own, Ebenezer loved reading. Poetry was his favorite genre. Hands stained from the dyes that colored the leather he handled, he frequently turned the pages of his favorite poem, "The Complaint, or Night Thoughts on Life, Death, and Immortality" (1742-45) by the English poet Edward Young (1683-1765), making out the words in dim candlelight. [80] The rather lugubrious work resonated with him and many other eighteenth-century people throughout America and the Continent (not, however, in England) who eagerly embraced the Romantic sense of melancholy that pervaded the verses. He memorized all of the poem's hundreds of lines and took pleasure in reciting them to others.

Ebenezer's ability to read, though perhaps unexpected given his background, was not an anomaly. In 1750 approximately 70 percent of men and 40 percent of women living in New England were reckoned literate. [81] His knowledge of the written word would come in handy as the political situation in Boston began to heat up in the 1760s and Ebenezer kept abreast of current events by avidly reading the newspapers. [82]

By 1759, when his father was once again disgraced financially, Ebenezer made a meager living as a shoemaker in South Boston's Twelfth Ward. That district lay south of the old part of town, encompassing the narrow strip of land called Boston Neck. The public gallows sat at the narrowest point of the Neck, reminding all who passed it that life could be short and brutal. The North End of Boston, where the town's upper crust lived, may have throbbed with merchants' activity and the bustle of the warehouses along the seafront, but the South End had its own attractions. There was a lively maritime presence with boisterous sailors and dock workers milling about. The owners of small shops lived in close proximity to "artisans", [83] creating a companionable social atmosphere and bonds that would be called upon before too long.

Ebenezer eked out a living and would never become prosperous. Even though Boston was by 1742 the principal manufacturer of shoes in the colonies, [84] by the time Ebenezer began working as a shoemaker Boston cobblers faced formidable competition from cordwainers in the Saugus area, John Mackintosh's first American home. New York and Philadelphia stole a considerable part of Boston's trade. [85] Faced with the depressing monetary realities of his job and possessed of an irascible, restless nature that became easily bored with the formulaic work of putting footwear together, it is no wonder that Ebenezer sought diversions. He soon found one.

The French and Indian War (1754-1763), as it was known in North America (Europe termed it the Seven Years' War), made uneasy allies of the British and the American colonists against the French and the native warriors who aided them. James Fenimore Cooper alluded to the testy relationship in his 1840 novel, *The Pathfinder* when he wrote, "…it would have been difficult to say, whether the Americans loved the English more than they hated the French…" [86] The crux of the dispute was French determination to retain her lands in North America and the East Indies, although eventually the conflict expanded to include countries around the world. Little did Ebenezer realize when he joined the fray that, because the hostilities directly threatened newly settled areas on the frontier, [87] he would be helping to safeguard land that would eventually establish the McIntoshes, including his grandson George, in northeastern Ohio.

Five months after the war erupted, Ebenezer joined Ward Twelve's "alarm list" militia on December 7, 1754. He remained in Boston until the spring of 1758 when he followed the call of a massive recruitment effort and enlisted in Captain Eliphalet Fales' company. [88] William Pitt (1708-1778), the British secretary of state, had instigated this push for recruits and supported it by promising to repay the colonies for outfitting and compensating the militias. That promise ultimately went unfulfilled, but it held out sufficient enticement to make Massachusetts, New York and Connecticut lawmakers agree "to arm more than 23,000 provincials…", men like Ebenezer.[89]

Serving during this conflict had three important implications for the young man's future. First, it provided the rudiments of the military discipline that he would use with great skill in the next decade. The experience also solidified his sense of unity with the other soldiers drawn from colonial households and third, it created an antipathy in him towards his British counterparts. The typical British soldier's use of obscenities and disregard for religious niceties offended many of the American-born men. Even more offensive to men who lived far from King George III's thumb were the inhumane floggings and other punishments inflicted on British soldiers by their own officers. Ebenezer retained memories of these incidents – about seven years later they helped shape his radical feelings against the British. Ebenezer Mackintosh was not the Royalist that John Mackintosh had been, but considered himself to be an American who was soon to join dramatically with some of his fellow native-born countrymen in attempting to break with the mother country.

His experience in battling both the French and their Indian allies to prevent the French from expanding their territory southward, thus threatening British colonial interests, was both short and, with one exception, fairly tepid. He served at Fort Edward which stood at a strategic spot [90] at the "portage between the Hudson River and the southern end of Lake George", [91] southwest of the more famous Fort Ticonderoga in New York. Small Fort Edward was the only impediment to the French marching "between Albany and the Hudson high road" directly into New York City. Allowing the French to establish themselves in New York City would cut the northern colonies off from the rest lying to the south. [92]

The French had defeated James Abercromby, the British commander-in-chief in North America, at Ticonderoga, forcing the English officer to retreat to Lake George. In July of 1758 the Marquis de Montcalm, Abercromby's French counterpart (1756-1759), sent about a thousand men to Lake George's eastern shore in order to interrupt any attempt Abercromby might make to try to make contact with Fort Edwards. [93] On July 20th several convoys sent out from the fort to obtain relief supplies for the hungry soldiers met with ferocious attacks by the French and Indians. Many of the colonists were killed. [94] According to at least one source, Ebenezer was among the soldiers attacked that day,[95] but, unhurt, he was eventually able to return to Boston.

In the end the colonists and the British succeeded in routing the French. In 1763 the parties signed The Treaty of Paris, an agreement ending all hostilities. The frisson of danger Ebenezer had felt made his return to the inherently sedentary task of shoemaking almost unbearably dull. But he would get another chance to shine. It, too, would involve an army of sorts and the beginnings of a much larger conflict between "nations" -- this time Ebenezer would act as a leader, not as a lowly foot soldier. This part of his destiny was very much linked to the section of Boston in which he lived and by the fires that plagued the entire town.

Boston had been dangerously ablaze many times. It was fire, the element that best matched his red hair and sometimes combustible personality, that gave Ebenezer his first opportunity to make a name for himself. He became a volunteer fireman with the South End Despatch Fire Engine Number Nine. [96] Stephen Greenleaf, (1704-1795), the recently appointed Master of Engine Number Nine, (in his later role as sheriff of Suffolk County of which Boston was a part, he would re-enter Ebenezer's life) "applyd for the Addition of one Man to Sd Engine…& proposed Ebenezer McIntosh who was by the Selectmen Approbated." [97] The position was one of many similar jobs offered to men who "although they held no taxable property [were] hard-working and reputable craftsmen who had established a permanent residence in Boston …" [98] Ebenezer's brave battling of fires showed off his mettle to certain people who, unbeknownst to him, were observing him carefully. He began to make important connections through his fellow firemen and the men who appointed them.

But before those connections bore fruit, Ebenezer's name had to become better known. He was a talkative man with a reputation for a flaring temper who fit well into the notoriously rowdy South End where residents found many reasons throughout the year to leave their employment in favor of noisy amusements. One of the most anticipated was Pope's Day, known in England as Guy Fawkes' Day, celebrated annually (in Boston from about 1685) on November 5 to give thanks for the foiling of the Roman Catholic Guy Fawkes' (1570-1606) attempt in 1605 to blow up the Parliament buildings in London. Young men from both the newer South End and the more established North End of Boston used the day as an excuse for enacting mock battles between effigies of the Pope and other unpopular figures that were paraded down the streets. From these high-spirited engagements in which the effigies were captured and then set ablaze Ebenezer Mackintosh emerged as the leader of his fellow firefighters who had joined together as a Pope's Day gang. [99]

It was after a fatal accident in November of 1764 that Ebenezer made his name as an admired leader of the mobs. John Rowe (1715-1787), a Boston merchant and cohort of Samuel Adams, recorded the incident in his diary: "A sorrowful accident happened this forenoon at the North End. The wheel of the carriage that the Pope was fixed on run over a Boy's head & he [John Browne] died instantly." [100] Boston authorities, hoping to curtail the throngs that had grown increasingly intractable over the years and who now had caused a child's death, ordered that the effigies be destroyed. [101] Disregarding the sad incident and not to be denied their entertainment, the determined North End hooligans returned to their part of town to make a new effigy. When the southerners got wind of this defiant act, Ebenezer led them north, too. A vicious battle broke out between the rival gangs, unimpeded even by a reading of the Riot Act. Ebenezer's "troops" prevailed.

Such civil disobedience could not go unpunished. As a result, Ebenezer and twenty-two others in what was now *his* mob were arrested. They included mostly young men employed in the laboring ranks: shoemaking, baking, ship building, and maritime jobs. On February 7, 1765 Rowe recorded, "Capt McKinntosh & others tryed before Mr. Justice [Richard] Dana [grandfather of the author of *Two Years before the Mast*, 1840] & Justice [William] Storey for the 5th of Nov. affair." [102] The justices held the proceedings to determine probable cause. [103] Although not all of the men were indicted, Ebenezer and a few of his friends were charged with rioting and assault, an accusation to which all pled not guilty. Boston authorities released the men from custody pending trials that ultimately never took place, suggesting that some political influence thwarted the path of justice.[104]

The crowds had by now embraced twenty-eight-year old Ebenezer, anointing him "Captain" Mackintosh, as Rowe calls him. He functioned as the acknowledged leader of the mobs in both ends of Boston. But in the pivotal year of 1765 his natural abilities found a more fruitful outlet than senseless conflicts. That summer things began to heat up in the colonies and not just because of the season. The British had proposed a Stamp Act, designed to raise funds for the maintenance of British troops in the colonies. The Act, passed by Parliament in March of 1765 and due to take effect on November 1, assigned a tax to *all* printed paper in the colonies. The act was so all-encompassing that it even included ephemera such as playing cards. The colonists had been not been asked for their opinions on the tax, neither had they voted on the matter. Despite circulating petitions of protest, they were unsuccessful in convincing the British to withdraw the planned tariff. A significant proportion of those who felt beleaguered by the Act belonged to the Boston gangs. Denied access to the political process because they did not own the land that qualified them to vote, they expressed their increasing frustration about the silence imposed upon them by rioting explosively. (It cannot be denied that some of them just enjoyed the thrill of physical confrontation). The government in London hesitated in the face of potentially violent American opposition. Parliament's faint heart only increased derision on this side of the Atlantic. [105]

Ebenezer now possessed an aura of fame and glory that generated new opportunities for him. On March 11, 1765 he was nominated to be a Sealer of Leather, one of only four such posts in Boston. A sealer inspected the quality of leather before it left the tannery, hammering an official seal on those hides that passed muster. [106] The offer hinted strongly at political patronage and the position became his when the city fathers approved the nomination. He was re-appointed in 1766, 1767, and 1768. (Note that these years overlap Moses' years as a Fence Viewer, implying that he, too, benefited from Ebenezer's connections). There are some suggestions that, because Ebenezer's name occupied the first position in public records listing the Boston sealers, he was considered the head of the group. [107]

Why, if Ebenezer had gained notoriety as a rabble-rouser who threatened Boston's civilized sectors, would the men running the town meeting agree to his appointment to *any* official post and perhaps reward his father with the fence inspecting position, too? It is likely that this office came to him through the influence of Samuel Adams (1722-1803), who spearheaded the radical Sons of Liberty in Boston and exerted some power over the Loyal Nine, a secret political organization made up of "merchants, distillers, ship owners and master craftsmen who opposed the Stamp Act…"[108] that decided to intimidate upholders of the proposed tax on paper through destructive acts. It was the Loyal Nine who "controlled the mobs and Boston elections" [109] and insinuated themselves into various positions in Boston's government without revealing their revolutionary leanings. Adams, a master propagandist, recognized that Ebenezer's charisma could be put to good use in propelling plans for political agitation.

It was to the advantage of these behind-the-scenes manipulators to keep Ebenezer both happy and in their debt. Their secret activities made them apprehensive of his unguarded chattiness, but they also realized that his influence could be useful to them. But Adams in particular seemed not always to be Ebenezer's ally. In the summer of 1765 Adams sued Ebenezer in a minor court and won a judgment of just over twelve pounds. Ebenezer did not pay the debt, probably because he was unable to. So, on August 12 Adams renewed the suit. But he never received the money owed him. Some speculate that the legal action was a ploy to obligate the shoemaker further to this powerful Son of Liberty, thus ensuring his compliance with the group's wishes. [110] Whatever Adams' motives, although Ebenezer's private fortunes seemed to be heading downward like his father's, his public life was about to hit its highest point.

On August 14, 1765 Ebenezer Mackintosh secured his place in American history (despite being sometimes mistakenly referred to as both Andrew and Phillip Mackintosh by various historians since). At the instigation of the Loyal Nine he and his mobs, now numbering in the thousands, strutted through Boston displaying effigies, not of the Pope, but of Andrew Oliver (1706-1774), the American lieutenant-governor of Massachusetts who had volunteered to administer the hated Stamp Act. Earlier in the day their ranks had been puffed somewhat by town merchants who were "patriots out of prudence"[111], but after these businessmen left the parade, the group's violent, destructive actions began. They first approached a building on the docks that they mistook for the Stamp Office, rapidly tearing it down. Then the men set off for Oliver's house, brandishing pieces of wood taken from the demolished waterfront shed. The commissioner and his family had escaped to the safety of Castle William, so did not witness the crowd smashing the precious, expensive windows of their home. The aroused mob even decapitated Oliver's effigy, tossing its head into the Oliver family's yard.

Ebenezer encouraged this plundering — witnesses reported seeing him swinging wreckage from the structure by the dock. His control of the mobs appears to have been nearly absolute and inspired grudging admiration even in Oliver himself who eventually described him as being "sensible and manly" and "dressed genteelly". Ebenezer's men moved in "two files" like an orderly military group. (His service in the French and Indian War apparently stood him in good stead here). If he heard a whisper coming from his followers, he had only to hold up a finger to hush them in a moment, so he certainly had the power to prevent much of the men's mischief. Accounts of the mob's frenzied destructiveness suggest that Ebenezer was willing to relax military control when it was convenient. "If Mackintosh had only been obliging a few merchants by destroying the evidence against them, the night's rampage might have ended there. Instead, the mob's two flanks joined forces and set out to wreak the greatest civil disobedience North America had ever experienced." [112] And, although Sam Adams may not have intended such massive destructiveness, Ebenezer's swarming, liquor-sodden men achieved the goal of forcing Oliver to announce that he would resign as Stamp Act Commissioner that day; August 14th became a holiday of "processions, feasts, and patriotic toasts" for the American revolutionaries for years. [113] However, although it could "be useful to be seen with [Ebenezer]", he was not invited to most of these fetes – no matter what his achievements were, class distinctions dictated social behavior. [114]

Ebenezer fully sensed his sway over the mobs and began to feel less and less need for approval from the Loyal Nine. He started to strike out on his own without their direction. On August 26, 1765 he targeted Lieutenant-Governor Thomas Hutchinson's (1711-1780) house, allowing the mob to break windows and plunder the home. But Hutchinson, away at the time, was not an eye-witness to the rampaging. The rioters later learned that the Governor was actually not entirely in favor of the Stamp Act and other laws that he viewed as injurious to the colonies.

This time Ebenezer had gone too far. Warrants were issued for his arrest and that of some of his followers. Sheriff Greenleaf, the same man who had headed the fire company in which Ebenezer served, was ordered by Francis Bernard (1712-1779), governor of Massachusetts, to seize the rebellious shoemaker in King Street, but Ebenezer's men thwarted him [115] and Greenleaf, who may have felt some loyalty to his former firefighting comrade, was chastised for not doing his duty. [116] Men who had been told to patrol the streets that night to fend off more rioting refused to obey unless their leader was freed, showing just how popular the shoemaker had become. Even Bernard's offer of a 300-pound reward to anyone who would come forward and finger the leader of the rioters did not produce results.

In the end, no one involved in the Hutchinson affair was ever indicted, let alone tried. The city fathers decided that a wiser course was to trust in

Ebenezer's ability to moderate the increasingly restive mob. He adapted himself admirably to that task on a rainy December 17, 1765 when Andrew Oliver made his way to the South End and a large elm called the Liberty Tree, [117] to swear that he would not enforce the Stamp Act. Ebenezer stood right next to Oliver, personally assuring that the mob did not seize the commissioner for tarring and feathering. From that day forward Ebenezer was known locally as the "Captain General of the Liberty Tree". [118]

Contemporary descriptions portray Ebenezer as a dashing, self-confident character. In November 1765 he had appeared for Pope's Day in full military regalia, wearing a blue and red uniform with gilt collar and a hat trimmed with gold lace. Completing his commanding image was a baton and "speaking trumpet", the latter used to convey his orders as loudly as possible. [119] The pomp and music that accompanied him and his mobs as they proceeded down the street aped practices of contemporary London mobs who used "Drums, and sometimes fifes and trumpets… to summon crowds, especially during the industrial disputes of the 1760s." [120]

A Colonel Brattle joined Ebenezer for the 1765 Pope's Day march. He belonged to both the Massachusetts militia and the Boston Council, so gave Ebenezer's men a certain sanction. Brattle linked arms with Ebenezer, praising his ability to keep his "troops" orderly. As Russell Bourne remarks, "In the most down-to-earth circle, Mackintosh was seen simply as the boss, not only the paramount leader of the town's violent waterfront gangs but also a force whose political power extended far beyond its South End base." [121]

Was his influence on Boston politics really that strong? If so, why did he withdraw from the scene after his triumph at the Liberty Tree? It seems that Ebenezer had little purpose after the Stamp Act had vanished as a target of patriot protest and it may be that Samuel Adams and others demanded that he leave the spotlight. There is no doubt that he would have done so unwillingly. Ebenezer returned reluctantly to shoemaking and his duties as a Sealer of Leather.

As the years passed Ebenezer's financial state began more and more to resemble his father's, especially when he lost his position as Sealer after 1768. He struggled against the worsening odds for a Boston shoemaker to make a living in the 1770s. [122] He was also assailed by further lawsuits. Between 1766 and

1773 the courts heard several cases against him. Failure to pay promissory notes was the most common complaint. [123]

Complicating fiscal matters, but otherwise enhancing his life, was Ebenezer's marriage on August 7, 1766 to Elizabeth Maverick, the eldest child of the Boston merchant Jotham Maverick (1717-before 1770) and his wife, Mehitable Banks Maverick, who came from Boston's North End. [124] It is not known how the two met or why Elizabeth's parents would sanction marriage to the twenty-nine year old whose straitened circumstances limited his ability to support a wife and family. His political leanings, viewed as traitorous by the British, carried great risk. Elizabeth must have been a courageous, like-minded woman to wager on a lifelong commitment to a man who had these drawbacks. The two were married by Elizabeth's pastor, the Reverend Andrew Eliot, the Congregationalist minister of the New North Church. Eliot had been responsible in the previous year for returning some of Thomas Hutchinson's precious manuscripts that had escaped the rapacious hands of Ebenezer's mobs [125] and thus would seem an unlikely man to unite the pair, but so he did.

Ebenezer and Elizabeth had two children: Elizabeth ("Betsey") (1767/68-1848) and Paschal Paoli (1769-1832). Ebenezer named Paschal for the Corsican revolutionary general, Pasquale Paoli (1725-1807), who was immensely popular with anti-British colonists. (In later years Paschal played an important role in the life of his half-brother, John, George McIntosh's father.) Ebenezer's new status as husband and father settled him down on the domestic front, but seems to have done nothing to temper his predilection for radical politics.

When Elizabeth married him, Ebenezer was still under threat of indictment for the violence of the previous August. The couple breathed more easily on December 6, 1766 when the Massachusetts General Assembly pardoned Ebenezer and the other participants, but there were those who viewed the South End shoemaker as a potentially very troublesome presence, particularly because of his assumed connection to Samuel Adams and the Sons of Liberty. Earlier that autumn the Tory George Mason wrote the following to his friend Joseph Harrison:

> You may please to remember I hinted to you formerly that if one Mackintosh in this town was apprehended—it would be a means of unraveling the whole scene of Iniquity. The man has already been threatened with Death in case he should inform. As to any Evidence

this side the Water it would weigh but little, but if Government should think proper to send for him Home, I am firmly persuaded it would answer the end. He was one that attended their night meetings, and knows more of their secret Transactions than the whole of what they call Torys put together. [126]

Was it because the Sons of Liberty had warned him that they would kill him if he denounced them, as suggested in Mason's letter, or because he was now a married man that Ebenezer thought it more prudent at this juncture to abstain from participating in the other riots that took place in Boston after his marriage? He certainly could take little time away from work because, not only was he now a family man, but he was also harassed with even more lawsuits. Sometimes he was the instigator. In one case he and three other Sealers sued a tanner for selling defective leather. [127] He was put out of commission entirely when committed briefly in 1770 (the same year in which his father was once again warned out of the town) to Boston's debtor's prison. [128] (Fellow shoemaker George Robert Twelves Hewes, "from the same group of frequently failed people as Ebenezer Mackintosh", was tossed in the same prison as Ebenezer. Their paths would cross three years later in a remarkable event that ensured their places in American history.)

Ebenezer's aloofness from politics didn't last long though. His anti-British passions rose once again on March 5, 1770, the day of the "Boston Massacre" when the general sorrow for those killed affected him and Elizabeth specifically. The affair is complicated and not nearly as one-sided as the propagandistic portrayal in Paul Revere's famous engraving of the incident. After a group of rope makers at John Gray's ropewalks establishment hurled insults at a British sentry standing guard at the Custom House, British soldiers ran to their comrade's aid. [129] A melee ensued between the soldiers and the crowd of men and boys who had gathered, some to throw insults and snowballs, others to witness the excitement as bystanders. One of the latter was Ebenezer's seventeen-year old brother-in-law, Samuel Maverick (1753-1770), Elizabeth's half-brother. [130] While eating supper at the home of the keg maker, Johnathan Cary, Samuel, an ivory-turner's apprentice, heard bells ringing, the traditional fire alarm in Boston. [131] Sensing some drama, Samuel raced toward King Street and found himself in the middle of a large, belligerent crowd where Captain Thomas

Preston, commander of the soldiers, was trying to deal with a potentially explosive situation.

After unsuccessfully ordering the mob to scatter, Preston told his men to fire. Five men, including Samuel, fell. A bullet had caromed off a wall, striking Samuel in the stomach and mortally wounding him. He was carried bleeding to his widowed mother's boarding house and died there the following morning after enduring an operation that removed the ball. [132] Someone would certainly have summoned Ebenezer and Elizabeth to the Maverick home, although contemporary descriptions do not mention their presence. Thousands marched in the funeral procession to the Old Granary Burying Ground, including John Hancock and Paul Revere. Ebenezer must have been among them, if not at their head. This family tragedy heaped fuel on his smoldering anti-British convictions. Soon he would once again be able to act upon them in a manner that suited his penchant for political theatre.

On December 16, 1773 he joined over a hundred other men whose ranks included apprentices, artisans and merchants, all disguised as Mohawk Indians. After meeting up with each other at various points around the town, the men assembled at the wharf by Boston Harbor. From there they boarded three tea-laden British East India ships and dumped overboard over 300 cases of tea, for which the unwilling colonists would have been assessed duty imposed by the British. The men took great care that the numerous onlookers did not make off with any of the precious substance. This rather juvenile playacting was a defiant exploit that many Bostonians deplored, even those who were beginning to hope for separation from England. But it solidified Boston as the eye of the revolutionary storm in British eyes [133] and greatly increased the peril for Ebenezer Mackintosh.

Some have doubted that Ebenezer was indeed a participant in the Tea Party, maintaining that the Mackintosh who dumped tea overboard that night was a fifteen-year old blacksmith's apprentice named Peter Mackintosh. But Peter denied taking part. The confusion resulting from haste and hidden visages, combined with the secret nature of the mission, made some positive identifications difficult; however, today most scholars admit Ebenezer's share in that night's activity. [134] It was just the sort of role he would have savored, full of intrigue and the white heat of men possessed by their abhorrence for what the tea represented. His connection to Samuel Adams who orchestrated the event increases the probability that Ebenezer was there that night, along with the likes of Paul Revere (1735-1818) and George Twelves Hewes (1742-1840), the man who shared the debtor's prison experience with him.

Thirty-seven years later Ebenezer told Schuyler Merrill, a ten-year old New Hampshire boy, the story of the Tea Party and asserted that he had been a member of the renegade group. He told Merrill, "It was my chickens did the job", perhaps conflating his earlier role as mob leader, but more probably claiming a larger, more prominent function for himself. (Merrill said that the comment "was a mystery to him…'how chickens could have anything to do with a tea party!'")[135] At the time Ebenezer spoke to Merrill he was once again suffering from money problems and likely felt the need to elevate himself in the eyes of neighbors who had not witnessed the glory years of their unfortunate neighbor.

Participation in the Tea Party made life in Boston even more dangerous for the now notorious Ebenezer. In London the reaction to such direct acts of rebellion was to plot punishments for those most directly involved. King George III (1738-1820) ordered General Thomas Gage (1721-1787), commander of British forces in the colonies, to find evidence against those involved so a trial for treason could be held. [136] The hoped-for guilty verdicts would then serve as an example to others who might be tempted to test the Crown's resolve. But Gage felt that such a prosecution could not succeed. [137] Rumors of possible retribution from the other side of the Atlantic abounded, some of which were actually substantiated by reports in London newspapers.

On May 19, 1774 *The Massachusetts Spy* reprinted an item that had previously appeared on April 7th of that year in a London newspaper. It was a report that must have caused alarm to the men mentioned, all well known to the British as agitators against the Crown: "It may be depended on that a sloop of war sailed from Plymouth 14 days since for Boston with orders to bring to England, in irons, Hancock, Row (sic), Adams, and McIntosh; the latter has been very active among the lower order of the people, and the other among the higher." [138]

As events transpired, it turned out that this particular report was false, but fear was in the air. Deportation to London meant much more than leaving American shores: the men faced the possibility of trial for treason and being put to death in horrific ways if found guilty.

Sometime between the Tea Party and the following summer Ebenezer, whose talkativeness created a real liability for him and his comrades, absented himself from his hometown. (Adams and Hancock had left Boston a bit earlier, in April of 1775, escaping Gage's June 12th imposition of martial law.) The widower (Elizabeth had died sometime before 1773) gathered up seven-year old "Betsey" and five-year old Paschal and set off on foot northward toward New Hampshire. Although people were far more used to walking long distances then than we are today, it is hard to imagine how the trio coped. They had to tote supplies, including Ebenezer's shoemaking equipment, and young Paschal also often ended up in his father's arms.

The approximately one hundred-fifty mile trip took them to North Haverhill, New Hampshire, a hamlet in the White Mountain area near Vermont's eastern border. Ebenezer might have remembered the region from his service at Fort Edward or he might at some point have encountered "his old army associate, Captain Ephraim Wesson" who now lived in Haverhill. [139] Their exact route is not known, but they probably traveled up the Merrimack River where it was possible to hitch a ride on a flat-bottomed boat. Then they would have walked about forty more miles into Haverhill.

Traveling posed many dangers in eighteenth-century America, especially the kind of journey Ebenezer and his children were forced to make. As they left densely inhabited urban Boston for wilderness with only sporadic settlements, they exposed themselves to dangers from both wild animals and human predators. The three of them had to make their slow way along rutted, often muddy tracks through heavily forested areas. Summer brought heat and exposed them to tormenting insects and malarial agues arising from the swamps they passed. The little family group would have been dirty, uncomfortable and probably frequently hungry because Ebenezer was a man of the city, not the outdoors. The trek required extraordinary tenacity, but it would be far from the only such mammoth walk undertaken by Mackintoshes, including Ebenezer's son, Paschal, and his grandson, George. Another such journey was even in Ebenezer's future.

They arrived safely in Haverhill sometime before September 27, 1774 when we know that Ebenezer witnessed and signed a contract involving the construction of a home across the Connecticut River in Newbury, Vermont. [140] Haverhill, founded just a decade before the Mackintoshes arrived, [141] was a newer settlement than any Ebenezer had lived in before. New Hampshire, like Massachusetts, had a reputation for its capable shoemakers and, in fact, some of its villages were called "cobblers' towns". [142] Many of them had backgrounds similar in many respects to Ebenezer's: "The pioneers were a literate group…many came because they held strongly to political and especially to religious doctrines that had made them unpopular or even persecuted in their home communities."[143]

North Haverhill was (and still is) a pretty place, one of five villages making up Haverhill proper. Ebenezer and his children settled in a densely forested area of North Haverhill known as The Plain. It must have seemed like a secure haven. Ebenezer resumed his trade as a shoemaker, but the brewing revolution lured him once again from his cobbler's bench. Even though New Hampshire, unlike its twelve sister colonies, did not suffer invasion by the British during the American Revolution, its residents could not have known that they would escape attack. Ebenezer was ready once again to serve the revolutionary cause.

Between August 18 and October 6, 1777 the forty-year old volunteered in a company led by Captain Joseph Hutchins.[144] His stint in the military was shortened when the company dissolved on October 6 without participating in any battles. Three years later, the British assaulted Royalton, Vermont, located just thirty miles from Haverhill. Ebenezer re-joined Hutchins, this time as a scout to determine if the British were approaching Haverhill. At the close of the Revolutionary War in 1781 Ebenezer was again making shoes in North Haverhill and the village selected him as its Sealer of Leather in 1782, 1783, and 1784. [145] Political influence was an unlikely factor in his selection this time, but his Boston experience as a Sealer recommended him.

It was in 1784 that at the age of forty-seven he wed for the second time. Ebenezer married a widow named Elizabeth Chase (1748-?), but found it difficult to support her and the family of three sons they had together.[146] Ebenezer was the unfortunate heir to his father's slippery hands when it came to holding onto money. North Haverhill, an almost completely agrarian community, did not offer the scope for employment that Boston had. Everyone, even the minister and doctor, supplemented their provisions with produce grown on their own land or garden plots and kept pigs, chickens and sometimes other livestock,[147] but Ebenezer did not take naturally to farming.

As his finances worsened Ebenezer sought various methods of relief. His children were the primary concern. Betsey entered service in the home of General Moses Dow (1746-1811), a 1769 graduate of Harvard.[148] When she was nineteen-years old, Betsey left Dow's home in 1786 to marry Jabez Bigelow (1764-1851), "shoemaker, tavern keeper and farmer". They moved about twenty miles across the New Hampshire border to Ryegate, Vermont, a town founded in 1773 by Scottish settlers. There they raised their eleven children. [149]

After the American Revolution ended, New Hampshire witnessed an influx of families determined to buy up any remaining plots of arable land. [150] Just as John Mackintosh had been unable to amass enough land to divide and pass on to his sons, Ebenezer could not provide acreage for his. Paschal, seeing the writing on the wall, found a better way to forge his way in life – in dramatic fashion. He also left North Haverhill in 1786, but was to travel a far greater distance than Betsey had.

While seventeen-year old Paschal probably relished the thought of escaping the small town with its limited prospects, his farewell to his cherished sister remained embedded in his memory. In an 1826 letter to Betsey, the only letter that survives from his hand, he wrote:

> I desire to see you, but it is not probable that I ever shall in this world, & if I should, time has made such alterations in your appearance, that I should hardly believe you to be that sister, which I beheld with a pleasing sorrow, at our last parting twenty three, or four years ago. Neither shou'd I appear to you like that boy, that bid you farewell, & left you in tears [at General Dow's] more than forty years since; to go and seek his fortune in lands to him unknown. You saw him no more, for six long years. [151]

Paschal had to steel himself both physically as well as emotionally for the hard journey out to the western frontier of America, to the Northwest Territory (also known as the Old Northwest) and what is now the state of Ohio. The land that beckoned to him lay in the northeastern corner of a vast tract of the Northwest Territory known as the Western Reserve. King Charles II, the monarch for whom John Mackintosh had sacrificed his freedom, had given the land to the Connecticut Colony in 1622, but Virginia, Massachusetts, and New York also laid claim to portions of the territory. Connecticut ceded much of the land to the federal government in 1786, retaining only the Western Reserve, the over three million-acre portion bordering Lake Erie's southern shore. [152]

The Land Ordinance Act of 1785 had already mandated surveying much of the Northwest Territory. [153] Congress's intent was a practical one. The young federal government needed money – selling neatly measured land to potential settlers realized some of those funds. The Congressional act represented more than an attempt to structure wilderness lands so as to attract a steady flow of settlers. It also communicated "national authority", forging a link between the government and its far-flung inhabitants who lived beyond the boundaries of the original thirteen colonies. [154] At the same time, however, the act completely disregarded the patterns of land use established over the centuries by natives; a similar disruption occurred in the 1860s in the Colorado Territory during George McIntosh's early years there. [155]

Paschal may have made the approximately 800-mile journey through the wilderness to the Western Reserve in the company of an advance guard of surveyors because it would have been unusual for the teenager to journey to the only vaguely charted lands entirely on his own. As he set off for the lonely, unfamiliar lands, he must have recalled something of the long walk from Boston about thirteen years before. But this time he was far more aware of his surroundings. As he left constricted North Haverhill with its tidy homes and farms he could not help but be awestruck by some of the sights along the way to New York where the real journey would begin. His wayfaring took him past sublime, Romantic, and as yet unsullied landscapes. He would have been an unfeeling young man indeed if he had had no response to views that would be celebrated just a few decades later by the Hudson River School of artists and by James Fenimore Cooper's *Leatherstocking Tales*. And if the religious enthusiasm that would come to dominate his life were part of his belief system in 1786, he perceived his surroundings as ample evidence of God's wondrous creations.

After navigating on and around New York's many waterways, Paschal and his companions followed the southern shore of Lake Ontario into the Northwest Territory, a journey of between two and three months, depending on the weather conditions, the availability of boats and successful interactions with the natives of each region. [156] They probably followed the southern shore of Lake Ontario until they reached the mouth of the Cuyahoga River. Then they canoed down the Cuyahoga directly into what was to become Portage County, where George McIntosh would be born almost four decades later. [157] Once in the area he assisted the few other early arrivals there in clearing their land and building dwellings. All the while he was earning money with which he would purchase land, just as his nephew George would do in another western frontier.

Paschal formed an intimacy with the less-than-hospitable countryside long before he was able to select his own acreage. He was well aware of the many unpleasant features of the area. There were "clouds of mosquitoes so thick that they looked like the forewarning of an August thunderstorm". He probably also suffered the torments of dysentery and endured swampy miasmas that caused malarial fevers. [158] But, in spite of these inconveniences, Paschal eventually took up a piece of land in the area. This dangerous wilderness offered him the fresh start that the more settled New Hampshire could not.

We don't know why Paschal left the Western Reserve in 1792 to return to New Hampshire. But he went back to the newly surveyed (in 1796 a group of land speculators called the Connecticut Land Company had sent surveyors led by General Moses Cleaveland, for whom the city of Cleveland would be named)[159] area in 1798, settling on lot number twenty-three [160] of the thirty-six making up the township of Mantua (pronounced man-ah-way) in Portage County. Early pioneer John Leavitt (who would help shape George McIntosh's father's early years) had called the township Mantua after the eponymous Italian town. Mantua may seem an odd name for an American village, but the frontiersman's perception of Napoleon as a heroic liberator of the Italian city of Mantua from the Austrians appealed to those for whom the American Revolution was still a vivid event. It was a perfectly titled place for Paschal Paoli whose own name recalled a heroic rebel from the Continent; however, the Mantua in Ohio showed itself during Paschal's life there to be less revolutionary than generally suspicious of opinions that varied from the norm. Although he was one of Mantua's earliest pioneers, Paschal found that his fellow citizens did not always respect him and he would suffer greatly in the future from their censures.

Paschal and his fellow settlers had, for the most part, no vision beyond their own acres, with little notion that their willingness to help expand the borders of the United States would lead to the establishment of the states of Ohio (admitted to the Union in 1803), Indiana (1816), Illinois (1818), Michigan (1837) and Wisconsin (1848). The people who followed in succeeding decades came to land divided into six-mile square townships further subdivided into thirty-six plots of land as neatly squared by those early surveyors as the irregular land would allow. But the regularity imposed upon the land was just about the only consistent pattern the pioneers found. Thick stands of trees and those mosquito-ridden swamps obscured their acreage, so much so that it was sometimes difficult just to locate the lines that defined one's property. David Hudson, for whom the Portage County township of Hudson would be named, spent six days searching before he found the elusive boundaries of his land! [161]

Hoped for stampedes of eager New England settlers did not materialize in the Western Reserve at first, although people did trickle slowly into the region, family by family, individual by individual. In the early years of the Reserve's settlement, single men like Paschal were far more numerous than families. Not until after the conclusion of the War of 1812 in 1815, when people felt that the government was indeed capable of protecting them, did the numbers of colonists become a steady stream attracted by highly inaccurate statements claiming that the Reserve was paradisiacal place, a notion that conveyed nothing of the true state of the undeveloped frontier. [162]

In spite of his isolation, Paschal was content with his surroundings, spending all of his time taming and cultivating the land. The abundant, thickly growing deciduous trees were difficult to clear, but otherwise benign. But within the dense forests lurked bears, panthers and wolves. "Wolves were everywhere. Few were the settlers who did not encounter them and hear their threatening howls...Bears were very plenty in this country up to 1815." [163] Orrin Harmon recollected in 1866 that "the wolves never did any bodily harm to any person in Mantua [they did, however, attack and kill sheep], although occasionally in the night time when one person happened to be traveling in the woods alone they would approach him in a threatening manner." In 1814 a Mantua man surprised by several wolves near Paschal's property had to defend himself by striking at them with a hand saw until they dispersed. [164] The populace of Mantua and surrounding areas immediately set about to hunt, trap and poison the packs of wolves into oblivion. The animals had almost completely vanished from the scene by about 1830, just seven years before George's birth, although rattlesnakes abounded well into his childhood.

Paschal had no other choice than to wade right into that forest and begin to chop down trees in order to clear room for a rudimentary shelter and farmland that he would fence with split rails from the trees he cut. Without draft horses to uproot the remains of a tree, Paschal and the others resorted to fire, accelerating the process by piling smaller branches and brush around the trunk and setting everything ablaze until little remained but ashes. Contemporary witnesses reported that all the Portage County townships were filled with the sight and smell of bonfires throughout the settlement years. The time-consuming process allowed for just two to three acres to be cleared in a year. Elias Harmon (1773-1851) noted on October 21, 1799 that he "helped McIntosh to raise his house", [165] (by this time Paschal had dropped the "a" in his last name and all further generations adopted this spelling), so Paschal did just manage to beat exposure to winter.

Although the tiny band of mostly male settlers aided each other in putting up cabins and socialized in the few free moments they had, Paschal led a secluded existence. By about 1800 more single men and several families had joined Paschal in the Mantua community, but the population remained sparse for years. The following anecdote highlights that fact. In January 1800 Paschal joined Abraham Honey and his wife on a trip to Cleveland, twenty-eight miles to the northwest. They rode in a sled pulled by an ox, camping by the side of the putative road (really little more than a rough path), enduring almost unbearably cold temperatures during the many days spent along the way. The trio's absence caused a precipitous drop in the number of Mantua's residents, leaving behind just three men and two women, Mrs. Elias Harmon and the wife of the Ottawa Chief Sawgamaw. Even by 1807 there were only about thirty people living in Mantua, *five* of them McIntoshes, including Paschal and the woman he married in 1802. [166]

The Mantua settlers did have some neighbors who were longtime, if transient, residents of the area. Native tribes included the Wyandot, Seneca, Ottawa, and Delaware. In her 1910 history of the Western Reserve Harriet Taylor Upton noted that "…just previous to the War of 1812 they [the tribes] began to disappear and at the close of the war they never returned in any such numbers or for any permanent settlement." [167] Her comment suggests that these long-established native groups vanished from the face of the earth when in fact they had been shifted by government agents or moved to reservations to make room for increasing numbers of eastern settlers. Paschal would have been quite aware of his native neighbors and, although not antagonistic toward them, almost certainly would have felt himself to be superior to them. He, like so many of his neighbors, probably regarded the Indians as tolerable nuisances. Nine-year old Emily Nash expressed the sentiments of most of the settlers in 1815 when she wrote the following in her diary: "before the war of 1812 there was six Indians living around the river to hunt and troubled people in Matua and hiram verey bad. They were wanting something all the time. If they would not have their wants gratified they would threaten to kill the people…They often wanted whiskey." [168]

Neighbors notwithstanding, Paschal began to feel an urgent expectation of something more than what his isolated surroundings provided. He had had limited interaction with women for several years. In fact, women were in short supply in the whole of the Western Reserve throughout the early settlement era. It was to be three years before Paschal would enjoy long-term female companionship.

The story of his unexpected winning of the woman who was to be his wife reflects either a measure of his desperation, the hot-blooded yearning of a man in his early thirties, or sudden, passionate love. Paschal most likely experienced both desire and affection. Because of the Reserve's predominantly virile composition, finding a mate was often a matter of luck and opportunity — and the ability to leave scruples behind, if necessary. Paschal jumped at the first opportunity with an impulsiveness leaving no doubt that he was Ebenezer's son.

In late March of 1802 Jotham Atwater, was betrothed to twenty-three-year old Hartford, Connecticut native Abi Clark (1779-1868). In 1799 she had accompanied her father, Ephraim Clark, and her mother to Burton Township in the Reserve's Geauga (pronounced jaw-ga) County, just to the north of Portage County. [169] There they joined three other Connecticut families who had formed the tiny community just one year before the Clarks arrived. Abi worked in nearby Nelson in the home of Delaun Mills and his family. That she was no longer living under family's roof may account for the events that were about to occur.

Jotham intended to firm up his wedding plans with Abi and took Paschal along with him for company on the supposedly auspicious trip. It would be auspicious all right, but not for Jotham. He introduced Paschal to the young woman he fully expected to wed. But the introduction led to complications Jotham had not foreseen. In a very short time Paschal and Abi hit it off well enough for him to "lead [her] astray" and on April 3, 1802, just a few days after meeting each other, the pair married [170] and returned to Paschal's farmstead.

At this point Ebenezer re-enters the story. He and his second wife had begun another generation of Mackintoshes, starting with Moses (1789-1863) who was born when his father was fifty-two-years old and his mother over forty. John (1791-1852), destined to become George McIntosh's father, followed two years later. Ebenezer's last child, David, (1794-1883) appeared three years after John. [171] Once again the impoverished McIntosh home was filled with hungry mouths. This time Paschal came to the rescue by first returning to his father's home in North Haverhill where his young half-brothers were now thirteen, eleven, and eight years old, respectively.

Had he been summoned by Ebenezer? It is an astounding testament to Paschal's loyalty to his family for him to have once again undertaken that long journey when he was a newlywed, leaving his young wife behind (probably in her family's care). He enjoyed seeing Betsey again, but the reunion turned out to be a side benefit of his real purpose: whether importuned by his father or not, Paschal was about to give his half-brothers the same kind of opportunity he had had. He accompanied his father and the boys back to Mantua. Ebenezer was probably a widower again at this point or he would not have made what turned out to be an extended trip. (Elizabeth Chase's death, like Elizabeth Maverick's, does not appear in local records nor is there a gravestone for her in any of Haverhill's cemeteries).

Once again Ebenezer was to embark on a stupendous feat of walking. Now sixty-five-years old, with three young boys and their thirty-three-year old stepbrother as fellow travelers, he had the exhilarating prospect before him of seeing the frontier. Paschal must have presented an enthusiastic picture of potential for economic prosperity in the West. The small group walked and boated from New Hampshire to Mantua Township, arriving in the autumn of 1802. [172] Such a dramatic removal no doubt appealed to Ebenezer's sense of importance. He remained in Mantua for at least three years, long enough to arrange his younger sons' futures before he left them forever. (Only David would return to New England to see his father once more before Ebenezer's death). Ebenezer also doubtlessly relished the novelty of his new situation, one that removed him from badgering creditors in the east and gave him new audiences for his stories of pre-Revolutionary Boston.

There is a fairy tale-like aspect to this image of an aged father accompanying his children through the forests, intending to leave them there in the wilderness, albeit in the home of close kin. Moses, John and David were just old enough to savor the adventure of the expedition while their friends remained behind to live a far more traditional way of life, but also young enough to miss the domesticity of their North Haverhill home. The future abolitionist John Brown (1800-1859) made a similar, if slightly more comfortable trip with his entire family just three years later, riding in a wagon from Connecticut to Hudson. The journey made a huge impression on Brown. He never forgot the "wilderness filled with wild beasts" and encounters with large rattlesnakes. [173]

Upon his return to North Haverhill in 1805, (the details of the return trip have gone unrecorded) in spite of divesting himself of most of his dependents, Ebenezer still teetered on the financial brink. Sadly, his fortunes never improved. Documents show that Ebenezer lived for a time with Betsey and Jabez in Ryegate where he might have enjoyed the ambience created by its heavily Scottish population, but the Bigelow's expanding family would have left little room for the old patriarch and he did not remain in their home for long.

North Haverhill citizens viewed Ebenezer, described as being "of slight build, sandy complexion and nervous temperament", [174] as a somewhat mysterious character who seemed to have had a celebrated past, but who was now merely an impoverished old man. The once proud patriot who had entertained youngsters like Schuyler Merrill with stories of his role in the Boston Tea Party, suffered a humiliating fate about six years before he died in 1816 at the age of seventy-nine.

Although some historians claim that Ebenezer spent his final years on a "poor farm", that is not precisely the case. Haverhill did not build an official "poor farm" until about 1838. [175] Ebenezer's ignominy occurred when he was auctioned off to a bidder who agreed to offer him room and board in exchange for unspecified "services". Elisha Hurlbutt(or Hurlburtt) "purchased" Ebenezer in what was surely a charitable act because the old man could not have done much in the way of service. [176] Ebenezer then lived in his benefactor's house until he died. It is easy to imagine that this proud man who had far exceeded the expectations of the three generations that preceded him would rather have died than expose his crumbling façade to this kind of end. Perhaps he found a kind of solace recalling lines 90-93 from part two of "Night Thoughts",

> "Thy purpose firm is equal to the deed:
> Who does the best his circumstance allows
> Does well, acts nobly; angels could do no more."

Ebenezer was buried in North Haverhill's Horse Meadow cemetery where, in death he suffered the added insult of being misidentified when the carver chiseled "Captain Philip Mackintosh, A Leader of the Boston Tea Party 1773" on Ebenezer's headstone and even this erroneous marker was not provided until 1913. [177] The error remains on the gravestone to this day. A historical sign near the entrance to the cemetery contains more accurate information about Ebenezer:

> Born in Boston and a veteran of the 1758 Battle of Ticonderoga. As a known participant in the Boston Tea Party, for his own and his children's safety, he walked to North Haverhill in early 1774. He later served in the Northern Army under General Gates in 1777. He was a shoemaker by trade and practiced his vocation here for the rest of his life. He is buried nearby in Horse Meadow Cemetery. [178]

Ebenezer Mackintosh had inherited John Mackintosh's indomitable Highland toughness, a toughness that sparked both bravery and bravado in this physically small man. That spark passed to his grandson, George, who managed to combine derring-do with the prosperity that had eluded so many in the clan's New England branch. But first it was up to Ebenezer's son Paschal and his three half-brothers, including George's future father, to make their own marks in opening up the wilderness to future generations. Each son's successful farming of the Reserve's rich acres helped turn the state of Ohio into an agricultural gemstone and provided the knowledge that helped George do the same for the northeast corner of what became the state of Colorado.

Historical marker commemorating Ebenezer Mackintosh. North Haverhill, New Hampshire. Photo by the author.

CHAPTER THREE

"Westward, Ho"

Paschal and Abi, bolstered by the young work force that had arrived on their doorstep, carved a productive farm out of the wilderness. Even though in his older years Paschal became increasingly eccentric and curmudgeonly, as a young married man he acted with a mixture of benevolence and practicality by housing his half-brothers (and for several years his father) in his frontier cabin. And, although Ebenezer eventually returned to his poverty-stricken life in New Hampshire, his sons faced much rosier futures in the Old Northwest.

What Abi thought of this bounty of boys is not known. Having come from a large family herself, she could have coped with the increase in her household and may have even welcomed the group as an antidote for the farm wife's chronic loneliness, but she bought companionship at the cost of losing privacy in her young marriage. Adding four people to the McIntosh log cabin at one fell swoop would have put a strain on the available living space. That space was pushed to its limits in 1804 when she and Paschal had the first of their own nine children. [179]

While the boys doubtlessly enjoyed the novelty of their surroundings, before long the harsh realities of helping Paschal and Abi shape their homestead catapulted them into adult roles. Before he left the region, Ebenezer apprenticed both Moses and John to local farmers. Moses remained in Mantua under the guiding hand of Amzi Atwater, the distinguished brother of Paschal's rival,

Jotham, and a member of two different surveying teams from Connecticut. John went to John Leavitt, the man who had named Mantua and who now lived in Warren Township, Trumbull County, about twenty miles from Mantua.[180] The miles between the two communities distanced John from his family more than we might think.

Today, when well-paved roads crisscross the Mantua region, there is nothing to show how rudimentary were the means of access through that area well into the early years of the nineteenth century. The first pioneers, consumed by the heavy physical labor of land-clearing, took full advantage of the paths laid down by natives as well as those established by large animals. Each new settler, eager to have some companionable links in this lonely land, made a trail to his nearest neighbor. Between 1801 and 1820 the industrious Amzi Atwater and others cleared several roads through Mantua, but "clearing" a road was a misnomer: it was just too difficult to remove all obstructions such as rocks and tree trunks. (In 1813 George's uncle David McIntosh became noted for the road he "cut...from Shalersville to Freedom", about a four-mile stretch cleaved out of the forest). [181]

His older brothers complied with Ebenezer's arrangements regarding apprenticeship, but David was contrary, perhaps because he had been more coddled as the youngest son. Echoing the hints of "disorder" in John Mackintosh's seventeenth-century home, the boy expressed unhappiness with "the treatment he received in [Paschal's] family." [182] Although Abi was reputed to be a good cook, famed for her venison and crabapple mince pies, and a "genial hospitable lady" [183] who probably did her best to care for the boys, she had a baby of her own in 1804 and David likely felt displaced by the infant.

Abby's pregnancy left her in a frightening situation. The few married women in early Mantua faced the prospect of giving birth unaided in a community largely composed of men. No doctor was eager to traverse the wilderness paths, especially during cold and muddy winter conditions, so the New England transplants resorted to an ingeniously frugal method of securing medical services. It was a plan that would have appealed about seventy years later to Paschal's thrifty nephew George. In the winter of 1804-05 two other Mantua pioneer women also expected babies. Their husbands clubbed together to engage a Doctor Thompson who agreed to live with each of the families in turn until a child was born. Then he would move on to the next of the three families. The man whose baby appeared last would be responsible for all of the charges. Paschal was one of the lucky two whose child was born free of charge: his son, John W., arrived first, on February 4, 1805. [184]

John W.'s arrival upset the balance in the small home and created new demands on Abi's time. Both Paschal and Abi were too busy and perhaps too unschooled themselves (although Paschal's letter to Betsey shows he was a lively writer) to provide what David wanted most — a good education. Mantua would not have its first school until seven years later. But yet again an empathetic member of the community stepped in to aid a McIntosh child.

David found refuge with Amzi Atwater and his wife, Huldah (1785-1845) in their Mantua home southeast of Paschal's place. One wonders what Moses, laboring in Atwater's fields, thought of his somewhat impertinent younger brother's arrival. Atwater, however, was David's kindred spirit. After helping to survey parts of the Western Reserve, Atwater had returned to the East to work briefly in New York before seeking out his uncle Noah for further tutelage. In 1800 he claimed his land in Mantua and began farming, but his education also enabled him to participate in other occupations. Elected in 1808 as an associate common pleas judge,[185] Atwater was also something of an entrepreneur as the proprietor of Mantua's first hotel. Because he knew firsthand the stultifying effects of poverty in his childhood and the uplifting effects of a real education, his financial successes inspired charitable acts that included taking David in and establishing Mantua's first school in his home in 1807.

Atwater sent David to school in Hudson, a town so small that he cannot have avoided rubbing shoulders with the eight-year old future abolitionist, John Brown. Even though Atwater paid for much of David's schooling, the tuition came at some cost to David, too. As a lodger at the Reverend David Bacon's (1771-1817) house, he was expected to help pay for his room and board by doing a number of chores. David's most onerous task was that of carrying Bacon's son Leonard (1802- 1881) on his back to school when the weather was bad. Those notorious stump-studded Western Reserve roads made David a rough mount and Leonard soon declined the piggy-back rides in favor of using his own legs.[186]

After attending another school in Warren (where John worked), David continued his studies in Vermont. He visited his father at least once before returning to Mantua in about 1814 to work on Judge Atwater's farm for twelve dollars a month until he was about twenty-years old. He also took more classes in bordering Shalersville where he would eventually make his home and then farmed on contract land that soon became his property. On November 2, 1818 he married Harriet Smith (1799-1884). The couple had five children, but only their daughters, Maria and Angeline, survived to adulthood. He supported his family by farming, but David's education opened other possibilities that could be realized and garner him local fame even as he farmed. [187]

David likely served as a role model in later years for his nephew, George, at least regarding real estate and agricultural practices. David thrived on buying, selling and owning land and was considered a canny farmer, all qualities that appeared later in his nephew. He displayed great interest in both civic and agrarian affairs, establishing the Portage County Infirmary in 1839 and founding the Portage County Agricultural Society of which he was president from 1848-1853. He also served as a member of the State Board of Agriculture (1852-1854). David's sense of duty included membership in the Ohio Militia, where he rose to the rank of Major General. During the Civil War the sixty-seven year old patriot helped organize Union army regiments. And, if you stroll the sidewalks of Mantua, Shalersville, Ravenna and other Portage County towns today, you will see American flags flying from lamp posts, flags still purchased with funds generated from an initial $1000 trust established by David McIntosh. [188]

As the McIntosh boys matured, Mantua began to turn into a small town that could meet its residents' most basic needs. The "roads" that connected neighbors gave rise to social institutions like churches. Paschal and Abi helped found Mantua's Methodist Church in September of 1807. Before 1825 Ohio Methodists made few inroads in creating church buildings [189] and therefore most often held their religious services in members' homes. The Mantua church's first congregation met in Abraham Honey's cabin that fall and consisted of the McIntoshes and four men. [190] They formed the nucleus of a Methodist congregation that was to flourish in Mantua. The Reserve's New England Calvinists competed with the Methodists for parishioners, but eventually the Methodist Church would predominate in Ohio [191] and in the McIntosh family. George grew up as a member of that denomination and at least two uncles on his mother's side were ordained Methodist ministers in the church George attended.

At the time of the Mantua Methodist church's founding, Paschal held deeply-felt religious sentiments that increased over the years to a point that jeopardized his relationship with his fellow worshipers. He may have been influenced by the popular open-air revival meetings conducted by traveling Methodist preachers in the Reserve in the nineteenth century. Often going on for days on end, the revivals attracted large numbers of people who prayed loudly, sang, preached, and confessed. Hysterical reactions were not uncommon. The result was a thorough cleansing of emotions, but revival-induced conversions did not always last. [192]

In some ways Paschal was similar to the character of Uncle Aleck in Albert Gallatin Riddle's 1873 novel *Bart Ridgeley: A Story of Northern Ohio*. Uncle Aleck, an otherwise likeable fellow, was prone to "constant conversations and mild disputations of Bible texts and doctrines, and sermonizing at the Sunday assemblies of his co-believers." Not only that, but his "sermons were faulty and confused, his language vicious, and his pronunciations depraved, so that he furnished occasional provocation…" [193] According to contemporary accounts, Paschal's religiosity bordered on the fanaticism Uncle Aleck exhibited. Paschal exercised "strict religious discipline" [194] that could be tough to sustain. He demonstrated the strength of his convictions and the self-torture caused if he felt himself wavering even slightly in his faith when he told his sister, "We join'd the Methodist Church nearly twenty years ago, but we have been unfaithfull, we have often turnd aside from the holy commandment deliver'd unto us, & we have not now that evidence of our acceptance with God that we have had in times past…" He despaired of modern developments: "There is reason to fear that the Methodist people as a body are falling, and becoming more & more conformd to this world…" He worried that his half-brothers had become religious slackers.[195] Few were swayed by Paschal's unequivocal religious beliefs, including John, who turned away from such severity to raise his family in a devout, but more open-minded atmosphere.

In 1825 Paschal suffered expulsion from the church he and Abi had helped establish, an event that could account for his despairing letter. It seems likely that he had been questioning the true devotion of his fellow parishioners to a point they found intolerable. Harmon recalled that Paschal had a "considerable amount of difficulty with his bretheren (sic) of the church, notwithstanding his professions of piety…" [196] But that unhappy event lay in the future. A far larger event disrupted all of their lives when the War of 1812 began.

The United States, tired of British meddling with American shipping and the country's habit of forcibly impressing American sailors into service, had declared war on Great Britain on June 18, 1812. The young United States suspected strongly that the British had aided the Indians in their run-ins with settlers in the Northwest Territory. Many felt that the only way to rid the area of the British was to "conquer Canada", [197] so the struggle came to be viewed as a second war of independence.

Moses McIntosh's name appears seldom in the public records, except as a voter and taxpayer. He owned a farm in Mantua that he left in 1812 at the age of twenty-three to serve in the War of 1812 when most of Portage County's "able-bodied white male inhabitants between the ages of 18 and 45" made themselves available for military duty.[198] Moses was the only one of the McIntosh brothers to enroll. John was probably completing his service to John Leavitt. Paschal, forty-five at the time, was ineligible for the draft. David still studied in Vermont.

Moses served as a corporal in Captain Hezekiah Nooney's company along with Amzi Atwater's son, Jonathan. [199] On September 15, 1812 Moses' company was among those "notified to hold themselves in readiness to march at a moment's warning." [200] The men lacked both training and sufficient weapons, recalling the conditions under which Moses' great-great grandfather John fought at the Battle of Worcester and those that Ebenezer experienced in the French and Indian War. The homespun soldiers knew how to fire guns – their lives as settlers depended on their shooting skills —but a professional army they were not. [201] Like the other state militias created to battle the British and Indian forces, Ohio's did not take well to military discipline and some refused to "fight outside the borders of their own states."[202]

Moses went on to serve for various stretches of time from September 28, 1812 until March 14, 1815 in the military company led by Nooney's replacement, Captain Thomas Delaun Mills, the same man who had employed Abi in his home when Paschal first met her. The company only got as far as Sandusky and Moses left the army in March of 1815, returning to his farm in Mantua.

It was Paschal's outspokenness early in the war that represented a misstep his neighbors were not to forgive or forget. He had never been one to hide his opinions behind a civil veil. The older he grew, the more impolitic he became. According to a contemporary who did not memorialize Paschal's exact words, he uttered views that his neighbors deemed antithetical to the interests of the United States government. Once again his intemperate behavior calls Ebenezer to mind. But while Ebenezer had directed his provocative actions at a largely popular cause, his son's strongly worded opinions apparently seemed near traitorous. Even though many in the Reserve shared some of Paschal's doubts about the need to fight this war, his inability to voice those concerns moderately made his neighbors distinctly uneasy when their nerves were already frayed by the idea of a battle that would come very close to their doorsteps. Paschal's fellow citizens "made it rather unpleasant for him to continue his residence there". [203]

But the farmer put on a brave front when he moved his family in late 1812 or early 1813 to the nearby township of Hubbard in Trumbull County close to the Pennsylvania state line. Residents of the Western Reserve had been advised to flee to Pittsburgh should the British invade the territory, so he could have saved face by using that excuse for leaving during this uncomfortable period. He did not abandon his well-established farm in Mantua, but rented it out for the duration of the war. In 1813 while reaping his fields in Hubbard, Paschal's misfortunes multiplied when a wheat-beard, the sharply bristled tip of wheat grass, flew up and cut his right eye. He lost sight in that eye. At the age of fifty-seven he wrote pathetically to Elizabeth , "Yes, my sister, I am now a poor, old, one-eyed man." [204]

Paschal was not the only one who feared that the federal government would be unable to protect them should the Reserve be invaded and that a reduced population of women and old men could not protect themselves. Their fears eased considerably when on September 10, 1813 Captain Oliver H. Perry and his naval force defeated the British at the Battle of Lake Erie on Put-In-Bay, Lake Erie.[205] Because most of the battles from then on took place in regions far-removed from the Reserve, relieved residents were finally able to resume their lives with some sense of normalcy. The Treaty of Ghent, signed in December of 1814, effectively ended the war, although one more engagement occurred early in the following month. The Americans could claim victory.

Paschal and his family returned to Mantua in the early spring months of 1815. It was not the best of homecomings because he managed to cause more estrangement from his neighbors, although this time it was not entirely his fault. His children suffered from whooping cough. Their germs spread rapidly throughout Mantua where the citizens had previously escaped the highly contagious and deadly childhood ailment. [206]

George's father John conducted his life in a much quieter, more self-effacing manner than did either David or Paschal. Twenty-one-years old in 1815 and freed from working for Leavitt, he bought the southeast quarter of Lot No. 24 in Mantua. The lot was situated close to the Cuyahoga River, making it a very appealing place. The house John constructed in 1822 remained his home until his death thirty years later. His decision to stay in the area to farm meant that all of Ebenezer's sons worked as farmers in Mantua. Even if they eventually moved, they never went farther away than neighboring Shalersville. Ebenezer's decision to deposit his sons in Portage County turned out to be the right one. All found stability in their flourishing farms, a stability that the turbulent era and urban setting in which Ebenezer grew to manhood had denied him. His sons knew all too well their father's financial failings; that image must have served as a perpetual goad to them to do better.

Paschal took some pride in his half-brothers' accomplishments, but his religious convictions reduced his praise for them by a notch or two: "All my Brothers have good farms near me, and are doing well, for this world, but they do not appear to extend their views beyond this world." [207] By the time Paschal wrote these lines, Ebenezer had been "beyond this world" for ten years. Although the old shoemaker had delivered his sons to the Western Reserve hoping that they might succeed where he had not, he would have been amazed by the degree of their success.

On February 18, 1818, two years after his father's death, twenty-eight-year old John, who had deferred marriage until he could represent himself as a man of property, married New York native Jerusha Ferris (1799-1874). They were wed in Mantua by Amzi Atwater in his capacity as a judge. A fragile, yellowed slip of paper is the only official documentation of their marriage. (Even so, the handwritten certificate is more than George and his wife would have – their marriage more than fifty years later would go unrecorded). Atwater recorded the event perfunctorily: "The State of Portage County S3[?] It is hereby certified that John McIntosh and Jarusha [sic] Ferris were this day joined in marriage by me. Amzi Atwater Just. Peace Mantua Fe. 1ˢᵗ 1818."

Jerusha was the daughter of John Ferris (1760-1841) and Jerusha Lockwood Ferris (1760-?) of Pond Ridge, New York. She had accompanied her brother Charles Grandison Ferris (1791-1867) [208] and some other members of the family to Mantua sometime before 1818. In the 1820s Jerusha's parents joined their children who had already settled in Portage County, living in Shalersville until their youngest sons, John (1801-?) and Joseph (1804-?), became ordained Methodist ministers in 1831. [209] The young men preached in the Mantua Methodist Church to a congregation that eventually included George and his family.

In 1826, eight years after his younger brothers had taken the plunge, Moses married Rebecca Bright (1806-1863) in Ravenna, Ohio. Their relatively small family (three children named Lovilla, Jones and Osman) farmed in the heart of what became Mantua Station, one of the three villages eventually comprising Mantua Township: Mantua Corners where George and his family lived, Mantua Station and Mantua Center. None of the villages was more than a mile or two distant from the others.

John and Jerusha's own family began with four children born in rapid succession at about two-year intervals (suggesting that Jerusha used breastfeeding as a natural method of birth control): Lorena (1819-1839), Ranson Ebenezer ("Eb") (1821-1896), Caroline (1823-1825) and John Henry ("Hen") (1825-1912). Four years later Joseph ("Jo") (1829-1873) and Caroline Lorinda ("Rind") (1830-1863) were born. Then it seemed that Jerusha's childbearing years were at an end, but seven years later she began the process again, giving birth to George Robin (1837-1924) and Newell N. (1843-1871). [210] Jerusha was thirty-eight and forty-four, respectively, when her last children were born. Just a little over ten years before John and Jerusha began to have children, the average size for an American Caucasian family was reckoned to be seven to eight offspring, [211] so the couple produced the statistical average, meeting the nineteenth-century expectation of producing numerous children, essential when farming was the family business and many hands were needed to accomplish all the chores.

George began his life in the same year that the young Victoria ascended the throne, Michigan became the nation's twenty-sixth state, and the future President Grover Cleveland was born. Other notables born in 1837 were the Ohio author William Dean Howells, financier John Pierpont Morgan, and

James Butler Hickok, otherwise known as "Wild Bill" Hickok. Charles Dickens' *Oliver Twist* had begun to appear as a serialized novel, Samuel Morse patented his telegraph invention, and Louis Jacques Mande Daguerre discovered a method of photography he termed the *daguerreotype*.

In 1837 a gazetteer characterized the Western Reserve's population as "an enterprising, virile, intelligent and homogeneous community of farmers with just enough millers, manufacturers, merchants and professional men to supply the local demand." [212] This cheery assessment ignored both the reality of the area *and* the many female contributions to the Reserve's development. Nonetheless, Mantua had begun to shed some of its roughness and started to appear more like a real town in the 1830s. A Greek Revival Town Hall, built around the time that George was born, was just one of the public buildings of which Mantua could boast.

Mantua, Ohio's citizens were justly proud of the buildings constructed around the time of George's birth that made their town a more refined place to live. The Mantua Town Hall, built in the Greek Revival style, circa 1836-1840, stands next to Christ Church (foreground) and would have been a familiar sight to George McIntosh. Photo by the author.

Mantua was also an economically stable town, at least until just before George was born and the situation changed. Martin van Buren (1782-1862), inaugurated as the eighth President of the United States on March 4, 1837 (just a little over two months before George was born), inherited a panic-stricken country from his predecessor Andrew Jackson (1767-1845). The financial bubble created by excited speculation in manufacturing, new transportation systems, and the rise of numerous new banks "resulted in an overextension of credit." [213] Both banks and shops failed in ominously large numbers. The Western Reserve counties felt the economic depression in the summer of George's birth when the price of commodities dipped precipitously in Ohio. By August of 1837 John McIntosh faced a 40 per cent downturn in the price of wheat. Only pork, a Reserve staple, held its value. [214]

Fortunately for the McIntoshes, while urban workers suffered, farms like theirs went on. They would have felt the pinch, but John could feed his children and keep them warm. The depression lasted well into the 1840s, so George's early years were tinged with a concern about finances that may have influenced his thrifty ways as an adult when he took carefully calculated risks with his money, but did not hesitate to cut his losses before they had too great a negative impact.

When George and Newell were born, they occupied a far different space than the one some of their older siblings had experienced. Lorena and Ranson spent their infancies in a log cabin, but their parents' hopes for the family demanded a larger and more enduring accommodation. They planned a house whose design was far from haphazard. Just as seventeenth-century Dedham citizens had built in the English village style they knew, so did Western Reserve families from New England reflect their architectural heritage in their frontier homes. John would likely not have had access to any of the several home design books in circulation at the time, so he and Jerusha would have relied upon rough sketches of their own, laying out the sizes and locations of rooms, entrances to those rooms, windows, and the all-important hearth before beginning construction.[215]

The home the young McIntoshes planned was a roomy two-story frame house built in a modified Federal style marked by a central doorway flanked by identical windows. "The impressive, symmetrical façade was meant for display to passersby and faced the road." [216] It would be many years, however, before their standard of living matched the home's façade. But, important for the people who built them, these homes evoked the character of towns like North Haverhill and connected the frontier populace to something evocative of the refinement that did not yet characterize towns like Mantua.

Transforming the frontier townships into surroundings more recognizable to Easterners helped further solidify the notion of the West as being part of the United States. The area's metamorphosis was astounding. In 1819 John Wright traveled through the Western Reserve, publishing his observations in *Letters from the West or A Caution to Immigrants*. He noted the presence of "many handsome and well cultivated farms, with large and convenient houses, the barns well filled and the cattle looking thrifty." [217] Wright's impressions were a bit misleading, just as were those of the 1837 gazetteer's author. In truth, visitors from the East were often dismayed by the Ohioans' rustic living conditions; they reported equally crude diets, clothing and manners. Foreign travelers, too, could exhibit disheartening condescension toward the pioneers. Frances Trollope, mother of the prolific English Victorian novelist, Anthony Trollope, made her own trip to Ohio (Cincinnati) in 1827. Her reactions to American demeanor (she misunderstood much of what she observed) appeared five years later as *Domestic Manners of the Americans*. Although she admired the landscapes she traveled through, she deplored Americans' casual familiarity with strangers like herself, their habit of leaving doors unlocked so as to facilitate social interaction, and the lack of proper observance of the Sabbath. Mrs. Trollope made absolutely no allowances for the necessity of the near continual labor needed to keep the wilderness at bay. [218]

Even had they known of them, John and Jerusha would not have allowed Mrs. Trollope's criticisms to affect them. They had justifiably high expectations for their new home. John created most of the lumber for the house by hand, even though by 1818 Mantua had a sawmill. He felled giant trees and then cut them into the shapes and sizes needed. [219] The marks of his axe are still clearly visible today on the mantelpiece and interior beams of the home, tangible and moving evidence of the sheer amount of physical labor that went into constructing a durable building whose longevity was virtually guaranteed by the care with which it was built.

Their neighbors who helped raise the house where George was born approached the event "in a spirit of fun and sport." [220] The dramatic and convivial community house-raising solidified bonds in an area where neighbors might not see each other for days on end. While the men worked at the taxing, dangerous job of hoisting heavy timbers and fixing the framework into place, the women served a bounty of food. Men and women alike eased aching muscles by drinking copiously of Portage County's staple product, whiskey. Thomas Pegram notes that "By 1820 American drinkers were enjoying a whiskey glut; whiskey and cider [Mantua excelled at the production of both] stood supreme as the national beverages." [221]

People expected the raw distilled and extremely potent liquor (the same that had been introduced so disastrously to the native tribes) to be served at such gatherings. Drunkenness became a real problem in the area, leading to the creation of the Portage County Temperance Society just seven years before George's birth. In spite of the temperance group, George still witnessed scenes of drunkenness in the Mantua community and in the McIntosh home. Influenced by Methodist teachings and the increased presence of the temperance movement in Ohio, George might have shunned the bottle anyway, but it would be alcohol's effect on one of his brothers that made George conclude decisively that he would never drink hard liquor.

John McIntosh's home was one of the first of its kind in that section. Standing today at the southeast corner of Highway 82 and Vaughn Road in the shade of huge old sugar maples and Norwegian spruces, it is still a family residence. A few windows have been added, but the house has otherwise changed little since the late-nineteenth-century. The Cuyahoga River, "until the mid-nineteenth-century…a clear stream winding through marsh grass and wildflowers",[222] once meandered across the lot and forests bordered the land John cleared to make room for cultivation. The river made it possible to irrigate easily the loamy acres around them. George lived for the first nineteen years of his life in that house, storing up memories of both its style and the water that coursed through his father's land. As an adult he would put both memories to good use.

Open fields extend along the now paved Vaughn Road (the Vaughns were close neighbors), recalling the small 108-acre farm once belonging to John.[223] The generally scaled-down Mantua farms continued the New England tradition of something like subsistence farming until the Ohio-Erie Canal opened in 1832, making it possible for farmers to buy and sell a greater variety of goods. But the ideal of small-scale farming promulgated by Thomas Jefferson in his

The exterior of the house John McIntosh built in Mantua in 1822 suggests comparisons with New England houses constructed in the Federal style. This is the home in which George McIntosh was born in 1837 and where he lived until he was a young adult. Photo by the author.

Notes on Virginia, published first in Paris in 1784, was still very much alive during George's formative years.

Jefferson said, "Those who labor in the earth are the chosen people of God, if ever He had a chosen people, whose breasts He has made His peculiar deposit for substantial and genuine virtue." [224] Jefferson's high-flown words had a profound effect on the American nation. His view of democratic ideals combined with agrarian goals to form an "'agricultural fundamentalism', a belief in the social, economic, and political superiority of rural citizenry", that grew to be an accepted philosophy in the United States. [225]   Portage County farmers might not have articulated Jefferson's theories in the same way, but they believed in his agrarian vision. George later rejected the model derived from Jefferson's words and thus rejected his own father's style of farming. George would deliberately acquire far more land to devote to agriculture while retaining the notion of the moral "goodness" of working the land. His vision would prove to be the more successful one.

The McIntoshes had to continue toiling mightily just to eke out a living from their small farm. The "substantial and genuine virtue" of doing so was probably not always at the forefront of their minds as they pursued their daily tasks. As the children grew older they joined their parents in the work, but at first it was just John and Jerusha. Besides clearing land, plowing, planting, harvesting, and hunting game John had to make their furniture, farming implements, barrels to hold produce, and more. Jerusha likewise labored to make meals and clothing for her increasing family, hauled water, laundered with handmade soap, (clean items had to be draped over bushes or on the grass to dry because there were no clothespins) and tended to a kitchen garden, in addition to her many childcare duties.

George grew up in a humble household where everyone wore homespun garments and were just as likely as not to go shoeless. Jerusha wove and spun flax to create tough "tow", the coarse part of the flax that she turned into pants for her boys. The scratchy material stood up to tree-climbing and rough games, saving her hours of mending time.[226] The family's food was equally plain, centered around corn the family grew. Cornmeal mush, Johnny cakes and Indian pudding were just three of the variants Jerusha cooked in a Dutch oven over the fireplace in the middle of the first floor (in the hot months she retreated to her summer kitchen, an extension at the side of the house).

Despite what seem to us today like fairly unappetizing meals, most people who were George's contemporaries recalled the tantalizingly delicious smells of such food and how much they looked forward to consuming it, especially after a hard day working on the farm. Salmon Brown (1836-1919), one of John Brown's twenty children, and Ohio native son and author, William Dean Howells, both savored memories of the corn dishes. Howells recalled a favorite meal prepared by his mother. "I think there can be no doubt that the new corn grated from the cob while still in the milk, and then molded and put in…to brown in the glow of…embers, would still have the sweetness that was incomparable then." [227] John and his boys could add some protein to a meal by hunting for the still plentiful game in the forests around them or by fishing in the river.

Eventually, the McIntoshes would raise chickens and dairy cows, livestock that gave them meat, eggs, milk, and butter and cheese. Just about everyone kept pigs, so pork became Mantua's other staple food in the first half of the nineteenth century. Jerusha hung smoked ham from hooks in the attic beams. Known as "razorbacks", landsharks" or "railsplitters", the hogs ran free until it was slaughtering time, gorging themselves during the summer months on nuts and roots. [228] They became almost feral (some grew six- to eight-inch long tusks) and had to be lured home with Indian corn for fall slaughtering. If the animals had confined themselves to the forests where they liked to root (and became tempting bait to hungry bears), all would have been well, but they ranged freely around the homesteads, too, raiding precious orchards and gardens.

The McIntoshes supplemented meat, corn, turnips and cabbage with the potatoes that still grow so well in Mantua. However, it was apples that both George and Newell savored as they were growing up. But even the simple apple was to cause irritated amusement at Paschal's expense for many in Mantua in an incident that solidified his reputation as a cantankerous eccentric. "[Paschal]…took great pains in the culture of…peach and apple trees [so]…at an early day he had a large supply of peaches and apples,…" [229] He became renowned for his bountiful orchards in a region famed for its apples. It was Abi who had provided the beginnings of the "first fruit bearing orchard" in Portage County from seeds from her family's Connecticut fruit trees. [230] Paschal's success, though, caused him to run afoul of his community again.

It is no wonder that George and Newell reminisced about Mantua apples while both were serving in the Civil War. Just the names of the kinds of apples grown in early nineteenth-century Mantua make the mouth water: Sops of Wine and Yellow Transparent, (summer apples); Wealthy, Maiden-Blush, and Nonpareil (fall apples); and, in the winter months, Baldwin, Northern Spy, and Mammoth Blacktwig.[231] Paschal planted his apple trees on higher ground than most in the town, so their fruit withstood the frosts that sometimes came late in spring. [232] The abundance of fruit on his trees tempted many to pilfer from them. His standing as a cranky, miserly man who was already something of a pariah because of his unpopular views made him an attractive target for those who would not normally have robbed a neighboring farmer.

But that is precisely what young ruffians were about to do. Stealthy nighttime attacks on the trees occurred regularly. Paschal became enraged about the nocturnal raids. He sat up at night to guard the apples (an almost impossible task for a farmer who had to rise early) and, when that became too difficult, paid others to keep watch. It is some measure of the enduring community antagonism toward the aging farmer that the sentries he hired had no compunction about charging people a small fee to enter his fields and gather fruit in the dark.

In the autumn of 1819 Paschal harvested his apples, storing the aromatic bushels in his locked barn. He felt that at last the crop was safe and he could enjoy this "richer, sweeter pause in farm life", as Riddle described it in *The Portrait: A Romance of the Cuyahoga Valley*, [233] an 1874 novel set in Mantua. But he hadn't reckoned on the impudence of the teenaged thieves Harvey Baldwin and Royal Taylor from nearby Aurora who managed to break into the barn and make off with some of the apples. And *they* had not reckoned with Paschal's iron-willed determination to protect his hard-won property. He spotted them (not bad for a man with one eye!) sneaking away from the barn and roused his neighbors to join in his pursuit of the miscreants.

Paschal seems to have been inherently unable to behave in measured ways. He responded with excessive vehemence to a relatively minor crime, although the disrespectful act did symbolize an assault on his livelihood. Perhaps he was afraid that he would be seen as a truly soft mark if he did not demand full prosecution of the thieves. Harvey and Royal eluded capture that night, but Paschal's frenzied demands that someone be found guilty finally convinced two justices of the peace to question a number of youthful suspects from Aurora. The Grand Jury indicted several of the boys, including at least one who was clearly innocent, but no convictions resulted from the ensuing trial, [234] an outcome that must have infuriated Paschal. Nothing in his half-brothers' lives suggested anything approaching Paschal's contentiousness and they must have felt extremely embarrassed about the incident.[235]

Paschal's battles were public ones, but women like Abi and Jerusha fought more quietly against the many threats to their families. They faced terrible diseases like cholera, diphtheria, whooping cough, and measles that menaced families before the advent of inoculations, antibiotics, and safe painkillers. Burns, cuts, and broken limbs, insect and snake bites were also a normal part of raising a family on a Mantua farm.

Jerusha grew medicinal herbs that could at least ease certain symptoms. But Jerusha faced an insurmountable challenge when she tried to treat young George's severe asthma, also sometimes called *phthisis* in the nineteenth century. Asthma plagued him his entire life. This chronic and little understood condition was a constant worry that created special demands on his mother's herbal knowledge. To ease George's considerable breathing problems she probably turned to plants such as thyme, comfrey, or pennyroyal for teas. But these decoctions would have given George only temporary relief.

His asthma represented a serious impediment to any child in the nineteenth century, but especially to one who lived on an Ohio farm. Because allergies can set off an asthmatic episode, dust from grains and freshly plowed fields, pollen, mold, poultry feathers, animal dander — all represented potential threats to George. Mantua's cold, wet winters and humid summers also did his lungs no good. During an attack George felt his chest grow tight. He wheezed and coughed. He struggled to expel his breath, causing sweating, anxiety and sometimes a feeling of drowning. The attack could last minutes – or hours. Nineteenth-century doctors tended to see asthma as another form of consumption (tuberculosis), so one can understand how worried the family was about George's illness.

The disease tends to run in families. George's cousin, Milton (1833-1917) was ineligible for the Civil War draft because of his phthisis, causing Hen McIntosh's wife, Maria (1829-?),[236] to accuse Milton in a letter to George (August 23, 1864) of malingering. [237] Maria's hypocrisy regarding Milton appears when, in the same letter, she mentioned that her daughter, Addie, "has the Phthisic to day she has it hard some times I am afraid she will always be troubled with it". And at least one of George's own children inherited the disease.

Alfred Beaumont Maddock observed in his 1844 *Practical Observations on the Efficacy of Medicated Inhalations in the Treatment of Pulmonary Consumption, Bronchitis, Chronic Cough and Other Diseases of the Respiratory Organs, and also Affections of the Heart* (a title that would test an asthmatic's ability to utter it in one breath):"The hereditary, the more frequent cause,[as opposed to accidental] descending from persons of a hectic constitution, usually indicated by a smooth, fair, and rosy complexion, light eyes, large transparent blue veins, fair or red hair, a narrow pointed chest, high prominent shoulders, long thin neck, and generally slender frame..." [238] Certainly not all asthmatics match this profile, but George possessed many of the characteristics mentioned above. Like his grandfather Ebenezer, he was thin and small of stature, with blue eyes and sandy-colored hair.

His sister Rind referred to George's poor health several times in her 1856 diary, recording on January 22 that eighteen-year old "Bro. George was sick" and on February 26 that "Joe got some medicine for George." The medicine Jo obtained for his younger brother was probably laudanum. Laudanum, an opium derivative mixed with alcohol, caused the desired expectoration, but it could also become an addictive narcotic. Even in the early nineteenth century many physicians viewed laudanum as a risky remedy for the asthmatic because an improper dose could suffocate the patient. [239] Nonetheless, the McIntoshes used both laudanum and quinine when they felt ill, as did many nineteenth-century families. Rind resorted to one or the other for those times when she felt "half sick", a recurring condition mentioned in her diaries.

Asthma derailed George sometimes, but his parents couldn't dispense entirely with his help. As Robert Jones has noted in his history of Ohio agriculture, "While farms varied in size, emphasis, and stage of improvement, there were chores for the men and boys on every one of them..."[240] If his lungs couldn't tolerate leading a horse repeatedly around a barn floor strewn with bunches of grain to be threshed by plodding hoofs, [241] or if he couldn't rake hay, he was capable of innumerable other essential tasks. A boy could plant potatoes, weed fields and his mother's garden (a job Howells despised as a lad), tend livestock, or harvest apples, among many other things. The chores may not have been fun, but they gave George much of the practical know-how required when he began farming on his own. He gained much of the rest of his agricultural knowledge by observing the rest of his family at work. Especially valuable to him was discovering that his father was "forced to make old tools serve new uses; to shape former habits...and ideas to changed conditions; and to find new means when the old proved inapplicable." [242] George learned these lessons well. Years later as a Colorado farmer he was highly regarded for his flexible responses to agricultural changes. Increased profits were his reward.

Agriculture may have been at the core of Mantua's existence, but transplanted New Englanders like John and Jerusha also placed a special emphasis on education. Even though learning was often a hit-or-miss proposition for families whose children had to work on the farm, George and his brothers and sisters all received a common school education – they could read, write and do arithmetic. Western Reserve schools, influenced by the high standards brought by its settlers, usually offered better educations than those in southern Ohio. [243]

Even so, farming demands on students' time meant that most did not attend school for more than three to six months annually.

Both George and Rind became teachers for short periods. Rind taught in a district school in Mantua or Hiram for several months in 1855.[244] Her diary records the ebb and flow of students – she never knew exactly how many "scholars" she would have on a given day. Although she was a mature twenty-five years old in 1855, Rind was tested severely on May 10 by the behavior of "some pretty wild children." Later in the month she noted that both boys and girls tended to wander off for hours, often "to the swamp". She did not hesitate to administer what seems to have been ineffective discipline, even when the miscreants were sons of neighbors. On June 18 she "feruled [smacked with a ruler] George Brigs and Henry Vaughn for putting pins under each other." George, who enjoyed good-natured pranks, may very well have been feruled himself occasionally.

George's much-loved older sister, Caroline Lorinda or "Rind", circa late-1850s. Rind's loyalty to her family endured even when it was tested severely by their brother Jo's alcoholic binges. Courtesy of Judith Rice-Jones.

When on March 9, 1863 Rind wrote a letter to her older brother Eb from Otoe County, Nebraska (Territory) where she and her husband Abner Clark Reed had settled after leaving Ohio seven years earlier, she gave several examples of the importance of education to the McIntosh family. She lamented the illiteracy of a fifteen-year old Missouri girl who had lived with the Reeds in the winter of 1862 because she "had never been to school but 3 wks. in her whole life." Rind goes on to boast that nine-year old Charley, Reed's son by his first marriage, "has been to school about 9 months last year…Ida [Caroline and Abner's firstborn daughter, almost five when this letter was written] went 4 wks last Fall. We have to pay $2.50 a term for schooling. But it is close by. There are many children in Nebraska that get no schooling at all."

When George was six Amzi Atwater donated land specifically intended for the construction of a traditional "little red schoolhouse". George's Uncle Moses "furnished lumber" for the construction [245] and Atwater's thirty-eight-year old son, Darwin, earned $14 a month as the school's first teacher. He would have tried to inculcate the three Rs into his students, but not much more. The choice of textbooks often depended on what was available to the teacher. Commonly used were the *Bible*, *A History of the Life and Death, Virtues and Exploits of General George Washington* by Mason Locke "Parson" Weems that underwent successive printings after initially appearing in 1800, a spelling book, the *Western Calculator*, and a grammar, although most early Reserve instructors did not have enough knowledge of grammar themselves to teach that subject. [246] Grammatical deficiencies and erratic spelling add character to the delightfully descriptive letters exchanged among George and his siblings. Rind was the best speller in the family. Some evenings she and Jo and Eb enjoyed attending "spelling schools" where lively, crowded competitions took place and Rind sometimes won. [247]

There was always time for reading in the McIntosh household, despite long hours of work. George became a lifelong reader whose family often gave him books as gifts. Rind was the same. Even after doing housework, quilting, making a carpet in many complicated steps, sewing clothes for the family and others, teaching, or working in a tailoring shop, socializing, going to church, and feeling ill frequently, she still squeezed in moments for a great deal of reading. In fact, it was unusual for her to be without a book. If the titles and subjects recorded in her diary are an indication, she read challenging, recently published nonfiction, such as the 1854 *History of Madame Roland* by John S. C. Abbott and *Female Life among the Mormons* by Maria Ward, 1855, as well as fiction. She also turned to books as sources of specific information. On January 18, 1855 her diary notes that she read "the law all the eveing"[sic], hoping to find a legal way of dealing with the liquor trafficking that threatened their family and friends.

Paschal may have fretted about his brother's beliefs, but John and Jerusha and their family spent most Sunday mornings at the Methodist Church in Mantua, although they did not set that day aside solely for religious thought. Especially as their children matured, the McIntoshes allowed them time on Sundays to read, write, visit friends, go boating or sleigh-riding, or even to sample other denominations, such as the Disciples of Christ or the Latter-Day Saints. [248] So they managed to combine their faith with open-minded attitudes toward others, instilling in George and his siblings a willingness to admit people who were not exactly like them into their lives. The tolerance fostered in the McIntosh household engendered curiosity in their children, enabling them to entertain new ideas and belief systems, although they certainly also evinced prejudiced viewpoints common to their social group and time. But George in particular sometimes fully embraced "otherness".

George and his siblings didn't just read and attend meetings and bees in their free time. They all enjoyed the wonderful outdoor world lying just beyond their doorstep. As the youngest children George and Newell probably enjoyed greater freedom than their older brothers had. The proximity of the Cuyahoga River gave George a chance to indulge in his lifelong love of swimming in the summer – in the winter he and Newell probably skated on the frozen river. Going for sleigh rides across the snow was a cold-weather joy for all of the McIntoshes. The boys also spent time fishing, hunting, and digging for Indian artifacts. In the spring there was fun for everyone when families tapped sugar maples to make syrup and candy, but the "warm sugar" the McIntosh children craved created problems for them, too: in her journal entry for July 24, 1855 Rind describes taking her false teeth to the dentist to be repaired.

George's partiality for country life did not preclude his interest in the great change that came to Mantua in 1854 when the Cleveland and Mahoning Valley Railroad Company finished grading for tracks in the town. [249] Not only did the work provide a spectacle for excited onlookers, many of whom had never seen a train before, but those tracks symbolized a faster exit out of Mantua than the slow boats on the Ohio-Erie Canal. By 1856 the train went all the way to Cleveland. Two years later George would use it to begin his exploration of a much wider world.

The advent of the train was only one mutation affecting the frontier township in the 1850s. Benefiting economically from the opening of the canal twenty years before, Mantua began to see a few more varied shops and services sprouting up on its main street. [250] Jerusha's nephew Osman, a physician, lived in a house "downtown" and had his office there, too. Dr. Ferris represented a rather different slice of Mantua life that marked a subtle shift in the township's balance of power, separating the township into the farm folk and the "townies", into those who earned a living by working the land and those who had a "profession", into those who had a common school education and those who enjoyed debates and talks given at the Mantua Lyceum. For his entire life George showed his allegiance to the farmers, although he enjoyed friendships with both groups of people.

Mantua's changes were, for most of George's boyhood, small ones and life went on in a rather ordinary, quiet way. There were, of course, deaths in the McIntosh family: Paschal died in 1832 and John and Jerusha lost their older daughter, Lorena, in 1839. Lorena, married to a carpenter named Erastus Young (b. 1813) the year George was born, had died after the birth of a daughter, Lorena E, [251] and George never really knew this older sister. But deaths occurred frequently in nineteenth-century Mantua. What was rare was the township's exposure to earthshaking events, so a superficial sense of unvarying continuity that accorded with the farm family's awareness of the regularity of agricultural tasks prevailed. Although Mantua and the other Portage County townships remained limited, slightly monotonous places at this time, they *were* home to a few people destined for fame, or infamy, or something in between, people who stirred the calm waters. Sometimes the waves they created passed very close to George McIntosh's family.

Five years before George's birth Joseph Smith (1805-1844) and Mormon convert and Hiram resident, Sidney Rigdon, (1793-1876) a former Baptist and then a Disciples of Christ minister who had preached in Mantua, [252] provoked some people from Portage and Geauga Counties to violence. [253] Believing that Smith intended not only to convert people to his beliefs, including polygamy, but that he was also going to buy land near Hiram for a Mormon compound, a gang of men from Hiram, Shalersville and Garretsville, all townships close to Mantua, yanked Smith from his bed in a Hiram farmhouse on the night of March 24, 1832. They tried to strangle, beat and poison him before resorting to the eighteenth-century barbarity of tarring and feathering both Smith and Rigdon. [254] The two men eventually recovered from their painful injuries and, with their families, sought a more welcoming spirit in Missouri.

An excited thrill must have passed through Mantua when it heard the news of the assaults because most people at least knew of Rigdon, although many, like the McIntoshes, would have deplored the excessive violence used against him and Smith, even as they deplored some of their teachings. Not only was Rigdon a familiar figure to Mantua and Hiram folk, he was also distantly connected to a young man who lived in Hiram and would later achieve national fame. For Rigdon had taught Greek and Latin to the father of Lucretia Rudolph who in 1858 would become the wife of James Abram Garfield (1831-1881), the twentieth president of the United States. [255]

Garfield briefly attended the Geauga Seminary in Chester, Ohio. After teaching in various district schools, he entered Hiram's brand new Western Reserve Eclectic Institute (now Hiram College), founded by the Disciples of Christ. After graduating from Williams College in Williamstown, Massachusetts, he became principal of the Institute, teaching there for the next five years. One of his students was George's cousin Alexander, who with some foresight, predicted that his teacher would one day become the nation's leader. Hiram became Garfield's "second home" [256] during the time Rind worked in a tailoring shop and lived there. It was such a small community that they must have known of each other. Her diary entry for January 28, 1855 records that she and a friend 'went to singing school at the disciple church in the evening." The Disciple Church she visited that night was one that Garfield, a devoted member of the Disciples of Christ, frequently attended.

Garfield often preached in Mantua and other Portage County homes. He visited Mantua frequently during 1852 and 1853, "speaking to the brethren". [257] One surname, in particular, leaps out when Garfield writes: "Today Bro. Foote and I received a letter from Bro. Darwin Atwater to go and speak at Mantua two weeks from yesterday."[258] He liked Darwin and spoke of the Atwaters (who lived near Moses McIntosh) as being "very fine people, and I feel very much

drawn to them…We (the young people) had a very fine walk through the pleasant groves of Bro. Atwater's large and beautiful farm. It seems that a person
might live a better life in such a place." [259] At this point in his life, when he was
struggling with a number of different emotions and directions for his life,
Garfield seems to have found some appeal in the signs of Jeffersonian agrarian-
ism all around him.

John and Jerusha did not aspire to the heights that attracted Garfield. But
during the nearly three and a half decades of their marriage they helped form
the backbone of the Western Reserve. Their long partnership sadly ended in
the late summer of 1852 when sixty-one year old John died on the 24th of
August "before sunrise" as Rind noted in her journal on the third anniversary of
her father's death. He left behind his wife and six surviving children. Jo, perhaps because of his addiction to liquor, still lived at home with his siblings Rind,
George and Newell. Eb and Henry were already married and living in their
own places. Under Ohio law at the time Jerusha was allowed to keep little other
than her own clothing and jewelry, a bed and linens, and a few "household
goods" to help provide for the remaining minors (George, fifteen, and Newell,
ten years old) in her household. [260] Anything that remained reverted to John's
estate, and, although Jerusha most certainly contributed to the accumulation of
family wealth and might very well have brought her own dowry to the marriage,
she was only entitled legally to the use of one third of the estate for her lifetime.

Ohio's laws regarding minor children allowed their father to entrust them,
even before they were born, to total strangers if he wished. Although such a
scenario was unlikely in the close-knit McIntosh-Ferris clan, the legal power of
determining guardianship lay entirely in John's hands. Had Jerusha been married to someone less caring than John McIntosh, she would have had no say in
the upbringing of the minor duo in her care. If John's death had come at the
end of an illness and were therefore not a sudden one, he and Jerusha might
have had time to confer about the best course of action to take for their children. We know from court documents of at least one decision made regarding
George and Newell.

They became wards of their mother's nephew, Dr. Ferris. The boys
remained at home with their mother, Jo and Rind, but the official guardianship,
"appointed on June 10, 1853" [261] meant that Ferris agreed to assume some
financial responsibility for the boys. The guardianship and its monetary help

did not obviate the need for the boys to work. Two years after the guardianship took effect George and Newell both helped with the family's income by doing agricultural labor on neighbors' farms. Until she married in 1856 Rind helped support her mother and George and Newell by teaching school sporadically and by her tailoring work.

The value of John's real estate at the time of his death was $2,825, a figure astoundingly close to the value of the average Ohio farm in that year — $2,495 for a farm that was about seventeen acres larger than his. [262] The disbursement of his estate took place a year after his death, on August 27, 1853. Jerusha's share amounted to $138.85. John's "personal property" sold for $257.32, he had notes worth $166.81, and his "cash on hand" amounted to $42.50. Assessed against John's worth were bills totaling $277.70 that included the fees for his doctor (Dr. Andrew Jackson Squires, a revered older physician in Mantua), for an attorney, and for the costs for appraising his personal property. Jo paid $6.00 for his father's coffin. [263]

John's death marked the advent of innumerable changes for his family. The beautiful home that John and Jerusha had so carefully crafted and where they had raised their close-knit family was sold to Chauncey Messenger, sometime between 1856 and 1860. Jerusha and Newell then went to live with Jo on his farm. Most of the McIntosh children remained in or fairly near Portage County, but two of John's youngest children set off on paths he could not have imagined. The loss of his father set in motion George's decision to leave Ohio on a circuitous journey that would lead him to northeastern Colorado where he made the McIntosh name one to be reckoned with.

CHAPTER FOUR

All That Glitters

John McIntosh had lived long enough to see two of his older sons take up their father's work as farmers, but not long enough to witness whether they accomplished as much or exceeded what he had done. Three years before his father's death Eb had married Affa Messenger (1825-1896), the sister of Chauncey Messenger who would later buy the McIntosh home. Only one of Eb and Affa's children, Otis, was born before George left Ohio. Rogenia "Genie", Milly and Cora followed Otis and might have been lost to George had he not come from a family where letters kept the family as close as possible. It is through those few existing letters and Rind's journals that the life of Eb McIntosh's family emerges.

Eb and his growing clan lived a hardscrabble existence, trying to manage even a subsistence level of farming, but eventually failing at that. Eb watched his brothers reap the benefits of raising crops and livestock where he was unable to — the experience turned him into a self-pitying man who sometimes sounded like Paschal, but without the latter's more elegant turn of phrase. It is tempting to attribute Eb's increasing inability to make a decent living to an innately impractical nature passed down from his namesake, but on February 23 and again on March 2, 1855 Rind's diary mentions "fits", sometimes two or three in succession, that afflicted Eb. Whether these were epileptic seizures or caused by some other condition, the fits disrupted his life and may have been at least part of the reason that he could not make the fertile soil of Portage County yield enough to support his family, no matter how hard he worked. And yet, until his failures beat him down psychologically, Eb was fun to be around. Rind and George both enjoyed their older brother's friendship and Rind's diaries speak frequently of going to Eb's place where she often spent the night, sharing a bed with one of his children.

Meanwhile, Henry, his wife, Maria (1829-?) left Mantua for Lorain County, Ohio in 1851, settling first in Napoleon and two years later finding a home in Ridgeville Corners. Henry and Maria had two children who died early. The five remaining to them were Alice Lorinda, Adelaide Lodiska, Mary Janet, Kate Rose, and Carl Tilden.[264] Henry's removal to another county, no matter its relative closeness to Mantua, made letters essential to maintain contact with his siblings.

In the 1860s and 1870s it was correspondence that bound the McIntoshes to each other; none of George's nineteenth-century letters survives, but we can hear his words reflected in replies to him from his brothers and sister. The importance to the McIntoshes of these communications is highlighted by Henry's brothers' responses to Hen's occasional dilatoriness as a correspondent — they did not hesitate to take him to task. "Henry McIntosh Does not write to me I have wrot a Number of Letters to him but Do Not get No answer from him," complained Eb to George on June 10, 1872. Industrious Henry seems to have relied on his wife to write the frequent letters his family desired.

Maria displayed an uncharitable attitude toward less successful members of her husband's kin (it was she who had complained about Milton McIntosh's seeming evasion of military service). When she wrote to George on August 23, 1864, calling his cousin, Darwin McIntosh (c.1829-?), wife, Adelia, and their young children, "a disgrace to our name...not any body nor you cant make any body out of them. I have never called on them I cannot associate with them nor I don't want my children to. Dar's wife and children are natural thieves. I don't feel safe to leave home as I used to I have lost soap and Pork and they have not bought any soap since they have ben here." Maria's birth into the Tilden family, prominent in Hiram, seems to have given her a feeling of superiority over the McIntoshes. George's reaction to her harsh words does not exist, but his generally mild-mannered and less judgmental nature probably was taken aback by Maria's nasty suspicions. Almost fifty years later his wife's sister would utter strangely similar words directed at George's children.

More charmingly candid is a letter from Alice, Henry and Maria's oldest daughter, to her "unkle[sic] george" on April 17, 1864 when she said, "I did not go to school this winter for it made me sick so i thought i would stay to home and tend my little sister for she is so good and fat that i like to tend her. her name is mary jerusha she looks like gramma McIntosh." Chubby little Mary Jerusha, possessed of her maternal grandmother's name and appearance, was one of Hen's children who did not live beyond childhood.

Jo, who was married to a woman named Rhoda at some point before the Civil War, wrote letters to George and Newell that reveal a responsible and compassionate personality, but it was one that contained a weakness that prevented him from fulfilling the family's high hopes for him. Three years (March 27, 1855) after her father's death Rind observed that, "Father thought more of him than any other child". He was the son who administered his father's estate, took in his mother and Newell after John's death, corresponded diligently and lovingly with all of them, and who did his utmost to prevent his youngest brother's premature death. And yet Jo, like Eb, had a bad problem. He was an alcoholic.

In the 1850s young men in Mantua and neighboring townships turned not to the whiskey of their fathers' generation, but to rum. Bingeing on rum and other alcoholic beverages represented a serious problem throughout Ohio and other states in the middle of the century. From Ohio's *Zanesville Daily Courier*, December 17, 1852 came this startling piece of information: "RUM – It appears by the census that the consumption of spirituous and malt liquors in the United States reaches the enormous quantity of eighty-six millions of gallons annually equal to six gallons for every adult person." Jo's increasing intoxication from rum created misery for the family. Rind's heartrending description of the result of one of his benders in 1855 deserves to be quoted in full, not only because it is so vivid, but also because it demonstrates how her deep love for her brother battled against the condemnation she felt he had earned:

Tuesday March 27
Jo went to Ravenna this morning – came home tonight –in such a light with what anxiety I have watched him when I saw him coming home from places where I knew liquor was sold and felt as though a load was taken from my mind when I saw that he was sober – but tis

of no use we must give him up – tis a hard thing to give up the dead, but oh how much harder the living – I heard him tell a dream at the commencement of this year – he said he thought he was surrounded by serpents that bit him & stung him & he lay powerless – had not ambition or energy to move – oh to feel that he must go to fill a Drunkards grave – what anguish in the thought – he had been the pride of the whole family – Father thought more of him than any other child – but little did any of us think he would ever come to this – as I write he lays insensible in the corner in the deep sleep of the drunkard – I have noticed for several days that he seemed out of humor with himself & everyone else & dreaded what I feared would follow, but I think I have said all I ever shall to him – no person in the world knows better than he does & ever has the degrading, damnable effects of liquor – thrashes round & groans – seems to be a fearful sick boy."

What makes this account particularly poignant is that immediately preceding it is this sentence, "A man was found dead in the road of a mile east of here", as if Rind were linking Jo's drinking with the distinct possibility that he could end up like the man in the road. She continued this entry by citing the examples of two other local young men and commenting that "there is no end to the victims of this diabolical rum traffick" – when her writing was interrupted by another groan from Jo. This situation is why she turned to law books for suggestions about what could be done to eliminate the enticements of liquor. Most of Jo's drunken collapses seem to have taken place at home, so it is no surprise that George's reaction was to become a teetotaler. Although George was sometimes absent from the family home in 1855 and 1856 while he worked for area farmers, he cannot have avoided witnessing Jo's alcoholic stupors.

While Jo struggled with his demons, Rind developed into a lively, affectionate young woman, full of intellectual curiosity. Her letters and diaries give a brief, but delightfully frank glimpse into her life as a young Portage County woman just before marriage. Each day, despite many hours of labor-intensive tasks, Rind managed to write at least a few lines. She paints a picture of a young woman in a small town, dependent on even insignificant social exchanges to relieve the drudgery of constant housework, of teaching in a district school filled with unruly, uninterested students, and of sewing garments for long hours in unheated rooms. She was a compassionate gossip, ever solicitous if one of her friends encountered trouble. And she adored her family. In 1856 when she boarded and worked in Hiram, she missed them constantly, although they lived just a few miles away.

Before her marriage to Abner Clark Reed, the name of her husband-to-be appeared only twice in her journals: once when she recorded the burial of his first wife, Dolly Andrews (1820-1855), on July 1, 1855 and again on March 30, 1856, a few days before she married Clark (as everyone called him) when she merely stated, "Abner Clark Reed was here this evening." Her earlier candor is here replaced by a certain shy reticence and we learn nothing about Clark as a suitor or about her family's reaction to the engagement. They were married three days after her March 30th entry.

Abner Clark Reed was a Mantua native, born to Limon (Lyman) Reed (1789-1873) and Rhoda Clark Reed (1794-1855). His first wife had given birth to a son, Charles ("Charley") Clark Reed, in 1854. As an adult Charley became a farmer and state legislator in Nebraska. Clark and Caroline's first child, Ida Lorinda, was born on May 20, 1858 in Mantua, [265] part of a generation of children born in settled areas of the United States who would grow up on the western frontier because their parents and, in Ida's case, also her Uncle George, sought more opportunities at a time when America's financial situation was again looking grim.

Another economic depression had hit the United States in 1857, spurred by events in Russia that rebounded to American shores. The Crimean War (1853-56) took thousands of British men away from their farms to be soldiers, so the British government turned to American agricultural products to feed its populace. [266] But when the soldiers returned, there was no longer any need to purchase American foodstuffs. "Hard money began to disappear" and credit was harder to obtain.[267] Rind's 1855 diary foreshadowed the economic bad times that were to come and there can be no doubt that the teenaged George registered what a financial downturn could mean for subsistence farmers. Disappointments for the McIntoshes and their neighbors began to accumulate that year. On February 2 Eb's well went dry, the weather was "uncommon cold", and the hay crop had not done well. A week later Rind recorded that hay cost an expensive "17 dollars a ton – some cattle will starve before spring & hope it won't be ours." On February 15 "we hear of cattle and horses starving to death & now & then e'en have accounts of human beings sharing the same fate." Hay became extremely scarce that spring. Rind noted on March 9 that there was 'no hay for sail – one man said he was offered $25.00 a ton." The price had been $20.00 a ton on February 26. So, even if the Crimean War had not affected American finances as it did, Mantua farmers would have found the 1850s to be financially challenging years anyway.

Clark, an ambitious man who had goals that looked for fulfillment beyond agriculture, found that bad economic times gave him a motive for leaving Ohio. His eagerness to relocate in the west took him, Caroline, Charley and the infant Ida away from Mantua and their families on Monday, June 2, 1858. Rind may never have seen any of her McIntosh family members again. She encouraged Jerusha to come visit, but her mother is unlikely to have made the trip. It is just possible that George stopped by their place two years later on his own way west, but no evidence remains to confirm that as fact.

After some overland travels, the Reeds caught a boat that took them to St. Louis, Missouri via the Ohio River. It was Caroline's first boat ride. Her impressions appeared in her journal entry for June 2. She enjoyed ascending to the pilot house to observe the passing countryside, and, like a true McIntosh, noted the "orchards all in bloom." Used to the rural quiet of Mantua she found that the noise of the boat ("sounds like a hurricane") prevented her from sleeping at night. They flowed south past Marietta and then Gallipolis. She admired the Kentucky landscape as the boat drew closer to the junction with the Mississippi River where they would veer north toward St. Louis. From there they battled the crowds of people trying to obtain a covered wagon and team of oxen to take them into Nebraska Territory.

The small family finally settled in Wyoming City, Otoe County, Nebraska Territory on the far eastern edge of the present state of Nebraska. There Caroline seemed happy, raising Charley and the children she and Clark had together: Ida was joined by Rhoda Adella (b. 1859), Harriette Estella (b. 1861) and Caroline (b. 1863) [268] But little Caroline would never know her mother. Rind died a month after the birth under possibly suspicious circumstances. But that story comes a bit later.

Newell lived in Jo's household until enlisting in the Union army early in the Civil War. Upon his return Newell followed the same route to a career as his Ferris cousin, Osman, Jr. According to Eugene H. Roseboom, it was the "'bright boy'" in almost every family [who] was regarded as the logical choice for the legal profession." [269] With all of the other McIntosh males either involved with farming or heading in that direction, Newell seems to have carried the McIntosh dreams for having a professional man in the family. On July 5, 1868 Jo wrote to George that "Newel is in Ravenna Reading Law with Raney [sic] and hatfield." Becoming an attorney in this manner was something of a hit or miss proposition, depending on how much legal instruction the attorneys had time to impart to their student. But Newell was fortunate in his choice of teachers.

Both Henry Clay Ranney (1829-1919) and Edward Hatfield (1843- ?), who was exactly Newell's age, were already well-respected members of the bar. Henry had served for two years as a captain in the Union army. Then he returned to Ravenna and resumed the practice of law. A "cheerful and sympathetic" man, he was well-known for mentoring younger lawyers. [270] In *Bart Ridgeley*, Riddle's novel about a young nineteenth-century Portage County lawyer, Ranney "plays" himself as a "shy and awkward" law student. [271] Raised in a gentle, nurturing family, Newell must have responded well to Ranney's genial, low-key manner. After his two years of study, Newell passed an examination on the law and was admitted to the Ohio bar on May 10, 1870. He was ready to set up his own practice.[272]

So John and Jerusha's children became self-sufficient adults. Except for service during the Civil War, all but one of the boys remained in the corner of Ohio where they had been born and raised. Rind's departure was determined by her husband. It was to be George, the supposedly frail asthmatic, who decided independently to leave Ohio the year before Rind and Clark did and who went on to conquer frontier after frontier. His father's death, coupled with the worsening economic situation in the 1850s, gave him the shove he needed to fly from the family nest. And this fledgling was more than eager to make that first flight because, although the canal and train brought more liveliness to the Western Reserve, Mantua remained in many ways a sleepy, backwater town where tradition would largely predetermine his future life.

Although Caroline, spirited away to the Nebraska Territory by her husband, and George, spirited away by his own impulses, were the only two of John McIntosh's offspring to leave Ohio for good, they weren't the only people pulled away from eastern states by the lure of a fresh start: between 1850 and1873 many Ohioans left for places like Iowa, Kansas, and other locales in the West. [273] And, although Ohio had led all other states in terms of "diversified agriculture" until about 1850, after that point its economic curve leveled off.

The western territories, especially those encompassing the prairies where a farmer could grow wheat with relative ease, offered emigrants new, potentially profitable opportunities. The 1857 financial panic changed the lives of many discontented Americans by hurtling them westward. [274]

It was at some point in about 1857 that George made the momentous decision to leave his fond family and Mantua friends, to venture off to Sheboygan, Wisconsin on the shores of Lake Michigan. There he hoped to find a climate that might help his asthma. At least that is the reason given in the sometimes erroneous short biography of him that appeared in *The History of Clear Creek and Boulder Valleys, Colorado* in 1880. [275] The brief reconstruction of his life, based on George's own memories and meant to celebrate one of the leading men of Boulder County, Colorado, would hardly allude to the perhaps more self-centered motives of a young man bent on acquiring wealth. But George's future activities provide more than enough proof of multiple reasons that might have taken him from his Ohio home.

After sometimes being sidelined by his caring family because of his asthma, George lusted after adventure, after the life-affirming exploits that might have been physically taxing and even downright dangerous, but that proved he was alive. The asthmatic Theodore Roosevelt (1858-1919) proved to be in some respects similar to young George McIntosh. According to the historian Peter Gay, Roosevelt's "picturesque and excessive vitality, his Faustian inability to be content with the worlds he had conquered…appear like a desperate struggle with an all-too-familiar sense of impotence, a reiterated (because never wholly convincing) proclamation of fitness that will enable him, the asthmatic, to survive the next attack." [276] George exhibited a Roosevelt-like restlessness for the next eleven years. And for the rest of his life he set about proving his capacity for overcoming others' lowered expectations because of his smallness and labored breathing. In this respect he was certainly Ebenezer's grandson, although he and Ebenezer had set about dispelling those diminished expectations in far different ways. Unlike his grandfather, George never sought the limelight, but as a goal-directed young man, he did find satisfaction in achievements that corrected people's mistaken notions of his abilities.

His decision to leave must have inspired farewell parties and tender goodbyes. Most of the McIntoshes wore their hearts on their sleeves and were not ashamed to show emotion toward one another. Even George's father allowed his feelings to emerge publicly when faced with the loss of family members. On the twelfth anniversary of John McIntosh's death Maria McIntosh wrote to George that when she and Hen left Mantua for Ridgeville Corners, approximately fifty long miles away, "tears stood in [John's] eyes as he bid me goodby for the last time."

George left a town much transformed since his birth. Riddle described Mantua just before the Civil War, a few years after George departed: "...I stopped at the Mantua Station, on the Mahoning Railroad...There was the old Judge Atwater mansion turned into a tavern, and save the Cuyahoga, a diminished but still a beautiful stream, my eye saw no familiar thing." [277] Although we do not have any account of George's leave-taking, at least some of George's family undoubtedly waved goodbye to him from the platform of the Mantua Station as he boarded the train for Cleveland, the first stage in his exodus from Ohio.

Why did George really give up Mantua for Sheboygan? Health concerns cannot have been the real reason because Sheboygan, situated on the shores of Lake Michigan just a little further north than Mantua, had a climate that represented no improvement over Mantua's, featuring the same cold, wet winters and hot, humid summers. Part of George's rationale may have come from a friend and neighbor, C. H. Ray (1835-?). In about 1856 Ray had embarked on a journey in a covered wagon with his older brother that took them many miles from Mantua. They stopped in Wisconsin, eventually going on to Kansas where they remained for two years and where the Rays, who held strong pro-abolition views, talked with former Portage County resident John Brown when he visited their older brother's store.[278] Ray clerked in that store and worked in a mill there. His mother paid neighborly visits to Jerusha and would have shared letters from her sons. George would have been eager to hear about his friends. C. H.'s tales of "camping out and sleeping in the wagon nights..." [279] and his description of their sojourn in Wisconsin stimulated George's craving for a change in his life. If he couldn't go to Kansas or someplace similar right away, at least Sheboygan held a certain allure.

Newly chartered as a city in 1853, Sheboygan was a boom town when young George arrived. It offered an unruly atmosphere that might appeal to this untested farm boy from a quiet small town. Located at the mouth of the Sheboygan River, the Wisconsin community boasted a thriving harbor, four weekly newspapers, and at least seven churches when it was chartered.

Workers constructed plank roads at a fast pace, trying to keep up with the rapid influx of population: in 1846 the town had almost 500 people — by 1853 that number had expanded to 2,000. [280] The rapidity of the town's growth spurred a call for workers of all kinds, so George found employment quickly. Following Ray's lead he clerked briefly in a store and then applied for and got a teaching position.

In spite of the urgent need for instructors in Sheboygan common schools, all teaching applicants had to demonstrate some level of competence in a variety of subjects. Sometimes competency examinations were waived when necessity dictated. However, even if the standards were neither uniform nor particularly high, George had to be at least literate and numerate to be hired.

His salary was low and the esteem of his students probably lower still. Male teachers earned an average of $15.22 a month – women earned less than half that amount. [281] George's already developed thrifty habits came in handy in Sheboygan where he was certainly squirreling away funds in preparation for yet another adventure beyond the borders of the Old Northwest. Teaching represented a stopgap measure. But, until he could save enough money to move on, George faced students in the classroom.

Knowing of Rind's experiences with rowdy students might have made him a reluctant instructor, but George's options, like his grandfather's when he opted to learn shoemaking, were limited. As a small young man with health problems George could not have worked in Sheboygan's shipyards or as a carpenter helping to put up the vast number of structures needed by the swelling town. Even so, he had chosen a job in which a commanding physique would have given him more confidence in front of a class. He was not the burly, muscled man that James Garfield was and even Garfield had had trouble controlling his scholars. Some of George's older students towered over the not quite five-foot, five-inch tall Ohioan. As Jo recollected on July 5, 1868, George had "no beerd nor Mustash" when he left home, so he appeared almost as youthful as some of his students. Lacking the size and age that at least would have demanded some attention from them, George fell back on his sense of humor to establish his presence in the classroom.

Like many sickly children, George had developed ways of personal interaction that depended more on levity than on physical abilities. Later in his life people remarked upon George's love of joking, an attribute shared by most of his siblings. Despite her hard life, Rind loved funny situations, even when the joke was played upon her and George shared that trait with her. The following story highlights his sense of humor. Once, when he was about sixty-years old, he visited his brother-in-law Richard and his wife Jane in their Longmont, Colorado home. He sat with his "feet to the kitchen stove", drinking coffee and eating cookies Jane had baked. A young boy who called "Mr. Mack grandfather" [282] climbed atop George's lap. Then the idea sprang into the boy's head to hook his toes on the chair rung, bend back without using his arms, "touch his head to the floor and come up again." The trick went awry when the boy flung himself backwards, toppling both himself and George to the floor. Instead of being angered at the sudden indignity, George "was calm, and his laugh was like the 'Ho! ho! ho! of a Santa Claus…" [283]

A good-humored approach toward life could ameliorate many difficult situations, but his asthma didn't yield to positive thinking and, unsurprisingly, did not really improve in Sheboygan. By early 1860 he had saved enough money to leave teaching and Sheboygan. So, "his disease becoming worse, he again decided to try another climate, and started across the plains for Colorado with an ox-team." [284] Again one has to wonder if his health problem was really the main reason for George's decision to depart from the Old Northwest for good. Colorado, then part of the Kansas Territory, certainly boasted a climate beneficial to those with respiratory ailments – dry air and hundreds of days of sunshine per year—and even in the mid-nineteenth century Colorado's salubrious climate was well-known beyond its borders. In fact, before the century ended it had spawned a sizeable health care industry. "An air more delicious to breathe cannot anywhere be found; it is neither too sedative nor too exciting, but has that pure, sweet, flexible quality which seems to support all one's happiest and healthiest moods." [285] In other words, *perfect air*!   But once again George's reasons for moving on were multi-faceted. One of them represented a sparkling dream.

There had been buzz about gold in the Kansas Territory as early as 1857 when the national economic depression made the chimera of striking it rich irresistible. And a chimera it was. Although some miners actually did realize their dreams and became rich men, most of the optimists flowing steadily to the western mountains would fail. It was an old story. Out of the thousands who tried their luck, "droves of miners gave up in disgust", [286] the poorer for their effort.

In 1859 the discovery of gold at several Colorado locations — Pike's Peak, Cherry Creek near Denver City, the foothills above Boulder, and in a gulch located near the current casino-dominated town of Blackhawk – triggered a great rush of men from all over "the States" (Colorado would not become a state until August 1, 1876). It was a Georgia man named John Gregory who found gold on May 6, 1859, less than a week before George's twenty-second birthday, in what is now known as Gregory Gulch. When Gregory discovered a lode of gold in that ravine between the present-day towns of Central City and Blackhawk, he unwittingly altered the lives of thousands of people, George McIntosh among them. News of the exciting find made its way east with startling rapidity.

Like so many other young men, in the fall and winter months of 1858-1859 George learned about the potential riches through an avalanche of positive publicity spurred by rumors of gold in Colorado. The reports had a factual basis, but too often originated from people who had not even seen the area themselves. [287] The *New York Times* contained this opinion on January 29, 1859:

> Ho for Pike's Peak! There is soon to be an immense migration, especially from our western states, [that is, states such as Ohio and Wisconsin] to the new El Dorado. The extensive failure of crops in 1858, the universal pressure of debt, the low prices realized or promised for the fruits of the husbandman's labors, the deadness of enterprise, the absence of thrift, render such a migration inevitable. There is scarcely a village west of Ohio in which some are not fitting for and impatiently waiting the day when a start may prudently be made for the neighborhood of Pike's Peak. [288]

Within weeks of hearing the news an onslaught of romantic hopefuls, adventurers and entrepreneurs of all stripes streamed into those Colorado hills. Egging them on were exaggerated newspaper reports and hot-off-the-presses guidebooks to the region. Those in the first wave of would-be miners dashed off enthusiastic letters about the relative ease of finding gold nuggets. When these accounts were added to those of the previous year about discoveries to the south of Pike's Peak, it must have appeared as if the Colorado area truly was an Eldorado. Only those with no ambition at all could possibly fail to amass riches in a very short time. Or so it seemed.

Stay-at-homes, too, saw the opportunity for increased wealth by promoting the mining adventure. For outfitters in Missouri River towns here was an unimagined chance to reel in the dollars. Council Bluffs, Iowa, where George most probably bought his oxen and supplies, had earlier established itself as the portal to the western territories when it outfitted large numbers of men bound for the California goldfields. Its position on the Missouri River made it a prime goal for those heading west. The proliferating guidebooks advised would-be miners about supply depots like Council Bluffs and also about necessary supplies, mileage, and the best routes to the gold fields. Unfortunately, much of that data, too, was false. [289]

In Thomas Warren's guide the author tempered his advice with a more realistic assessment of the ideal candidate for this mining gamble: "But the young man, whose hands are free—who has a strong constitution and stronger moral courage; who has not permanent paying business in the States – let such go and with industry and perseverance he may reap a golden reward...All will not be equally successful—some are doomed to disappointment." [290]

Except for not having a "strong constitution" George McIntosh fit the bill, but his hopes for that "golden reward" were twofold: perhaps he could improve his health *and* his wealth at the same time. He was single with little to lose. He saw the potential to make some monetary gains, but the attempt would require courage and a giant leap of faith. He was leaving a comfort zone: the people and places he knew and, in a much more fundamental way, the United States. The promotional literature did not skirt this issue nor did the letters from the men already staking their claims in the west. Both displayed an acute consciousness of living in a Territory and, therefore, outside "the States". Although a daunting proposition, for many this concept was also exhilaratingly freeing. What an opportunity it was for those who wished to escape the economic depression and, sometimes, their own identities. It gave George the chance to re-define himself as a young man who could stand on his own two legs.

He followed at least one piece of advice promulgated in the various guidebooks by timing his departure for early spring, leaving in March of 1860,[291] (the year when so many went out to seek their fortunes in the Colorado mountains) so as to make progress during relatively good weather.   Not until he reached Council Bluffs would he invest in the equipment and provisions needed for the long journey.   In Council Bluffs he would have purchased an assortment of mining tools, such as a pick, a wide-rimmed metal pan large enough to hold three gallons of water, and a shovel with a long handle. He provisioned himself for the long trip with large sacks of flour, sugar, beans, coffee, and so on. Maybe he also took along some seeds, heeding the advice of more cautious men who offered up the compelling thought that agriculture might, in the long run, reward an ineffectual seeker of gold with so much more than empty dreams and empty pockets.[292]   By 1859 gold hunters had already opined that the area that was to become Boulder County, Colorado had "the best farming land in the country."[293]   So, there was always the thought for some that, if a man failed at mining, he would at least have something with which to start a farm. In fact, as George would soon discover, the region's arable fields held far greater promise than the gold fields.

Victorian apprehension about the immorality of easy riches versus the inherent decency of earning a living by farming prompted one writer to state in the *New York Tribune* on October 2, 1858 that a man had "better dig gold than stand idle, but better plant corn, shoe horses, build houses or make fences than do either of these…the young man who can earn $100 per annum over the cost of his board and clothes should do it rather than court the risk of goldhunting."[294] The Jeffersonian ideal that equated the agrarian life with morality was still very much alive in the mid-nineteenth century. The notion that looking for gold was a somewhat scandalous way of making a living probably never occurred to George or, if it did, it did not trouble him enough to give up his dreams. Perhaps because he always had at the back of his mind that any money he earned by mining would ultimately go to the purchase of good farmland he was able to justify a questionable method of accumulating that money.

Determined on his course, George bought a covered wagon and a team of well-matched oxen to transport his belongings.   He would test his endurance by walking most of the distance (another huge McIntosh march), approximately twenty miles a day, while his team pulled the wagon.[295] Some, who perhaps had been more impatient and less provident than George, had to resort to walking behind wheelbarrows or riding a horses without benefit of a wagon to haul their belongings. [296]

George placed a chair inside his wagon, an item that few other young men embarking on such an adventure would have made room for in the tight confines of a covered wagon. But it was this single object that made the trip feasible for George. Because his asthma made sleeping in a prone position nearly impossible – he just could not breathe – the chair enabled him to sit upright and slumber relatively comfortably during this long, fatiguing journey.[297]

It was during this trek westward that George took the step that transformed his face into the one his family would not have recognized. Like most of the other young would-be miners he gave up his razor and grew a beard that remained on his face until his death sixty-four years later. There wasn't time for niceties such as shaving on the arduous trek, but the beard also made obvious his newfound maturity and his bond with the predominantly male contingent marching to the gold fields.

Did he stop at Rind and Clark's place as his route took him very close to their home? The answer is probably yes. George's fondness for the sister he hadn't laid eyes on for several years would have made passing up a chance to visit unthinkable. But it wouldn't have been a long stay. The wagons and men passing through Wyoming City reminded him of the urgency of reaching the mountains. When he reached Omaha, Nebraska Territory's capitol city and one of the last opportunities to replenish his supplies, he probably stopped briefly and then was on the road again, walking behind his steady team. They reached the South Platte River nearly three-hundred miles after leaving Omaha. There were certainly other routes that would have taken him to his destination, but the Platte was the most heavily traveled and reckoned to be the least risky of the three major trails heading west. [298]

The farther west George travelled, the wilder and stranger his surroundings became. Houses and trees disappeared, to be replaced by vast spaces abounding with wildlife. Cheyenne and Sioux Indians made frequent appearances to conduct mainly cordial exchanges that involved trading guns or whiskey for moccasins or buffalo robes. Sometimes the natives camped near the travelers. Every once in a while a stage station popped up, but otherwise it was endless plains of buffalo grass. The boundless landscape could have become monotonous, but not the risky trip itself. The wind whipped up sand and thunderstorms threatened. Equipment broke. A wagon wheel might break in a deep rut. As the days became warmer and dryer, the arid atmosphere made the wooden wheels shrink away from their spokes, so they had to be refitted. [299] Numerous accidents occurred along the trail to humans and livestock proved to be just as vulnerable. Horses stampeded when spooked by noises or rattlesnakes and oxen might drink from alkaline water that could poison them. [300]

More mundane were the regular chores each man had to do just to ensure that he could continue the journey. Every day George had to find both pasturage and clean water for his animals. Good water was sometimes hard to locate. That was another reason a spring departure was advisable — creeks dried up quickly once the summer months arrived. He had to cook his own meals after gathering buffalo chips for fuel. When ignited, the chips gave off a stinky odor, but the travelers' appetites were undoubtedly so great at the end of a long day that they did not care. As his oxen pulled the wagon slowly westward, George used his boyhood hunting skills to shoot antelope, deer, and buffalo, but there were days when fresh meat was not available.

When George arrived at Fort Kearney, still a long three-hundred-eighty miles from Denver City where he could set off for Gregory's discovery, the would-be miners scented both novelty and some measure of safety in what was for most of them their first view of a fort and soldiers. They were moving into landscape that was becoming grassier and more elevated. The grass encouraged both man and beast, but more inspiring was the first glimpse of the Rocky Mountains, causing some to wax poetic: "At first glance they appeared like clouds pending from the sky in blue and black shrouds…the emotions produced in the mind of the young tourist, sweltering in the midsummer sun, as he views those snow-capped mountains, can be more easily imagined than described." [301] George had to have been astounded by the mountains, such a contrast to Portage County's gentle hills.

At North Platte, Nebraska the Platte River separated into its north and south branches. George followed the latter, soon entering present-day Colorado at Julesburg, in the farthest northeast corner of the state. Julesburg, founded in 1859 by the French trapper Jules Beni, was a hub for westward-bound travelers and represented another opportunity for renewing supplies. The contact with civilization, rudimentary though it was, reassured the tired men. Less encouraging were the markers all along their road that pointed out the graves of those who had not survived the trip. But George remained an optimist — and something of an opportunist. Despite the lure of the gold, his keen eyes were always on the land. Walking past the river-hugging land of the Cache la Poudre Valley close to Fort St. Vrain (near the present-day city of Greeley) he noted that the land held potential for farming. But Denver City and the gateway to the gold were almost within view, so he trudged on to the crude community that was metamorphosing into something much grander.

Even in 1859 the still nearly treeless Denver City was becoming a town with a sense of permanence about it. When George entered the town the following year its unpolished frontier structures were already giving way to frame- and brick buildings. Denver City's accelerated transformation occurred thanks in large part to the advent of the miners. It became the pre-eminent "gateway" town where they could obtain essential supplies and "…Denver, with its earlier start, its newspaper, its aggressive founders, and its advantageous location, emerged to the fore…" of other towns competing for primacy. [302]

Miners and other immigrants were everywhere, their numbers enormous. Approximately a thousand people arrived every day in May 1859, as well as wagons loaded with supplies for the mining mills and miners. [303] They camped all up and down the Platte River before moving up into the hills. Getting into those beautiful mountains along rugged, treacherous tracks that had not evolved into real roads yet was not for the faint of heart or for the unprepared. It would have been difficult for George to be patient and make the brief halt to re-provision while the constant stream of new arrivals heightened his anticipation of reaching the gold fields.

George learned to his chagrin that he was already a latecomer, having followed in the footsteps of the thousands and thousands who had stolen a march on him. And many disheartened men had already thrown in the towel. Known as "Go-backers" or "Stampeders", they were returning to the States in large numbers, but their places did not remain empty for long, so George had plenty of competition. He could not have known that, by the time he finally arrived in Nevadaville where he staked his claim, "the easy pickings were over." [304] In fact, there were to be just a few more years of feverish mining activity in the Colorado gold fields. By the mid-1860s the intoxicating speculation had imploded[305] and the fever of war replaced gold fever. [306]

The surest route to the area around Gregory Gulch was via Gold City (now known as Golden), about fifteen miles from Denver City. Everyone along the way was alert to methods of making money from the men who thronged the way, even charging the miners a toll to use the road that led into the mining areas spread all around the mountain town of Central City. The road was just barely large enough for the miners and their wagons, tents and livestock to pass, but from its heights one could see spectacular scenery. However, most ignored the view to pay closer attention to negotiating the rugged, steep, rocky path so as to avoid losing life or limb.

George and his companions on the road had to have abundant self-confidence (or mental blinders on) to ignore the dirty, exhausted and downhearted "Stampeders" trudging in the opposite direction.[307] Getting up into the mountains was one thing, but George's asthma was an additional concern and it is easy to understand that he might have begun to doubt the region's much-touted health benefits as he watched the physically wrecked figures straggling past him. Nor did the weather exactly live up his expectations of a dry climate as rain *and* snow fell on the area in late May and early June 1860, just about the time he arrived in the mountains. [308] But on he went.

From Gregory Gulch mining claims sprouted like weeds in a very wild garden. The numbers of men (and some women) led to the creation of boom towns like Central City. Founded in 1859, Central City fit the boom town bill perfectly with its saloons, gambling establishments and brothels. George, however, trudged beyond these attractions, climbing up about two more miles to Nevadaville, a mining town set in what had been a scenic valley before the miners had deforested it in their frantic search for ore. It possessed a very different character than Central City and had a code of conduct drawn up by the Nevadaville Miner's Court. One of the regulations stipulated that "...there shall be no Bawdy houses Grog shops or Gambling Saloons within the limits of this District..." [309] Laws such as the ones formulated by miners in Nevadaville benefited its diverse residents; moreover, they created an underpinning for the development of Territorial regulations and for the eventual creation of the state of Colorado itself. [310]

The largely impermanent populations of these towns were far from homogeneous. Yet, in spite of the miners' varied backgrounds, there was a uniformity to them, too. They were all after gold, most of them found the process tedious and disagreeable and most of Nevadaville's residents were male. On June 1, 1860 just over 400 men aged twenty to thirty lived there – there were forty women in the same age group. These young people dominated the total population of 750 men and one-hundred-twenty-four women. Many of those female inhabitants were widows who operated boarding houses. Miners, not surprisingly, made up the largest employment category in 1860 – there were as yet no freighters and no "gentlemen" as were to be found in Central City. The greatest numbers of Nevadaville's miners came from Ohio and New York, so George was in at least somewhat familiar company. [311]

Nevadaville was the topmost of the quartet of Gilpin County mining towns (Blackhawk, Central City and Mountain City constituted the other three) that burst into being around Gregory's find. It presented an ugly face. Dubbed "The Little Kingdom of Gilpin", [312] the community's sudden growth represented a 21st-century city planner's nightmare. Hundreds of structures spread higgeldy-piggeldy beyond the center of what became the main street. And the mines lay no more than a quarter of a mile from town, on hillsides "pitted with prospect holes, abandoned shafts, and mounds of tailings and refuse". [313] It was a far cry from Mantua's pretty farms bordered by large, ancient forests. George might well have been especially dismayed by the sight of the few small lodge-pole pines and aspen that remained growing on the hills around him after the miners had cut down the rest to make rooms for claims and cabins. One observer thought that the gulches appeared to have been "turned inside out." [314]

George and the other men lived in tents or built "cockeyed raw-pine cabins" [315] all over the uneven ground near their claims. Eager to strike it rich, they had little time for amenities. The typical one-room cabin, constructed in haste, had bare ground floors and a "sod or canvas roof". [316] The men gave only the most rudimentary attention to weather-proofing, a neglect that caused many an uncomfortable night. Rain or snow could creep in, but worst were the ferocious winds that could blow up suddenly and tear down fragile structures. With bedding brought from home or purchased in Denver City or even made from pine boughs (known as "Rocky Mountain feathers"), the miner could protect himself from some drafts, but it was far from a comfortable existence. And yet for eight months George wagered double stakes on both wealth *and* his health.

He established a claim on the north side of Quartz Hill at the Kent County Lode. George must have talked to other miners or was lucky in his choice of a claim site. Quartz Hill was "one of the grandest depositories of wealth that the world possesse[d]…a network of mineral veins, spurs, and feeders, and a great number of lodes, such as are rarely seen in any country." [317] Even allowing for the exaggeration common to such descriptions, Quartz Hill really was ripe with potential and the Kent County Lode was a rich one, discovered just the year before George arrived. [318]

Because George, like so many of the men around him, was not a professional miner, his efforts at extracting gold were limited largely to placer mining and sluicing. It was difficult, boring, uncomfortable, and wet work. Standing up

Nevadaville in 1860, the year George was there. The mountain in the background is Bald Mountain. George mined near the Kent Lode on Quartz Hill where the wagon in the left foreground is traveling. Courtesy of the Denver Public Library, Western History Collection, X-11265.]

to his ankles in frigid mountain water for hours on end, George experienced great discomfort for little reward. Patricia Limerick has characterized placer mining as "… labor that most of the ambitious miners would never have chosen as wage work." [319]

George had to use either a pan and water to shake down the gold from the material he had gathered or he had to run the mucky mixture through a sluice box, a slanted, shallow wooden box with grooves on its bottom to catch miner-

Nevadaville today, looking toward Quartz Hill. Photo by the author.

als. The sluice box, too, required the addition of water and sometimes quick-silver (liquid mercury) that attracted and adhered to bits of gold, setting it off from dirt in the pan. Although just as wet and cold a process as placer mining, sluicing made it relatively easy to separate the gold from the clayey stuff in which it hid. But gold often appeared in the form of small flakes that really didn't add up to much, so a day of labor frequently produced only a miniscule amount of ore, if that.

Placer mining, also known as "poor man's diggings", required minimal financial outlay. No grand vision guided placer miners as it did mine owners who were willing to stake substantial sums on the large-scale and more technical extraction of ore from quartz in the Nevadaville hills. But enterprises both small, like George's, and large co-existed there until the bubble burst in the mid-1860s and the Civil War intervened. Even by the autumn of 1860, there were indications that it was becoming more and more difficult to find gold by hand. The *Westerner Mountaineer* reported on September 6 that, "…the miners…have no resource left but more fully to prospect their claims, not on the surface, but down into the 'bowels of the earth'."

In November the quartz-crushing mills began closing for the winter, although the *Daily Rocky Mountain News* stated on November 20, 1860 that "Great numbers of miners are at work upon their claims, and will continue to get out quartz nearly all through the winter…The supply of good paying quartz is not equal to the demand for the mills, but a large quantity will be accumulated during the winter months."

The thousands who labored in close proximity to one another (some shafts were "sunk almost side by side.") [320] ultimately caused their own failures as veins grew too narrow and claims on single lodes too numerous to support the effort. After just a few months, George's prospects began to discourage him. Matters grew more complicated as the months wore on and the water necessary for sluicing and general mining operations wasn't always available. [321] But still he kept at it until the late fall.

Most of the miners worked seven days a week. Despite Nevadaville's emphasis on morals, business of all sorts went on as usual on Sundays. Stores remained open and the stamping mills continued their noisy crushing. It was a largely monotonous life dominated by unpleasant mental and physical circumstances. Later in his life George maintained that the Colorado air had indeed provided some relief from his asthma. But the conditions in Nevadaville were not otherwise conducive to promoting good health – his, or anyone else's.

George had come from an altitude of twelve hundred feet in Mantua and about six-hundred-fifty feet in Sheboygan; Nevadaville lay at just over nine thousand feet. Before becoming acclimated to these heights, George and the other miners suffered pretty much universally from what we now call "altitude sickness." Physical labor, even the exertion of climbing up to the camp, was wearying. The men complained of headaches and dizziness, sometimes feeling severe symptoms such as a retarded heartbeat and sleeplessness. [322] The conditions often produced health problems that only appeared years down the road. One of the most common afflictions to hit the miners later in their lives was rheumatism; many believed it was caused by all those hours standing in cold water. George was troubled by its pains from about the mid-1880s on.

The community's lack of water for mining processes meant that there wasn't much water for sanitation either. The populace of Nevadaville had not paid much attention to such concerns, but with the men living and working so close to one another, the town was a breeding ground for various fevers and agues. Physical problems competed with compromised mental states, too, when the miners' hopes of striking it rich were repeatedly raised and dashed. Of little help to the men's depressed moods was the lack of female companionship.

George's first foray into mining lasted just about five months. He saw placer mining was probably for him a futile exercise and he could not have recognized then the great potential that existed for Colorado mining in general. But historians would later find that, "…no industry had a greater impact on Western history than did mining…[it] took a comparatively gradual process and accelerated it…It called territories and states into being and forced them to an early maturity." [323] His role in advancing the Territory's development would hardly have been likely to console him at that moment. What might have made him happier in the midst of a sense of failure was the feeling that he had found a place in the Territory where he could put down roots.

George's part in pushing Colorado toward statehood would come from several endeavors, another of which was just about to develop. In October or November of 1860 the young pragmatist cut his losses, at least for the time being, and left Nevadaville. He was not a person who looked back with regret; the mining venture had not succeeded, but he was not a quitter and would not return to the comforts of Ohio. He was ready to try something entirely new, far more profitable, and more dangerous than gold mining had been.

CHAPTER FIVE

War in the West

News of unease in the nation's capital wafted across the plains to Denver in the early months of 1861. That unease was soon to become all-out civil war, but George could never have suspected how quickly and how deeply he would become involved in this distant conflict between the "States". Even less did he suspect how many years he would give to the war, years that could have been devoted to establishing a farm in this frontier territory. The war hadn't caught up with him yet, though.

George's mining experience had been a disappointment. But he didn't give up entirely on extracting wealth from the hills of Gilpin County for profit. He just turned to a different method. George had made an important observation: the amount of effort he had expended standing in cold water removing bits of gold could be put to better use by freighting supplies to the men locked to their claims by their frenzy for the ore. The venture was a money-maker for George, but freighting, like mining, was also essential for the entire region's growth. The miners were intent on one thing and one thing only: finding gold. By depending on freighters to bring them provisions, those who were taking gold out of the hills were able to continue their work, so the entire economy remained stable, at least for a while. [324]

George never viewed freighting as a long-term proposition. He had come to the realization that northeastern Colorado's true riches lay in agriculture and decided to settle down sometime on his own farm. Gold mining, however, had not produced enough money for the land, seed, and livestock needed to make a good farm. Although employment as a freighter may seem far-removed from George's ultimate career as a farmer-rancher, in fact, "many a ranchman got his start in hauling hay to the mines, where it was badly needed for the draft animals used in transporting timbers for mine work and for conveying ores and supplies." [325]   For George this interval after mining allowed him to make money quickly, but, perhaps more important, the routes he traveled gave him the opportunity to scout for promising farm land.

While freighting back and forth from the Cache La Poudre Valley where he had first noticed rich acres on his way out to the gold fields, George discovered a quarter-section in Larimer County that looked promising. He claimed the land by squatting on it. [326] Although the term now connotes a disreputable act, it was legal and even encouraged when George did it. The Pre-emption Act of 1841 allowed people to squat on and claim unsurveyed acreage; after about fourteen months, George would have been legally entitled to purchase his quarter-section for $1.25 an acre. George erected a log cabin in which he lived when not transporting goods;[327] several years later he sold both cabin and acres to another freighter.

He freighted loads of hay, the first crop for many of the settlers in northeastern Colorado where tall grass grew naturally in abundant quantities. Because the resilient pasturage retained its rich nutrients through cold winter months, farmers could allow it to dry in the fields where it fell and still be assured that it would later be nourishing feed for livestock. George bought the hay for about $25 a ton. [328] The young bullwhacker used a team of oxen to carry the bales up the treacherous roads to the camps. After delivering the hay or other goods to places like Black Hawk, Central City and Nevadaville, George returned with an empty wagon, ready to take on a new load. It was grinding, dangerous labor for both George and his team, especially when they were hauling a shipment over those notoriously rough, nearly impassible mountain roads. But in typical McIntosh fashion he persevered.

Members of the Arapaho tribe frequented the routes George traveled. He told his grandson, Neil, that "the Indians at that time were working back and forth over the high country." George showed Neil his old haunts from those years before the Civil War. Much later Neil recalled a trip he had made with George to Denver sometime in the second decade of the twentieth century, stating, "...one time we walked up and down the street...[there were] Indians standing in doorways, all decked out in feathers…and I'd be damned if the old boy couldn't talk to them. He'd stop and talk to one young man…They talked awhile… [George said], 'Don't see very many Arapahoes. He's an Arapaho.' He talked to him and seemingly understood him." [329]

The anecdote reveals George's rather uncommon habit of befriending of people on the fringes of nineteenth- and early twentieth-century society. He probably did not view the young Arapaho man as his equal, but George seemed not to care what others thought about his relationships with "outsiders" and these marginalized people responded warmly to him. That he had troubled to learn some of the Arapaho language and retained it in his old age shows that he was willing to go to some lengths to be amiable. But during his freighting period he was also prudently cautious when natives were in the area he traveled through and made it a habit to sleep at some distance from his wagon just in case the Indians tried to make a surreptitious attack. [330]

In the late summer of 1861 George found himself back in the Cache La Poudre area, a fact confirmed by the appearance of his name in the *Territorial Voters' Rolls* on August 19, 1861. The young Territory's male voters were selecting a delegate to the United States Congress and choosing its territorial legislators. After being sworn in by a judge, George voted at "Ole Nelsen's [sometimes spelled Nielsen] House" in the Cache La Poudre, [331] exercising the civic responsibility he had learned as a boy in Mantua. Shortly after the election George returned to mining in Nevadaville. He left behind no explanation for his decision to try mining again. Perhaps the upcoming winter months made freighting hay to the camps too risky a proposition. In any case, he spent no more than about six months in the camp before the Civil War swooped down on him and changed him into something other than either a freighter or a miner.

When the American Civil War broke out on April 12, 1861 with the Confederate bombardment of South Carolina's Fort Sumter in Charleston, the action, though far-removed in distance, had almost immediate repercussions in the new Colorado Territory (created out of the Kansas Territory on February 23, 1861). President Lincoln had just appointed William Gilpin (1813-1894) governor of the young Territory on March 22. Gilpin was an impatient, emotional man, prone to impulsive actions that would before long end his gubernatorial career. [332] But, when he arrived in Denver in late May 1861, he faced a situation that left little time for careful consideration.

A small but vociferous Confederate element in the Territory found the attack in South Carolina heartening to their cause. They took action. Sometimes they were brazen. For example, on April 16 a southern sympathizer raised a Confederate flag "over one of Denver's largest stores." [333] The flag, although not allowed to remain aloft for long, symbolized the divided loyalties that threatened the young Territory. Rind's stepson, Charley, told a similar story:

> On July 3, 1863 Mother [Rind] and two neighbors sat up and made a big flag to hoist over the Post Office. Next morning, Father and other Union men put it up. The Southern Sympathizers threatened to take it down. Union men stood out with guns declaring they would shoot any man who molested the flag. Someone hurried to Neb. City for Officers of the Law. The Officers came and disarmed them and arrested all and took them to Neb. City. At the hearing, the Judge gave them a good lecture. Later he called Father aside and asked if he knew the gun he showed them. Father, "Yes, it's mine." "What were you going to do with it?" Father replied, "Protect the old flag." "Take it, protect the flag with your life if necessary. [334]

At times in Denver those with antipathy toward the Union acted more covertly, gathering secretly to assemble caches of weapons. The possibility lurked that they might seize guns from Denverites, so Gilpin ordered all gun-buying Confederates arrested. [335]

West Point-educated Gilpin was ready to react with military force against the obvious Confederate presence in his Territory and to more serious belligerence emanating from Texas and New Mexico. Colonel Edward S. Canby (1817-1873), Union army commander of the Department of New Mexico, (promoted to Brigadier General in 1862), knew that Confederate troops were massing to take advantage of the fact that Fort Union, located northeast of Santa Fe, was vulnerable. However, he did not have enough men to repulse an attack by the southerners.

He asked repeatedly for reinforcements. By the time the request was granted, not only had Gilpin already ordered the formation of a regiment of Colorado volunteers, but those men were marching south to come to Canby's aid.[336] The threat was real. The rebels had set their sights on securing

Colorado and California mining wealth to increase their war coffers. They had sundered the New Mexico Territory, gaining control of its southern regions that were loyal to Texas and the Confederate cause. And they were readying themselves to move north.

Governor Gilpin faced a significant defense problem. Federal troops had already departed from the Territory to reinforce Union positions in the eastern states, leaving the trails that connected the Territory with the "States" unprotected. The Territorial citizens' pervasive fear about Indian attacks made the situation urgent. Rumors abounded that the natives, disgruntled by their displacement by white settlers, would ally themselves with the southern rebels. That sense of urgency encouraged him to act recklessly in raising the funds necessary to outfit a volunteer army that would be known as the Colorado First Volunteers. He issued unauthorized "drafts on the U. S. Treasury" for $375,000. [337] Unluckily for him, the Treasury eventually refused to recognize the legitimacy of these drafts. Before too long Gilpin would lose the trust of his constituents, particularly those storekeepers who had provided guns, ammunition, uniforms and other equipment on the basis of Gilpin's promises of reimbursement. Even the soldiers, who became known as "Gilpin's Pet Lambs", (after his later dismissal they became simply the "Pet Lambs") received no pay "as U. S. troops until eight months after their enlistment."[338]

In July of 1861 Gilpin called for recruitment offices to open. He hoped to fill a proposed regiment (about 1000 men) made up of ten companies. George responded to a notice like the following, issued by Josiah Hambleton, who was to be his first commander:

> "SOLDIERS WANTED — The Undersigned having been authorized by the Governor to raise a company for the its [sic] Regiment of Colorado Volunteers, to serve for three years or during the war, has opened Recruiting offices in Empire, Nevada[ville], Central and Missouri cities, and at Black Hawk Point. Only able bodied men, who answer the requirements of the regulations of the War Department, will be accepted. J. W. Hambleton, Captain Co. G." [339]

George enlisted on October 10, 1861 in Nevadaville where he stated in his enlistment papers that his occupation was "Miner". He also declared that he was twenty-four years and five months old, single, childless and otherwise suitable to serve. He underwent a physical examination performed by one of the authorized doctors and was deemed to be free of anything that would incapacitate him from serving as a soldier. Either George's asthma was not apparent or the doctor was none too rigorous in his assessment of George's true health. Lack of rigor could be explained by the fact that, as of September 5, 1861, Governor Gilpin had appointed just three physicians for the overwhelming task of scrutinizing the health of all potential soldiers in the regiment. [340]

George was small like his grandfather, but also fully prepared like his grandfather to engage in battle for what he saw as a good cause. He fortified his courage with the same anti-slavery, pro-union convictions shared by his family in Ohio; Jo, Hen and Newell all served in the Union Army. (Eb, forty years old and hindered by those mysterious convulsions, was unfit for service according to Army regulations). George was not a hypocrite – he believed in the above ideals. But he and many of his fellow miners also had another, less lofty reason for enlisting. They wanted to protect their future interests in the Territory and that was a goal best served by supporting the federal government in the war.

Gilpin's call for volunteers attracted large numbers of miners like George. "Down out of the mountains they came in tens and twenties..." [341] All judged fit for service were made part of Gilpin's dreamed-of regiment. George became part of the Colorado First Volunteers' Company G, composed almost entirely of men who came from "Nevadaville, Empire City and neighboring Clear Creek mining camps." [342] They gathered first at Empire City (now simply Empire), undergoing some basic drilling exercises until there were enough men to fill out their ranks. Company G sought eighteen more volunteers as late as October 18, 1861. [343] The men formed an enthusiastic, if rag-tag, bunch used to the uninhibited lifestyle of the mining communities. Unlike the professional soldiers who had left the Territory to serve on other fronts, these would-be warriors were untrained and, until regulation equipment arrived, their weaponry consisted of a motley assortment of arms matching the men's appearances.

The regiment's commander was the prickly John P. Slough, a Gilpin appointee. Slough was an unfortunate choice. Born in Cincinnati in 1829, at the time of his appointment the thirty-three year old worked as an attorney in Denver. [344] He had been a politician in Ohio, but his "belligerent tendencies"[345] and a physical altercation with a fellow lawmaker caused him to be tossed from the legislature. [346] This non-career officer turned out to be no more popular with his soldiers and fellow officers than he had been in Ohio. The men soon developed such hatred for Slough that some in camp began to plot his demise – designs to kill him continued as long as he remained in charge.

But before any of those negative feelings came to the fore, the recruits congregated at Camp Weld, located close to Denver where there were scenes familiar to George. The Camp Weld inhabitants provided endless entertainment for Denverites who enjoyed watching the raw recruits attempt their often unintentionally comic drills and marching exercises, so George relived his great-great-great grandfather Mackintosh's experience of becoming a spectacle for others to view. Visitors could be present at the camp during these activities, but had to leave by nine which was lights out time for the soldiers. [347]

The newly minted soldiers adhered generally to their abiding desire to preserve the Union, but lacked the discipline necessary to form an effective fighting body at first. Life in the mining camps had done nothing to instill much more than a dogged preservation of personal freedom. The commanding officers had their work cut out for them. The large numbers of "cocky, free-dom-fancying" miners were not easily molded into self-controlled soldiers who would immediately and unquestioningly obey an order. [348] Chafing under the new lifestyle imposed on them, they were insolent to their officers and far more interested in making mischief than in learning what must have seemed like pointless and even childish military exercises. Many of their antics were harmless, designed more to taunt authority than to do real damage.   At one point a group of men learned that a guard detail was to be selected from among their ranks. The officer in charge lined them up, intending to choose men for the detail from the left end of the line. Learning of this tactic, the men foiled the officer by arranging themselves in circles. [349] The "Pet Lambs" resembled not in the least the meek animals for which they were named.

Some of them began to make their own fun – and it wasn't always legal. The men whiled away the time by enhancing their meager Army diets with hens and hams pilfered from local smokehouses. The drinkers among them (not George) "broke into saloons to get whiskey and champagne." [350] Tired of looking like scarecrows, some of them also broke into haberdashery shops and took clothing. Before long the Denver public had decided that the soldiers were no longer quite so diverting, but rather behaving disgracefully. It is not beyond possibility that the good-humored George participated in some mischievous acts. And if he had inherited any of his grandfather's personality along with his Scottish coloring, it is likely that he found irresistible the opportunity to twit the officers. Joining in such antics helped him forge the bonds soldiers need to feel when they are going to be fighting together against a common enemy.

A number of the men reacted to Camp Weld's unprofessional atmosphere by deserting. Spurring them on was the knowledge that some in Denver interpreted their wild behavior as lack of ability and believed that the Colorado First "was a failure." [351] Some of the troops began to believe this assessment themselves and deserted so as to join a regular Army unit in the "States". This defeatist spirit infected George's company when its Captain, the very same Josiah Hambleton who had advertised for men, deserted briefly and refused to be mustered in again when he returned. [352]Captain William F. Wilder assumed command of Company G in Hambleton's place.

Before long, reports of Texas Confederate advances on Fort Union in the New Mexico Territory made it clear that the Lambs, prepared or not, would soon have to show what they could do militarily. Canby ordered the Camp Weld men to move south as soon as possible. The *Daily Rocky Mountain News* reported on February 13, 1862 that,

> Orders were read to the entire regiment at Camp Weld this morning, to prepare for an immediate march to Santa Fe, to join the command of Col. Canby. It was hailed with joy by all, and each set about with alacrity to prepare himself for the march. All hail the rising star of the Colorado First, and may the God of battles watch over and protect them, and enable them to add new luster to the fame of the American army. They have the valor to do it, and only want the chance to display it.

"Immediate" did not mean that the Volunteers set off the next morning or even the one after that. It was difficult to get this army organized for a long foot march. The urgency to do so increased though, when people in the Colorado Territory learned that Texas Colonel H. H. Sibley had successfully led his forces against the northerners at the Battle of Valverde on February 20 and 21. He and his troops had to be stopped.

It was a distinct relief to citizens and restive soldiers alike when, on March 1, 1862, the First Colorado Regiment marched out of Camp Weld along the Platte en route to meet the Confederates in New Mexico. The men sang as they started out. Their lyrics mingled bravado with the camaraderie engendered in camps like Nevadaville:

> "Way out upon the Platte, near Pike's Peak we were told
> There by a little digging we could get a pile of gold,
> So we bundled up our duds, resolved at least to try
> And tempt old Madame Fortune, root hog, or die!" [353]

When not singing, the men spoke with each other about meeting the Confederates, bragging outwardly and probably worrying inwardly about how brave they would be in battle.

But music and chats didn't last long.

Four hundred of the men made up a mounted cavalry unit led by Major John M. Chivington (1829-1894), a blustery Methodist minister popular with the troops. George was among the remaining approximately 500 soldiers who went on foot. The rest had been sent earlier as a detachment to Fort Wise (soon to be renamed Fort Lyon), located in southeastern Colorado on the Arkansas River. George, whose asthma had so often cast him in the role of an invalid, was about to face enormous tests of both endurance and courage, beginning with the forty-five miles they are said to have walked south that first day.

The following evening they camped in view of Pike's Peak. If George's lungs hadn't already been strained by the long march, they suffered greatly when one of Colorado's notorious winds blew snow and ice at an estimated speed of fifty miles per hour into their encampment. No tent could protect them from that frigid wind that covered their heads and beards with stiff ice. The men must have wondered if they had come this far only to die before even meeting the enemy. Some were frostbitten so badly in the three-day storm that they were in no shape to fight, so had to be taken to a Colorado City (now Colorado Springs) hospital. [354]

The terrible weather caused Slough and Chivington to rail at one another. Slough wanted to return to Colorado City (which he did for a few days) while the swaggering Chivington accused Slough of cowardice and dereliction of duty. Slough's desertion of his troops, even for just a few days, coupled with his decision to ride in a coach for the entire journey from Denver to Fort Union, located ninety-four miles northeast of Santa Fe, cemented their disdain for him. From then on they would give all their loyalty and trust to Chivington whom Slough had accused of being a "crazy preacher" with a Napoleonic attitude,[355] an impolitic characterization that, however, contained some kernel of truth in it.

The storm lasted for three days. Only on March 6 were they able to begin to make their way through the deep snow. Famished and exhausted, they were finally allowed to camp for the night. It was then that Chivington learned that the Texans had taken Albuquerque and Santa Fe, but had still not arrived at Fort Union, so there was a chance that the men of the Colorado First could forestall such an occurrence entirely. The news was exactly what the soldiers needed to hear to reenergize them. Once again they headed south, at Chivington's command dropping everything but their weapons and some blankets on the brutal, increasingly fast-paced march. [356]

They arrived at Fort Union on the night of March 11, bone-chilled and bone-weary, receiving a rousing welcome and a much-deserved rest. In under a two-week period they had covered about 400 miles under the harshest of conditions. All the men, including George, survived, but Colonel Slough was a near casualty for a different reason. His procrustean, overbearing ways continued to nettle many of the independent-minded men he commanded and once again some plotted to shoot him.[357] The disgruntled soldiers abandoned their deadly intentions, but any small confidence some might have had in Slough eroded away.

At Fort Union the fatigued soldiers quickly regained enough energy to misbehave in much the same way as they had in Denver, "generally staying drunk and defiant for the entire time." [358] A Sergeant Darius Philbrook overdid it with his loud, intoxicated behavior, so Lieutenant Isaac Gray arrested him. The simple arrest became violent when Philbrook, enraged at the attempt to take him into custody, shot Gray several times, wounding him in the face. A court-martial ensued, at the end of which the presiding officer sentenced Philbrook to death. The sentence must have shaken George and the other men and awakened them to the seriousness of their commitment to the army. [359] They would not have to witness his execution by a firing squad on March 27th because five days before the event they would be out of the fort, soon to face the guns of the enemy. Before that day, though, their commanding officers knew that the soldiers needed as much extra training as they could drum into them.

These still unshaped recruits had proven their mettle in getting themselves south, but would they have the discipline necessary to fight the Confederates effectively? Their arrival at Fort Union signaled the resumption of about ten days of drilling to whip the seemingly carefree men into shape. The men might have exhibited some nonchalance because rumors abounded of panicky Rebels scrambling to leave the Territory because they thought the Union forces out-numbered them. In fact, the Confederates were the dominant force. [360] In any case, the rumors exaggerated the situation and there were large numbers of southern soldiers in the area.

While his troops worked towards becoming a fierce fighting team, Colonel Slough showed his own brand of aggression in unilaterally supplanting the authority of Fort Union's West Point-trained veteran senior officer, Colonel Gabriel R. Paul, despite Paul's protests to those higher up the chain of com-mand. [361] Paul was under the impression that he *and* Slough were to wait at Fort Union until they received further orders. But, as Slough slightly later related in an official report dated March 30, 1862, he understood his goal to be that of "annoying and harassing the enemy" [362] with his army of over 1,300 men, including not only the Colorado First Volunteers, but also some New Mexico volunteers and some regular army men. [363] Slough prevailed.

The Volunteers and the other troops set out to meet the enemy on March 22. George and his fellow soldiers spent about three days marching approxi-mately forty-five miles to Bernal Springs where they arrived on March 24th or 25th. Confederate Major Charles H. Pyron, underestimating the number of the Federal troops, known to the Texans as the "Pike's Peakers", decided to engage them. The two armies were soon to confront each other at Glorieta Pass, "a high, constricted part of the Santa Fe Trail that twisted through the southern rim of the rugged Sangre de Cristo Mountains."[364] The clash would become known as the "Gettysburg of the West". Although not everyone agrees on the details of this battle and the events that led up to it, it is an inescapable fact that the maverick Chivington [365] created a center-stage role for himself at the time.

As a scouting party the Major and his men encountered an advance party of Texans at Johnson's Ranch in Adobe Canyon on March 26th, engaging, against Slough's orders, in a three-hour fight with the southerners who retreated at its conclusion. Chivington's success assaulted the previously over-confident southern troops psychologically. They now had to face the sober truth that their push north through New Mexico and on into Colorado might not be as simple as it had once appeared. Pyron asked Chivington for a brief truce. He also requested that W. R. Scurry join him with reinforcements. Scurry complied, joining Pyron at Johnson's Ranch where their combined forces amounted to nearly 1000 soldiers.

On March 28th Scurry led his men back up Apache Canyon, having left the Confederates' supply train under a small guard at Johnson's Ranch. [366] This was the Texan's fatal mistake, but he wasn't to know it until the Battle of Glorieta Pass had concluded. Little did he suspect that, just before the battle, Chivington and his men had proceeded along the sixteen miles to Johnson's Ranch where they overpowered the guard detail, took them prisoner and destroyed the supplies and livestock without which Scurry and his men could not survive.[367] Meanwhile, Slough had arrived with about 850 men to add to Chivington's force. The two armies met each other in the hills at the narrow pass where a deep gorge loomed below. The engagement began at about eleven a.m., the canyon raked by bullets fired from behind trees on opposite banks of the canyon. The noise of cracking shots and soldiers' battle cries echoed as the men fought in the swirling smoke that grew thicker every time they fired their weapons. It was not battle of the anonymous sort, but soon became a very personal form of combat. A Texan later recalled, "On they came to what I supposed certain destruction but nothing like lead or iron seemed to stop them, for we were pouring it into them from every side like hail in a storm. In a moment these devils had run the gauntlet for half a mile, and we were fighting hand to hand with our men in the road."[368] The miners and their comrades were a force to be contended with, driven on by a sense of patriotism and "itching for a fight." [369]

By about two in the afternoon "both forces…formed battle lines across the Santa Fe Trail a half mile west of Pigeon's Ranch." [370] Although they hauled out their artillery, both armies found that individual men armed with rifles were more effective on the uneven, tree-covered terrain. George and the rest of the men in Company G "came up on the double-quick", Captain Wilder leading his soldiers to join other companies where they "stubbornly held their ground, only yielding, inch by inch, to an overwhelmingly superior fire." [371] Although out-numbered and having to retreat step by step, the "Pet Lambs" kept firing vol-ley after volley at the Confederates. By dusk both armies were exhausted and stopped shooting at each other. Mild-mannered George, who would later share so many memories with Neil, did not like to talk much to his grandson about the battles in New Mexico. Although he would fight valiantly with the rest of them, he did not savor killing men, no matter what their convictions were. Slough led his men back to Koslowski's Ranch, located southeast of the battle-field. Martin Koslowski, the Pole who owned the ranch, extended unstinting hospitality to the Union soldiers whose cause he supported enthusiastically. [372]

Scurry may be forgiven for believing that he and his men had reigned supreme at Glorieta as he surveyed the retreat of the Union forces. But the vic-tory did not belong to the Confederates. Upon his return to Johnson's Ranch Scurry discovered the devastated state of his vital supplies and livestock. Instead of leading a victory celebration, Scurry had to send an emissary to Koslowski's with a request for another truce. [373] Without food, medical equipment, or ani-mals the southerners had no alternative but to attempt a demoralized return to Santa Fe. The exultant Union troops followed Slough back to Fort Union, jubilant about their oddly achieved victory. Although the significance of the win was not lost on those in the Colorado and New Mexico Territories, the rest of the country paid little attention and even today the Battle of Glorieta goes largely unrecorded in standard histories of the Civil War.

Colonel Slough, still hated by most of his men, unhappy about the hor-rors of combat, and finally having to admit that perhaps he had made a mistake in overriding Paul, resigned his commission on March 31, 1862. He rode off immediately to Denver. [374] The men who held Slough in such contempt peti-tioned for the appointment of Major Chivington to replace him. Their officers supported the request. Chivington received a promotion to Colonel and Regi-mental Commander of the Colorado soldiers in the New Mexico Territory. [375] Alonzo Ickis, later a scout for Kit Carson, echoed the simple sentiments of many of his fellow soldiers when he wrote in his diary on April 12, 1862, "Chiv-ington is in command of the Col 1st — he is a brave man and a preacher". [376] Chivington's overweening confidence probably did not endear him to George, but the younger man might have felt a connection to the older because both hailed from Ohio and both were Methodists.

The two armies engaged one another once again on April 15, 1862 at Peralta, eighteen miles south of Albuquerque. Confederate Colonel Thomas Jefferson Green and his Fifth Texas Mounted Volunteers, in retreat after the Battle of Glorieta, had camped all around and inside Territorial Governor Henry Connelly's extensive adobe house there. [377] The disillusioned Texans released steam by plundering Connelly's wine cellar and seem to have felt little threat from the northerners. Meanwhile, Chivington and Paul and their men quietly surrounded the relaxed Confederates. Eager to rid the area of their foes once and for all, the impatience of the Colorado First and their compatriots was at last assuaged when they received the order to begin firing. The Texans, jolted from their carousing, used the village's adobe fences and irrigation ditches as defensive points as they returned the intense shooting.

Somehow Alonzo Ickis found time to record events of the Battle of Peralta practically as they were occurring. He noted at eleven a.m. on April 15th that, "Pauls [sic] battery is at work on the west   ours on the NE   the enemy is in a warm place...firing round shot   they are coming thick and fast around our co.....3 (P.M.) Paul has driven them from the Governors [sic] house   the strongest building." [378]

The relatively minor battle (four Confederate soldiers did lose their lives) ended when a sandstorm blew in at two in the afternoon and obscured visibility for both sides. Canby ordered the Union soldiers to stop firing. Eager to thoroughly rout the enemy, they blamed him for halting matters prematurely. But his decision turned out to be correct. The Confederates, weakened physically and emotionally and without faith in their leaders, fell apart and continued to make their way painstakingly back to Texas. About 3,500 of them had embarked on the quest to conquer the New Mexico and Colorado Territories — more than a seventh of that number died in battle or succumbed to wounds or illness; "another 500 were missing or in Federal prison camps." [379] Peralta was another casualty, virtually destroyed, the bullets and cannon balls making short work of fragile adobe and cottonwood trees.

The Battle of Peralta was the Colorado Volunteers' final encounter with the Confederates, except for rounding up a few prisoners of war. Their days of action were not over, but first they had to get back to Camp Weld, by way of Fort Craig. Their physical condition was not that much better than the enemy's, another reason for Canby to give up pursuing the southerners as they fled toward Texas. Rations at this point were barely edible. Both George and Newell had similar experiences with respect to their Army diet. On December 21, 1862 Newell, serving with the Union Army in the South, complained to George of having to eat "corn on the ear" and "rancid bacon.....[and] that the soldiers would not eat unless drove to it by Starvation." But far worse than hunger and exhaustion for the men in New Mexico was the knowledge that over a hundred soldiers from the Colorado First had died and 171 had been wounded. [380] George and all of his Ohio brothers who served in the Civil War escaped physical harm, a remarkable fact, considering that it was not unusual for several male relations from a single family to be wounded or killed in this war.

The Colorado First finally arrived at Fort Craig on April 19th and stayed there for some months, just in case the Confederates managed to regroup and attack again. Later that summer the bulk of the First, including George and Company G, began to move out, camping first along the Rio Grande River amid stands of cottonwood, where they weren't able to fend off the mosquitoes as well as they had the Texans. [381] Mosquitoes, sandstorms, heat – all combined to make the men's journey uncomfortable. They had many miles to go before reaching Fort Union, across desert areas where the only water to be found was "brackish, covered with lice and green slime." But they pushed on, arriving at Fort Union on September 4. [382]

Not until December of 1862 did the men return to Denver and Camp Weld.[383] According to Colorado First Volunteer Ovando Hollister, "They tramped back over that weary interval in mid winter, destitute of fuel and with little transportation. Such service does not look big in print, but it requires more patriotic self-denial than almost any other. " [384] By the time they reached Denver, they had been renamed. On November 1, 1862 the Colorado First Volunteers became the Colorado First Cavalry and would soon have new duties that required them to become horsemen.

Denverites anticipated the men's return with excitement — and some trepidation. The *Weekly Commonwealth and Republican* of January 15, 1863, announced "The Arrival of the First":

> Back again to the scenes of their first enlistment, and to the camp which was their first home as soldiers came the glorious First Regiment of Colorado, the heroes of three victorious engagements.

Yesterday the tops of the houses were crowded with spectators, and
the streets lined with eager crowds to greet those men who have by
their prowess saved two territories to the Union, the 'Pet Lambs of
Colorado'.

Chivington led them triumphantly into town. Observers noticed that the
young men who had left town the year before now appeared worn and dirty, but
also that their suntanned faces displayed the joy they felt upon returning safely
to the town's ovations.

Grateful Denverites, well aware of the men's brave actions, were more tol-
erant of their presence than they had been during the training period at Camp
Weld. Reported the *Daily Rocky Mountain News* on January 15, 1863, "They
have been so long in camp and on the march in the desolate regions of New
Mexico that the pleasures of town were duly appreciated...It was a good night
for 'blue coats'; they could be seen everywhere about town, full of fun, but civil,
and as quiet as could reasonably be expected."

The men of the Colorado First were in no mood to comport themselves
nicely and felt they deserved some time to drink and gamble and carouse. Chivington allowed the revelry to go on for a short time, but eventually reined in his
men. A week after their arrival, most of them camped quietly on the southeast
side of Camp Weld where they read and wrote letters, mended clothes and gear,
cared for livestock, cooked and slept and behaved much as they had during free
time in the mining camps. They probably felt at something of a loss: like
George, most of them had enlisted for a period of three years – now that they
had routed the Confederates, what did the Union army have in mind for them?
Their new name might have given them a hint.

Various Indian tribes had taken advantage of the troops' absence from the
northern parts of the Territory by attacking unguarded settlers and stages. It
was now time to tackle this challenge to the Territory's security with the new
mounted cavalry. But George was not to be a part of any army actions against
Indian people, not because of scruples he might have had, but for health reasons. His weakened lungs that had withstood so much finally succumbed in
January of 1863 when, in his own words, he was "taken down with the Pneumonia. I remained in Camp Weld near Denver Six month [sic] before I went
into active service again." [385] In June while Newell was simmering in the heat
of Vicksburg and Port Hudson, Mississippi and Chivington "began mobilizing

troops for the largest Indian expedition yet mounted from Colorado" [386]
George remained in camp, recuperating. His Company G, now under the command of George W. Hawkins, was notified that it should "be ready to march on
a day's notice." [387] George was not to be among them, but the Army found tasks
for him as soon as he was well. One was mundane, but the other involved participation in government acts that had historic import for opening the west,
although those acts were not always honorable.

By August of 1863 the First Colorado Cavalry muster rolls show that
George found himself in an entirely new role in his brief army career. Because
of his fragile health, instead of participating in skirmishes with the native tribes,
he served as the camp's cook! But his culinary position ended for an assignment
with a bit more cachet when he was detached from his company to become part
of an armed guard for the new Territorial Governor, John Evans (1814-1897).
Evans had replaced Gilpin when those shaky financial transactions on behalf of
his "Lambs" finally caught up with Gilpin and the public's trust in him began to
wear away. [388] As early as the summer of 1862 even the military successes of his
troops could not forestall mutterings that the governor was off his head and had
nearly bankrupted the country. Gilpin defended himself vigorously in Washington, but was soon dismissed, to be succeeded by Evans who served as governor of the Territory from 1862-65.

Evans faced his own crises early in his term when he had to deal with the
tribal uprisings against settlers. Deputed to appease the agitated natives, on
August 27th Evans rode east from Denver to the Red Fork of the Republican
River with George as part of his armed escort to meet with representatives of
the Arapaho and Cheyenne nations. His goal was to convince them to live on
the land reserved for them by the Treaty of Fort Wise (December 5, 1861). The
land lay along the Arickaree River where the government expected that these
proud people would become docile farmers. The Indians, however, had no
intention of capitulating to Evans' offer of a restricted area of land for a permanent residence. They simply did not appear at the meeting at all.

A dispirited Evans rode back to Denver and in October, again accompanied by George and other mounted soldiers, he turned south toward Colorado
Territory's settlement of Conejos to meet with the Tabeguache Utes. Evans and
John G. Nicolay, President Lincoln's private secretary, occupied a wagon, with
their escort riding alongside. [389] Conejos, located a few miles from the New

Mexico border, took George back along the route he had walked under such adverse conditions just the year before, but this time there were no blizzards and he had a horse securely under him.

At Conejos George witnessed extraordinary scenes. The Utes, determined to display their own disciplined military might, organized themselves into "squadrons" [390] and marched into the Indian Agency compound on October 7, 1863. Evans, Nicolay and a few others enjoyed the display from the roof of an adobe structure. [391] George viewed the Utes in their full regalia from atop his horse and witnessed Evans presenting medals to seven of the leading Utes.[392] The Tabeguache Utes, persuaded by Chief Ouray, were more amenable to reservation living than the Arapahoes and Cheyennes. They signed the October 7th treaty, known originally as the "Treaty with the Utah-Tabeguache Band, 1863", ceding enormous areas of valuable land to the United States government.

An observer to the gathering remarked upon the cavalry that was in attendance "against any trouble that might arise…there were never less than 500 soldiers to preserve peace." [393] There was no disturbance during the event and Evans and his party left for Denver satisfied with the way matters had transpired. In a weird side note to this historic meeting at Conejos, a pair of sociopathic brothers terrorizing the area thought that this was their opportunity to assassinate Evans on his homeward journey. Felipe Nerio Espinosa and Jose Espinosa, known as the "Bloody Espinosas", were local cutthroats who preyed upon settlers they viewed as squatters on their Conejos County land. [394] They already had killed and mutilated over thirty people before targeting Evans who to them was a symbol of the government that had taken "their" land and given it to the Utes. They had threatened to kill Evans (who was completely unaware of the two men) and the others in his group unless Evans restored the land to them. In the middle of October Evans and Nicolay, surrounded securely by the Army guard, rode unconcernedly back to Denver. Instead of harming Evans, the Espinosas kidnapped two people who were not fortunate enough to have their own bodyguards. [395]

His escort duty complete, George was then dispatched approximately one hundred-fifteen miles south to Pueblo in March of 1864 to retrieve Army horses. Although he would not muster out until the fall of that year, the most exciting and perilous parts of his military service were now over. He had defended the western region that he now considered to be his home. Unlike

George, each of his soldier brothers served in a different location in the South. Like George, their passions for preserving the Union and for living in a country free from slavery had been bred in them. Their feelings seemed clear, but those of their native state were more muddled. The Northwest Ordinance of 1787 and Ohio's 1803 state Constitution both specified that Ohio was to be a "free state" without slavery. [396] But the state also adhered to the Fugitive Slave Act of 1850 that mandated the return of runaway slaves, so by mid-century there was a schizophrenic aspect to Ohio's position regarding slavery.

Northeastern Ohio, influenced by its New England heritage, had long held anti-slavery sentiments. In the 1850s Portage County witnessed a number of public protests against the abhorrent practice. The teenaged George and his siblings may have been present at some of these events; even if they hadn't attended in person, they would have heard much discussion about the protests. Their personal associations with black people were limited. Mantua's first African-American residents, a married couple, had arrived as early as 1816, but few others joined them. By and large, whites in the Western Reserve coexisted peacefully with their black neighbors whose small numbers caused little "racial hostility." [397] But, even if the independent-minded McIntoshes knew few black people, they believed strongly that one person should not be held in thrall to another. And they believed that the states that their relatives and grandfather had helped settle and fight for must remain united.

Their feelings became public when David McIntosh ran for state representative as an anti-slavery Whig in 1845. A pro-slavery Democrat won that election, but the times were changing quickly. Moral opposition to slavery had come to predominate in Portage County. The sentiment grew even stronger with the outbreak of the Civil War. Portage County men did not just pay lip service to their convictions: over 2000 men from the county served in the Union Army during the Civil War; 312 died. [398]

In northern Ohio there was early and heavy enlistment among those men without farms, businesses or families. Memories of their "revolutionary inheritance" [399] played a part in their decisions to defend the Union. Besides Ebenezer's story, the young McIntoshes had before them the examples of their uncles — Moses' service in the War of 1812 and David's early participation in the Twentieth Division of the Ohio militia where he rose to the rank of Major General. [400] Mantua was no different than other Portage County townships in terms of offering up its male citizens for service. C. H. Ray, George's neighbor and contemporary who had so admired John Brown in Kansas, enlisted in the Union army, as did his five brothers. [401] One of those brothers, Mart Ray, served in the same regiment as Newell and figured in some of Newell's letters to his brothers during the war.

Young Newell was the first of the brothers to enlist, on September 20, 1861, just twenty days before George. He served in Company A of the Ohio 42nd Infantry Regiment, under the command of none other than James Garfield who drew many of the recruits for this regiment from "his former students at the [Hiram] Eclectic Institute." [402]

Three years later, on October 3, 1864, Jo left Rhoda and Jerusha in charge of the farm and enlisted in the 177th Ohio Volunteer Regiment. He reported his enlistment in a letter to George that November, noting that he had received a $600 farm bounty in exchange for his signing up. Jo underwent a brief training period at Camp Cleveland, "the largest of Cleveland's seven Civil War camp sites". [403] It was at Camp Cleveland that he spotted Newell who had been mustered out just a few days earlier, on September 30, 1864. Newell was at that point a sadly battle-seasoned young man. Jo was relieved that his young brother was going back to Rome, Ohio to live in Jo's house with Rhoda and Jerusha that winter. Jo wrote to George from Tullahoma, Tennessee where he did guard duty, but that was not all he did, for Jo was the third of the McIntosh brothers to participate in battle. From December 5th through 12th of 1864 the 177th successfully defended Murfreesboro, Tennessee and participated in several other fights in Tennessee and North Carolina. When Jo was officially discharged from duty at North Carolina on July 7, 1865, he made his way back to his family and the farm in Ohio. [404]

Late-enlisting farmers like Jo received a sympathetic defense from Ohio newspapers. The editor of the *Athens Messenger* on February 27, 1862 asserted that, "There has never been a time in the history of our government when so much depended upon the energy of our farming community. Our extensive armies are to be fed by the hands of the farmers..." The writer also provided justification for Jo and Hen to remain on their farms and not participate in military duty at all. "All could not become soldiers. It is just as necessary that some should stay at home, as that others should take up arms, and many could better serve their country by staying at home than by becoming soldiers in the field." [405] When Jo enlisted, however, there were approximately half a million "farm laborers" who *had* entered the army, a number that caused one commentator to remark, "In this the agricultural class has exhibited a most creditable patriotism." [406]

Hen waited until early 1865 to join the army. On February 21, 1865 Hen became part of the 184th Regiment, Ohio Volunteer Infantry, organized at Camp Chase in Columbus. Soon thereafter he was sent to Tennessee where the regiment engaged primarily in guard duty of various sorts. [407] The men returned to Camp Chase after being mustered out in September of 1865 and Henry returned safely to Ridgeville.

Newell's time in the Union army paralleled George's only in terms of the number of years he served. Even though George fought bravely in those important, but largely ignored clashes in New Mexico, he did not experience the unrelenting carnage that his younger brother did. The bookish twenty-year old participated in numerous fierce battles in Kentucky, Tennessee (Battle of Chickasaw Bluffs, December 26-29, 1862), Arkansas, and Mississippi (the Battle of Port Gibson on May 1, 1863, the Siege of Vicksburg, May 25-July 4, 1863, and the Siege of Jackson, July 10-1, 1863).

Rind worried greatly about both of her younger brothers and corresponded as often as she could with them. Just a few of their letters survive, but from even that small sampling one gets a distinct sense of the affectionate bonds that linked the siblings in that terrible time. Rind's letter to George on February 27, 1863 repeated some of what Newell had written to her:

> He was them [sic] at Memphis Tennisse was well but Tiared of the war — he says they are fighting to no purpes for the southern confederacy will have to be acknowledged. Says that we lost 900 men in a single assault upon the works at Vicksburg — out of his brigade of 2700 they lost 1200 so you can see that death was busy around him – he has seen very hard time for a boy as he is – he says he has seen the elephant…says he shall never see home again.

It was common for people in small towns to be amazed at the exotic animals paraded down main street by traveling circuses and they spoke of "seeing the elephant" to express their wonderment. The phrase drew currency in the Civil War, but the awe, in this case, applied to the horrors of battle. [408] Indeed,

Newell *had* seen the elephant. But battle was only one threat to soldiers on both sides of the conflict. When he wrote to Rind from Memphis on August 17, 1863, Newell reported that he was healthy as opposed to other soldiers in his unit, some of whom Rind knew from Mantua days. "We left M Ray and H Briggs at Vicksburg sick Mart had a furlough and will be home longe before you get this." And on September 6 of that year Jo told George that "Mart Ray cam home last week sick with cronic diarea he looks Hard."

Jo, the older brother who seems to have taken seriously his role as the looked-to head of the family (perhaps he had kicked his drinking habit), chided George gently on December 21, 1862. He noted that George's December 10th letter was the first word he had had from his young brother for eight months while "New" wrote almost twice a month. Even though George's letters did not arrive as regularly as Newell's, this one must have had a positive tone because Jo remarked, "I am glad to hear that you stand camp life & that you was out of the Servis."[sic] Jo probably meant that George was out of the fighting because his younger brother was obligated to two more years in the Union army at this point. Jo also informed George that their mother "frets a good deal about you."

In the same letter Jo informed George about Newell's participation in the June military maneuvers led by Brigadier General George W. Morgan at Cumberland Gap, where the road led through the Appalachian Mountains. Losing patience with the Union army's ability to feed and clothe the men who were fighting so valiantly, Newell had written comments that Jo characterized only as "not very patriotic." Caroline, to whom Newell had written similar sentiments, was more understanding about his possible motivations for penning words that disturbed Jo, who was as yet untested in battle when he received Newell's letter.

Not all of the news conveyed by the letters was war-related. Jo sensed that his siblings would want to hear about Mantua, both the bad and the good. Foreshadowing an event with less dire consequences that would occur in George's life sixteen years later was the message that their neighbor, George Vaughn,

> was killed by a horse running away six weeks ago he had been to a [illegible] Bee started home about 5 OClock & as soon as he drove into the road his hors took fright & ran about ½ m...they found George with one leg hanging in the shaves tangled in with his Buffalow robe he had dragged about 100 Rods his skull was fractured & had Recd internal injuries that cased his death in about ½ hower.

Newell, too, provided interesting social observations from the south for his siblings to enjoy. On August 17, 1864 while George was on daily duty in the cavalry yard at Camp Weld, Newell wrote to Jo from his encampment near Carrollton, Louisiana on August 17, 1864. Just a few nights before, Newell and his fellow troops had boarded a steamer that took them to Natchez, Mississippi (taken by Union forces in 1863) where the men gorged on fresh fruit sold by dockside peddlers. "The boys were rather greedy," wrote Newell. "The result was Collic— many a poor beloved paid dearly for his intemperance". Was this latter allusion a gentle reminder to Jo to stay away from drink? Perhaps. In any case, the sight recalled for Newell "sweet aples", those Mantua pleasures that the McIntosh family raised with such success.

On September 22, 1864 the youngest brothers awaited their discharges from service. Newell had been promoted to the rank of Corporal on May 4, 1863 and became a Sergeant a month before mustering out. George remained a Private throughout his service. Newell wrote to George that day, addressing his brother in the formal style that marked much of the correspondence between them, "Dear sir two days ago I recd a letter from you stateing that you was at Denver city." His thoughts often turned to home and he told George that "The country through here [Louisiana] is level and swampy with bayous runing in all directions as thick as brooks in olde Portage", an image that must have stirred George's heart.

George surely empathized with his brother's privations and terrible battle experiences, but it is unlikely that, after his own long, frigid march, he felt impressed when, in the same letter, Newell told him that his superior officers had informed the troops that they had a "twenty five days march before us and that our safty depended upon the rapidity of our movement and the ammunition we carried. well the order scared us into leaving evry thing behinde but our blankets." While Newell wrote of these events, George once again found himself out of action and under medical care. In late September 1864 he suffered from severe intestinal problems; on October 8-11 "Tertian Intermittent Fever", or malaria, kept him bed-ridden.

George mustered out of the Union army on October 27, 1864. Unlike some others in his Company, he did not re-enlist and it was this decision that allowed him to avoid participation in the Sand Creek Massacre on November 29, 1864. Any admiration he may have felt for his former commander, Colonel Chivington, dissolved upon hearing the news of the indiscriminate slaughter of hundreds of Arapahos and Cheyennes camped north of Fort Lyon. Late in his life George told his grandson, Neil, that the massacre was a terrible event.[409]

By the time the Civil War had ended in 1865 Hen, Jo, and Newell had all returned to their northeastern Ohio homes. But Rind, the faithful recorder of their lives together in the 1850s, did not survive to see the end of the conflict. Untouched directly by battles and settled in a small farming community only occasionally harassed by Confederates, Rind devoted her attention to raising her stepson and daughters. Her husband owned many acres of land, worked as the postmaster of Wyoming City, and ran a grocery store where, after the county gave its permission, he was able to sell liquor in 1862.[410] Caroline's strong anti-liquor stance must have been put to the test with this direct affront to her beliefs by someone so close to her, but no recriminations appear in her surviving correspondence.

Rind and Clark's most intimate connections to the Civil War were through their respective brothers. On February 27, 1863 Caroline wrote to George, telling him that "Clark's youngest brother is taken prisoner – he was in Tenausee." Clark added a postscript: "Brother George as Lorinda has given you all the news I here Send you my respects you halve my Simpathy and Should you ever become a prisoner as my brother is be composed take it cool for their is policy in it."

On September 14, 1863 Caroline Lorinda gave birth to her fourth child, a daughter named for her. A month later she died, followed in death shortly thereafter by the infant. George's sister was thirty-two years old. The boiler-plate newspaper obituary gives no cause of death. It contains the requisite platitudes and no more. And there the sad tale would end were it not for a postscript attached to a letter from Jo to George five years later, on July 5, 1868 when he said, "Oat Waite [a former Mantua native who then made his home in the Nebraska Territory] was here last Spring and staid over night he thinks that Clark Reed Poisened Lorinda But I cant Believe it."

There is, of course, no way to know if Waite's suspicion was true, but something odd about the circumstances of Rind's death must have stirred his suspicions. Maybe he had heard some gossip in Wyoming City. Although in some ways Clark was insensitive (opening a liquor store in the face of his wife's temperance and his quick third marriage to a nineteen-year old after Rind's death) and perhaps even criminal (after an allegation in 1872 that he destroyed a registered letter, he took his wife and children to Sterling, Colorado),[411] nothing remains to indicate trouble between him and Rind that might have prompted murder.

The Civil War touched the McIntoshes in various ways, as it did all American families to some degree or other during the conflict. Some of the soldiers were able to resume where they had left off. Hen and Jo made improvements to their farms, rebuilt their herds, and looked forward to the post-war years. Newell rejected farming in favor of studying law, but he, too, was moving forward. Only Eb, who might have found a way to prosper after the war when farmers were even more essential than ever, could not gain an advantage.

But George could. For the first time in three years he was once again an independent man. The Colorado Territory burst with opportunities for young, energetic people with vision. George fit the bill perfectly. The idea of life as a miner had lost its luster for him. Supplanting dreams of finding gold was the dream of having his own farmland, extensive acres to support the kind of thriving enterprise he had in mind. Even though he had lost those three youthful years to the war, the magnet of acres of fertile soil ready to be transformed by a gifted man gave George the impetus to establish a McIntosh farm in the West.

CHAPTER SIX

The Farmer Takes A Wife

George needed money in 1865 – badly. Almost twenty-eight years old when the Civil War neared its end, he, like others all across the country, felt an urgency to take charge of his own destiny again. He certainly hadn't gotten rich on Army pay, so he had to find some other way of financing that farm of his dreams. George was a hard worker, but also a lucky young man. More fortunate than most who had mustered out of the army, George had three sources of money.

In the fall and winter of 1864 both Jo and Newell had written to their brother with news of money due him, almost surely his share from the sale of the family home in Mantua. Jo's letter suggests that he expected that George might return to Mantua that year to collect the money and, of course, to see his family again. But George remained in the Colorado Territory, so on December 24, 1864 Newell wrote to him from Jo's farm in Rome, Ohio. The letter's stiff tone relaxes only when Newell returns to family matters.

> I received a line from REM [Eb] to day in which he states that he had heard from you, also you wished the money due you from Jo…I suppose you know the money was deposited with Mother about the 1st of Sept. and is there yet. Eb stated that you wished it sent not specifying whether at your own risk or not… I would like you to write me stating clearly how you want it sent and if by mail to

what address. Although I have no disposition to advise, I should consider it the safer way to send you a draft in lieu of the money and let you get it cashed. If you conclude so to do let me know against who it shall be made out if you have any National banks [412] in your vicinity I could get a draft on it and it would be perfectly safe. The money deposited is in one hundred dollar bills.

The receipt of this money gave George the courage and the means to move forward with his plans.

Then in early 1865 he sold his Laramie County quarter-section that was located west of present-day Fort Collins. Today that land, lying just north of Fort Collins' Old Town Historic District, is fully developed. A young Norwegian named Peter Anderson (1845-1927), who had arrived in Colorado four years before, bought the property. He moved into George's cabin in January of 1866.[413] The dual windfalls of inheritance and the sale of his property were easy gains for George, but he had to earn the rest through hard labor. Anderson had worked as a freighter during the last two years of the Civil War and may have encouraged George to turn once again to transporting goods.

Freighting hay to the mining camps had been difficult and dangerous, but it yielded huge profits. This time George enlarged his vision to carry cargo back and forth from Denver to Kansas City, Missouri. The first transcontinental railroad, still in the early stages of construction when he resumed freighting, would eventually spell the demise of such work, but George needed the job only until he could build up a sufficient bankroll to purchase land.[414] He could have gotten a job with a major freighting operation, but he had no desire to share his profits with a large business concern where he would have little say in what was required of him. After all, the Army had told him what to do for three long years. He was now more than ready to be his own man.

However, George was also prudent, so in 1866 he entered into a freighting partnership with William C. Denton who lived in the Cache La Poudre Valley near the future town of Greeley in Weld County. Denton, like many of the other area pioneers, raised small numbers of cattle whose beef steers were destined for Omaha markets.[415] This early exposure to raising cattle stimulated George's interest in the practice and, as he observed the livestock and their habits, he began to see how he might manage them more effectively. But it was only when he had a herd of his own many years later that he could test his ideas.

Although he was almost always on the road, George found time to take up a piece of Weld County land close to Denton's at Latham, near the Cache La Poudre River. (He sold it in 1870, two years after he had settled in Boulder County). During freighting's prime years, Latham was a hub, with wagons coming and going in many directions from there. [416] The traffic created an exhilarating atmosphere for George and his comrades, but became an intrusive nuisance for hungry Arapaho and Cheyenne people whose traditional lands were now occupied increasingly by white settlers. The natives sometimes raided homes or the wagons conveying goods. Neil Lohr remembered George telling him that there were times while freighting when he "had to leave his team and head out of sight because the Indians were around." [417]

All along the way to St. Louis stood stations like the one at Latham, positioned at intervals of about twelve to fifteen miles. George sometimes halted on the return to Denver from the east at the station called Church Ranch, built by George Church. The name now belongs to a major Westminster, Colorado thoroughfare (Church Ranch Road) where drivers speed by the site where, in 1868, President Ulysses S. Grant and his daughter stayed in the twelve-room house built specifically to accommodate less famous stagecoach passengers and bullwhackers like George.[418]

On his return trips west George followed the Platte River on into Denver, crossing the river by ferry or urging his oxen to pull the wagon through shallower waters. In Denver he stopped at a large loading dock known as the Elephant Corral, its name referring, as Rind had used it in her 1863 letter to George, to an amazing scene. In this case, the very scale of the transportation depot and its constant, noisy activity made it a place of astonishing sights and sounds generated by the freighters, farmers, and others who gathered there. When fire destroyed the original cottonwood log building in 1863, the owners built a warehouse on the site and there George and others unloaded and loaded goods, dickered for teams, and exchanged news.[419]

A freighter using oxen as George chose to do could make two to three round trips per season. Mules and horses moved more quickly than oxen, enabling their teamsters to get in an extra round trip. [420] But, even though the oxen were slower, they were the more reliable animals that George had come to value on the road west to the gold fields. They were inexpensive to buy and didn't require special feed, but grazed happily on just about any grass along the route. They were also strong animals with the stamina to survive the lengthy journey. The freight George carried from St. Louis back to the Colorado Territory and stops along the way varied enormously, ranging from "mining equipment and farm machinery[to]…grocery items, liquor and tobacco…firearms and ammunition." [421]

While George and his team traveled back and forth along the rutted trails he came to know all too well, others, novices to overland travel, were beginning to move west to take advantage of a momentous decision that had occurred in Washington, D. C. on May 20, 1862 when President Lincoln signed the Homestead Act of 1862. Although the federal government had failed earlier to lure settlers west, with this legislation it succeeded.

When Paschal and then his half-brothers took up their lands in the Western Reserve, they proved just how far men desperate for their own farms will go. The word *perseverance* inadequately describes their dogged, backbreaking efforts to establish a foothold in the wilderness. They did not see immediate rewards, but had to wait for years before markets opened to lift them from the world of subsistence farming. It was not a lifestyle that just anyone was suited for. But before the Homestead Act, the federal government wanted people to do exactly what the McIntosh brothers had done. It lured those who were discouraged by the scarcity of land in the East to turn to the Territories beyond the United States, but without providing the infrastructure needed to support such ventures. There were vast swathes of land available, all owned by the federal government (if one ignored tribal claims) that viewed these enormous reaches as sources of revenue. Why not offer portions of them for sale to pioneers willing to fork over the rather high price of two dollars an acre? Sadly, that uncleared land, far from markets, and without the public institutions that support a community, required so much commitment of money, energy and time that few could even contemplate such an effort. As a result, speculators entered the picture, buying up large areas and further reducing the chances that families with gumption but not much money could obtain land. The hoped-for opening up of Western lands bogged down even after the government dropped the price and size of tracts offered for sale. [422]

But Jeffersonian agrarian hopes did not wane, despite such setbacks. Land reform advocates like *New York Tribune* editor Horace Greeley, who would give his name to the town of Greeley, Colorado, despised the speculators who retarded the West's agricultural growth and prevented decent, ordinary folk from participating in that growth. After many years of advocating a means of providing virtually free farmlands, the Homestead Act's backers finally succeeded when Lincoln signed it into being. Potential homesteaders could begin to claim land on January 1, 1863, [423] following Greeley's exhortation to "Go west, young man, and grow with the country."

The rules were straightforward. The potential homesteader had to be a citizen of the United States or on the path toward citizenship and twenty-one years of age or head of a family, meaning that a single woman was also eligible to procure land. Each homesteader could acquire a quarter-section, one hundred-sixty acres, free of charge. After living on the land for five years and "improving" the property with a dwelling and so forth (some homesteaders' definitions of these structures were highly elastic and questionable) the settler had only to pay a small amount to file for title to the land. [424]

George approached the procurement of land with open eyes and pragmatism. He might have hesitated, knowing firsthand the vagaries of Colorado weather. He could have had few illusions about the almost too-dry climate and what the high winds and sudden snowstorms, hail, and extreme dips in the temperature could do to crops and livestock. However, he also knew that northeastern Colorado featured hundreds of sunny days each year. He had confidence in his own ability to make the most of those days.

George also was savvier in two other respects. Having observed his father and other Mantua famers struggling to support their families on relatively small amounts of land, he knew that a quarter-section was not sufficient to create a farm that went beyond self-sufficiency. He was also selective. Although he might have raced as others did to grab up some of the free acres, he continued to freight patiently, keeping his eyes peeled for just the right location.

It was on one of his freighting trips that he pastured his team of oxen on the Boulder County land (about forty miles north of Denver) identified officially as Section Three, Township Three, North Range 69 West in the Saint Vrain River Valley. This was land divided according to the same rules established when the surveyors partitioned the Western Reserve into townships.

The government surveyors had completed their first measurements of the St. Vrain Valley at the end of 1863. Near the tracts they established lay a tiny community called Pella where a small ferry carried people across the St. Vrain Creek at a point known as Laramie Crossing.[425]

The surveyors' official subdivisions once again set in motion the displacement of native tribes. In the words of pre-1860 Boulder County pioneer Morse Coffin, "Of course, the first settlers in this whole region were squatters on Indian lands…we used to hear that the Indians desired very much to retain this portion of the country as a permanent reservation and so we were uneasy about it and many declared they would never vacate, if so ordered, without being forced to do so. But when surveyors came in the fall of '63 we felt at rest." [426] Even early on when he had squatted on the land in Weld County, George had assumed he had a right to choose land from the vast acres spreading across the American West and likely gave little thought to the desires of local tribes.

One day when he had allowed his team to graze near Pella, George's practiced eyes spotted the oxen munching on grass that "grew high enough to hide a buffalo bull". [427] Here at last was what he had been waiting for — rich pasturage that could feed livestock and ground that he could transform into fields of wheat. He recognized that the bubbling up of moisture beneath his feet meant that he could irrigate this land, remembering, just as Newell had, the "brooks in olde Portage". He heeded St. Vrain Valley pioneers who had settled there just a few years before and who had bitter memories of watching their first grain crops wither and die due to the dry conditions. Some had taken extraordinary means to save their crops. Morse Coffin watered his young grain by hauling hundreds of pails of water from the creek. "We soon learned the soil was all right if it had water," he commented with wry understatement. [428] The men quickly began to dig the irrigation ditches that still crisscross much of Boulder County.

George was correct about the water below the ground. "Along the banks of the streams was low, level land, where the water table was so close to the surface that *wild hay grew luxuriantly.*" (my italics) [429] Here was land that could be made richly arable. Some of the liquid burbled up from what would become Lake McIntosh, formerly a small body of water that was enlarged early in the twentieth century.

The ready presence of water was vital in Colorado's arid climate where an average of only about fourteen to fifteen inches of rain falls annually in Boulder

County. And those wild grasses – gramma, buffalo and bunch — were ideally suited to the climate because they withstood both dryness and winter frosts. Instead of collapsing under the weight of ice in winter, the nourishing grasses remained standing, so livestock could have easily consumed, fattening feed all year round. [430]

There is somewhat conflicting information about how George obtained this land that was bordered on its northern edge by a rough track that had been used as a path by the area's Utes and came to be known as the Ute Highway. It is most likely that in 1868 he homesteaded the quarter-section described above *after* buying lots One and Two of the northwest quarter-section from a man named Norman E. Parker. We tend to look back on the Homestead Act with some degree of romantic nostalgia – free land for hardworking pioneers is a compelling image. In fact, however, "much good land was already in the possession of the railroads and states", so many potential homesteaders were left with little option but to buy. [431] On August 10, 1867 George paid Parker $500 for the two lots.[432] The sale did just what the federal government had hoped to end with the Homestead Act – it turned Parker into a speculator even if that had not been his intent. Parker used the commutation clause of the Homestead Act to sell his land: after living on the land for six months or more, he could sell it legally. He was then obligated to repay the government $1.25 per acre, giving him a profit in the deal with George. Parker had probably taken up the land shortly after the Homestead Act came into being, so had occupied it for about four years — selling it was likely not his original aim. Like so many others, he just may not have been able to support his family by farming. [433]

George abandoned freighting and hitched his wagon firmly to the star of farming in Boulder County. His timing in acquiring Parker's quarter-section and homesteading his own could not have been much better. Focused on finding gold and fighting the Civil War, other people were slow to take advantage of the Territory's agricultural possibilities, so good land was still available when George was on the lookout for it. Latecomers would not be as fortunate. He joined a small community of earlier settlers, people like Morse Coffin and his brother Reuben, Matt McCaslin, William H. Dickens and his half-brother Alonzo Allen, George and Mary Zweck (whose descendants still farm in the area). Ohioans, the majority of whom came from farming families, comprised the largest group of people settling on land in northeastern Colorado in the nineteenth century. [434] Like George, the farmers among them began the home-steading effort with a distinct advantage over people less experienced with farming practices — most avoided the pitfalls of greenhorns and turned the area into a rich agricultural region. But not every Ohioan could triumph over the land.

While George began forging his way as a farmer-rancher in the Colorado Territory, one of his brothers in Ohio floundered. On July 15, 1868 Jo wrote to George that Eb "lives at Plank Road station six milds from Cleveland — he has a small place & hardly makes a living." Just four years later on June 10, 1872 Eb wrote to his "Well wished Brother" George to say that he and his family resided in the small iron manufacturing town of Niles, something over twenty-five miles southeast of Mantua and close to Youngstown. Eb had lost his place on Plank Road and was reduced to laboring in a stone quarry for two dollars a day. Remembering the loss of his earlier place, he lamented, "It keeps me a homping to keep up having the humiliation of watching it auctioned off."

The auction was a bitter pill for Eb to swallow. He wrote, "I did Not know of the Sale till the Day It was Sold." Eb moved his wife and children to Ashtabula, practically on the shores of Lake Erie, where his family all "Did Chores and thrashed Oats for our keeping..." Somehow Eb managed to give his daughters the opportunity to go to school that summer. He continued, "I Stil Live and Shall Live til my time Comes. I did almost give up the Ship but I Come to the Conclusion It wase No use to Mourne for Spilt Milk but to try It anew. So I have. I worke all the time." George undoubtedly felt pangs for the almost fifty-year old Eb, but his brother's travails did not shake George's belief in his own ability to make a go of farming.

Henry continued to till the land in Ridgeville and Jo was busy improving his farm. Before he left for service in the Civil War, he had had to sell his dairy, but on July 15, 1868 he wrote to George that he had assembled a herd of nineteen cows and employed several farmhands to whom he paid "from $2 to $3 a/day". While he rebuilt his dairy business in 1868, Jo also repaired his house, so, as he told George, his family and Jerusha had to "liv[e] in the chees [sic] house" in the meantime, a phrase that tells us that he engaged in Portage County's famed cheese-making industry. He had planted ten acres of corn and potatoes, "6 acres of Rye, 4 of wheat, & 6 of oats. My haying & harvesting is coming together. Crops look well." George already owned more acres than his father had possessed. Now that he had the land, hearing of Jo's thriving crops made him even more eager to start preparing the ground and doing some planting of his own.

It would have been an almost impossible task for a single man to accomplish on his own. But George was not alone. While on what was probably his final post-war freighting trip, he had encountered an ex-slave whose name is known to us only as "Darkey Jim". [435] Jim was sick and weak. Empathetic and all too familiar with the debilitating effects of illness, George saw potential where others did not. He also undoubtedly felt some need to help this man who had been a slave, so George nursed Jim back to health and took him to Colorado with him on the return leg of the trip. [436]

George's association with Jim was a rarity in the St. Vrain Valley, although there had been small numbers of African-American men and a few women in Boulder County since at least 1860 when the Colorado Territorial Census counted just forty-six "free colored" (that is, not escapees from slavery). By 1861 the number had nearly doubled as African-Americans began to move westward for some of the same reasons that their white counterparts did. Gold was a lure, ranchers needed cowhands, and the Union army needed soldiers.

The two men sheltered and ate together. This kind of physical closeness between the races was common enough on trail drives where discrimination took a distant back seat to the hard work that united all the men, so it would not have been that unusual for George and Jim to live in this way. The same was not always true in towns. Even in Colorado towns, though, "...racial tolerance seemed to be the rule. The state's relatively liberal racial climate may have been attributable in part to the fact that large numbers of Southern whites did not establish residence there in the wake of the Civil War..." [437] That Jim was known only as "Darkey" Jim to others in the community (George was extremely unlikely to have used anything other than his first name) shows that tolerance could be a limited concept.

Jim became George's indispensable associate. He helped drive the oxen that pulled the handmade plow to prepare fields for planting. Then he and George planted that first crop of wheat. It was a logical choice. Wheat had proven to be a viable crop in Boulder County for about eight years before George and Jim sowed their first acres there. [438] They could expect to harvest about twenty-five bushels of wheat per acre [439] and within less than a decade George would be reaping many more bushels than that. The men would discover in the future that diversifying their crops and raising livestock would increase profits and form a buffer against losses to the climate and pests.

The fields they plowed and planted would not flourish without water. Already running across part of George's land and originating out of the watery basin that had first attracted him to the spot was a rudimentary conduit known as the Oligarchy Ditch. It had been decreed – regulated as to the amount of water that could run through the channel and how much a farmer could divert for his fields – in 1866. To make the ditch more effective George and Jim would have enlarged it, using oxen to pull a plow fitted with a sharp, pointed implement that scraped away the hard ground much more easily than a man with a shovel could.

As settlement increased, ditch-digging became a communal effort that joined each owner's ditch segment with another's. The Oligarchy Ditch passed through several quarter-sections, allowing farmers to control to a certain extent the watering of their fields. Later diversification of crops required them to develop more sophisticated systems than just forcing ditch water to stream slowly over the planted ground. Approximately a decade later, when George added an apple orchard, he would have had to direct the water's "flow constantly a few feet distant"[440] from the trees rather than keeping the entire plot wet.

George and Jim solved the problem of irrigation, but finding enough wood for constructing a cabin, outbuildings, and a fence was another matter because, "Except along the streams, where wild hay grew, the land was a tree-less waste…" [441] In fact, George faced a problem quite the opposite of his father's monumental task of felling large numbers of ancient trees in order to build his home and clear his land. Although some willows and cottonwoods grew on George's property, there was no other available timber. It was from Dave Lykins (1828-1898), who lived northwest of George between St. Vrain and Left hand Canyons, that he sought assistance.

Lykins had come to Colorado in 1859 in search of gold, but soon gave up that endeavor in favor of ranching and raising Shorthorn cattle. He had a gruffly direct personality that contrasted with George's gentler demeanor. One day when the rancher had given George and some others permission to chop down trees from his land, a huge, violent thunderstorm arose. So the men made their way to Lykins' cabin to seek shelter and the older man told them to come in. He surveyed his dripping visitors from head to toe and asked, "What would you have done if I told you to get the hell out instead of inviting you in out of the storm?" George, unruffled and agreeable as ever, replied, "Well, I'd go along. What else?" [442]

George and Jim and their neighbors worked their land and, at first, thought of little more after a hard day's labor than getting some sleep before the sun came up the next day. But within a few years they were to face a new breed of pioneer settling within about five miles of their homesteads. Just as Mantua's professional class had created a sort of cleft in the town's society, the new arrivals would similarly alter George's world. On November 22, 1870 a group in Chicago investigated the idea of attracting a number of people to northeastern Colorado where they would become known as the Chicago-Colorado Colony. An exploratory committee arrived at Burlington, a tiny community just to the south of present-day Longmont, on January 23, 1871. Even though the number of people already farming in the area dismayed them slightly, the committee members ultimately advised those awaiting word in Chicago to pack up their belongings and take the train west to the 2,300 acres the committee had purchased for $5 an acre. Each colonist paid $155 toward the venture and received in return a small amount of land for farming, in addition to a lot in the small community that was to become the city of Longmont. [443]

While the Chicago colonists laid out a town with regularized streets, George and Jim ignored the increasing presence of city folk in the area and went on with the hard work of improving the homestead. But something else was about to occur that would impact both of their lives significantly. Satisfying though the work and the friendship with Jim was, George's life lacked something essential. With the exception of Newell, George's brothers had all been married for quite a few years and George was now ready to take a wife of his own. Early in 1872 he met a young widow named Amanda Jane Lee Noble. Amanda's brother Richard almost certainly had a hand in the matchmaking. Richard lived on a farm near George's with his wife Mary Jane (known as Jane), daughter Hattie, and his fourteen-year old brother Simpson. George and Richard had first met in about 1869, becoming close friends. Amanda's brother sensed rightly that both of these people dear to him were well-suited to one another.

Amanda was born in Grove Township, Davis County, Iowa, the fifth child of Joseph Lee (1811-1871) and Malinda Lee (1810-1882). Joseph and Malinda shared the surname Lee and were probably cousins. Amanda's parents had married on June 27, 1832 in Vernon Township, Jennings County, Indiana. Like so many of their fellow citizens in Iowa, the Lees were hard-working farmers who brought their children up in that lifestyle.

Malinda, like Jerusha McIntosh, bore her children at approximately two-year intervals and continued to give birth when she was well into her forties. Her children's names bear mentioning because several of them played a part in the lives of George and Amanda. They were Francis Marion (1833- ?), Celia Lucinda (1835-1842), Richard Mark (1837-1906), John Braxton (1839-?), Amanda Jane (1841-1913), Matilda Eveline (1842-1855), Elizabeth Emily (1845-1855), Catharine Maria (1847-1934), Joseph Jennings (1849-1855), James Wesley (1851-1896), and Simpson Asbury (1855-1933).[444]   The last two boys bore names with strong Methodist associations.

Living near the Lees was a young man named William S. Noble, born in New York City in 1823. He had come to Iowa sometime before 1859 when he taught school while living with the family of Nutter Rogers whose farm lay next to Joseph Lee's. [445] Amanda was a student in William's class; he was eighteen years her senior. The pair fell in love and married in Stylesville (now Stiles), Iowa on December 4, 1859 when Amanda was eighteen-years old. Almost exactly nine months later on September 5, 1860 their first son, William Guest, was born in Davis, Iowa. Two years later Amanda gave birth to Joseph Lee. It was Joe who would sadly complicate George's life.

When the Civil War began, their father was thirty-eight years old. Even though teaching was his first love, he had turned to agriculture in order to support his family, but enlisted on May 10, 1864 and mustered in as a corporal in the Union army as part of Iowa's 45th Regiment Infantry Volunteers, Company D. He had to lie about his age, swearing he was thirty-nine years and eleven months old when his actual age was forty-one and thus over the legal limit. Like George's brother Hen, William was a "Hundred Days Man", recruited to help end the war in a final, all-out effort. He was not an infantryman, but became a medical attendant/nurse, a job he later blamed for causing the tuberculosis that would kill him seven years after his discharge on September 15, 1864. [446]

After mustering out, he returned to Iowa and resumed farming. William and Amanda had two more sons, but these boys did not live long. Neither Simeon, born in October of 1867, nor Cassius, born in August of 1869, survived to see a first birthday. [447] Their names, such departures from the family names given the first two boys, indicate their well-schooled father's close familiarity with both the Bible and the classics.

By 1870 restlessness seemed to have seized the small Noble family. The 1870 Federal Census shows them living in Douglas Township, Montgomery County, Iowa. Whether it was William's inability to make a living farming because of his worsening health, grief over the loss of the children, or some other reason, about a year later he and Amanda picked up stakes yet again and moved to Clarinda Township in Page County, Iowa. Other members of the Noble clan, including William's sister Martha, lived in both of these counties in the 1870s, so their move took them closer to support from the Noble family.

But, like George's asthma, William's more serious and rapidly progressing consumption demanded an immediate change to a sunnier, drier climate, so Amanda and her two young sons accompanied the dying man on a train bound for Colorado in November of 1871, arriving on the 17th. [448] It was a desperately futile last resort. Because he was so close to death, there was no time to find a home of their own. Amanda's younger sister, Catherine, had married a Littleton, Colorado rancher named Levi Palmer (1840-1898) [449] and their ranch accommodated her sister and family during this crisis. Their number fell by one just five days after their arrival when William succumbed to the tuberculosis.

Joseph, nine years old when his father died, recalled in later years that William had resisted death to the very end, "lifting himself haltingly from his bed, crying out that he could not die" because he needed to take care of his family. [450] Joseph revered his educated father whose death and subsequent events combined to scar Joe for life, making him an embittered, angry adult. Amanda's loss was especially keen. Her life's companion had wasted away in front of her eyes as she struggled to keep the family going. She was now left with two fatherless boys to raise. The impact of William's death was magnified because it was the second grievous blow she had suffered in 1871—Amanda's father had died in a terrible event earlier that year.

The gold fever bug had bitten not only George and David Lykins, but also Joseph Lee. In 1863 he had journeyed out West and mined a claim near the South Platte River in Park County, Colorado Territory. This adventure could account for the fact that all of his surviving children and their families eventually settled in Colorado. Then, as with so many of these peripatetic mid-nineteenth-century families, there is no record of his whereabouts until about 1870. The following year Joseph and Malinda were living in the Montana Territory. No longer farming or mining, the sixty-one year old carried mail destined for the post office at Fort Benton, located on the banks of the Missouri River.

In May 1871 Joseph rode on horseback along with two other men, Drew Denton and Charles Williams, transporting bags of mail. On about May 10th they drew to within ten miles of the safety of Fort Hawley. Alarmed by signs of Indians in the area, the three men hid quickly in a willow thicket that did not shield them well enough. A roving band of Teton Sioux spotted them. Later estimates place the number of Sioux at forty-five, a number that may have been wittingly or *un*wittingly exaggerated by Denton and Williams, who had been traumatized by what they had experienced. In any event, the Indians most definitely outnumbered the mail carriers.

Joseph, shot and killed outright, died in one of the first skirmishes staged around the thicket by the whooping Sioux. Williams and Denton defended themselves with rifles. Despite being wounded and outnumbered, the pair managed to inflict injuries on their attackers, too. As the Sioux retreated to gather up their dead and wounded, Denton and Williams made their escape using the thick brush along the river as camouflage. It was too dangerous to try to retrieve Joseph's body. Ten days later, reinforced by locals, the men returned to the scene of the initial conflict where they found to their horror that Joseph had been scalped. His companions buried him where he had fallen. [451]

So Malinda and her daughter both became widows in 1871 and Amanda lost her father, too. Malinda was probably already taking refuge with Catherine and Levi when Amanda and her family arrived. It cannot have been an easy situation for Catherine to have had so many sad, needy people descend upon her. She had a six-month old infant, Harry (she and Levi had lost their first-born, Loren in 1869; Harry died in 1874). And the sisters grated on one another, then and to the end of Amanda's life, even though they continued to socialize occasionally. Two contentious themes emerged: their children and their relative social statuses, with the younger Catherine assuming superiority in both areas.

She was certainly something of a social climber. While George and Amanda became enormously successful in their joint farming endeavor, they were not much interested in tea parties, clubs, or women's groups. Catherine was. She belonged to Littleton's Christian Women's Club, attended and gave tea- and card parties, and, after Levi's death, moved into town where she could entertain more easily. She built a fairly lavish home whose construction progress the *Littleton Independent* chronicled. And she made sure that her older sister knew every step of her upward mobility while simultaneously managing to denigrate Amanda and her offspring. It is no wonder there was friction between the two of them.

George and his siblings endured their own losses in the early 1870s. In 1871 George learned of an unexpected death that made him even more susceptible to the comfort of a lasting attachment with a woman. Newell died suddenly after months of ill health exactly on George's thirty-fourth birthday. Jo wrote on May 15th, three days after the death, to inform George of the young man's passing. Jo's tendency to write run-on sentences increased in this letter, the urgency of telling the sorrowful story making his pen fly. It was probably a cathartic exercise, but he also knew that George would need a complete account of his youngest brother's death.

Newell had set up his law office in Kent, about twenty miles from Mantua. Jo informed George on December 7, 1870 that Newell had "thirty cases in court of common pleas and has on an average two cases a week before a J. P." Just five months later, on May 15, 1871 Jo reported to George that their little brother was unwell and feeling depressed by his undiagnosed illness, telling Jo that, "if he had to be sick all the time he mint as well be dead." The young lawyer's worries about the amount of money he had expended in setting up his office seemed to aggravate his condition. Jo described Newell's ailment as "Billious fever".

Jo's guess about what troubled Newell was a good one, although ultimately probably incorrect. Bilious fever was an infectious disease that Newell could have picked up while serving in the South. It caused abdominal pain, vomiting, and bleeding from various orifices and body parts, including the stomach. Newell definitely felt miserable for months before his death. As early as March 1st he had left Kent and returned to Jo's house, unable to care for himself and certainly unable to conduct business. Despite Jo's pleadings, the proud young man refused initially to see a doctor because he could not pay the fee. Even when Jo offered to pay, Newell was obdurate. For a time he seemed to improve and walked twice to the creek with Jo and even helped him prepare a garden, taking "a good deal of interest in my [Jo's] work."

But as Newell's condition worsened he maintained that he was not really that sick and he began to make plans to return to work in Kent. Jo told him flat out that "he was not able to do business in an office." As Newell's health deteriorated rapidly, he finally allowed Jo to run to a neighbor who summoned the physician. When Jo got back to his house, he found that Newell was delirious (or "insane", as Jo phrases it), tossing back and forth violently in the bed. By the time the doctor arrived, Newell had calmed down. Death followed shortly after. The doctor's examination suggested that Newell had, not bilious fever, but stomach cancer. Newell's demise meant that George had now lost the sister and brother closest to him in age and experiences.

The grieving George and Amanda needed one another for consolation and for practical reasons, but their typical pioneer workaday attitudes mixed with a real attraction to one another. They married on July 21, 1872, with a justice of the peace officiating. No official record of the ceremony was ever made.[452] George, thirty-five years old to Amanda's thirty-two, was a good catch — pleasant-natured, generous, owner of hundreds of acres, and able to take Amanda to an already much-improved homestead. Except for the bouts of asthma that must have reminded his wife of her former husband's lung problems, George was hearty and strong. Amanda was an attractive, capable woman. Slim, and fair-haired with large blue eyes, Amanda's only slightly displeasing feature was a downward-turning mouth that marked several of her offspring, too. (She had inherited the mouth from her mother. Malinda also had high cheekbones and a rather exotic face, leading some of her descendants to believe that she might have had some Native American blood).

Because of George's longish beard, it is hard to say exactly what he looked like when they married. He had a large, straight nose and close-set ears. His hair had already begun to thin – in later life he was bald — but all except the most formal photographs of George show him smiling, his round, apple cheeks emphasizing a mouth that turned in the opposite direction from his wife's.

Amanda's remarriage less than a year after her husband's death would not have raised eyebrows because everyone understood that finding someone to head her family again was essential. But Joe Noble always felt that his aunt and grandmother had reasons for pressuring his mother to accept George's proposal. Perhaps Catherine wanted to get Amanda and her brood and the wrangling they provoked out of her house. Malinda may have desired to make her

Malinda Lee, George's future mother-in-law, date unknown. Courtesy of Cindy McIntosh.

Amanda Jane Lee Noble, the widow with two sons, circa 1871, who became George McIntosh's wife in 1872. Courtesy of Cindy McIntosh.

own escape from Catherine's tyrannical ways. It is true that around the time of the marriage Malinda and her son James went to live in a cabin on the McIntosh homestead, so maybe Joe was correct. It is, however, also probable that he had to justify what he perceived as his mother's all-too-quick betrayal of his father's memory.

In George's first few years of married life his family expanded considerably and contentedly. Although both he and Amanda came from large clans, for the fourteen years since he had left Mantua he had led a bachelor's existence living in largely male communities or with Jim.   Suddenly, with the words of the justice of the peace, he was a husband and stepfather, soon to have his mother- and brother-in-law living very close by and other Lee brothers settling on land around Pella.   McIntosh family reminiscences suggest that Jim left when George married. But perhaps he had departed the scene a bit earlier — the1870 St. Vrain District Census does not record Jim's presence in George's household at all. Instead it shows that a James Chocran (Cochran), a farm laborer, and his wife, Grace, lived with George at that time. They were temporary boarders, looking for land of their own.   All of a sudden, Jim seems to have disappeared from George's life.

George no doubt regretted the departure of his erstwhile companion, but the void filled quickly. Neither William nor Joe was present at the marriage ceremony, but shortly after the wedding the couple sent for Joe (but apparently not for William who remains an elusive figure with only an occasional mention popping up in a census or similar official document). [453] But ten-year old Joe was anything but elusive.

Joe joined his mother and new stepfather the same month they were married, traveling alone on the train from Littleton to Erie. There he boarded a spring-wagon, riding shotgun with the driver, Eben White, who was kind to the boy and remained his friend. White (1845-1922) had moved to the St. Vrain Valley as a member of the Chicago-Colorado Colony the year before, earning his living for three years by driving the stage approximately six and a half miles between the train stop at Erie and Longmont. [454] He had served in the Civil War at the tender age of sixteen and no doubt had exciting tales to share with Joe who yearned for an adult male with whom he could bond. It was an auspicious beginning to Joe's new life, but the situation soured quickly after he reached the McIntosh cabin.

Although Joe eventually achieved some kind of accord with his stepsiblings whom he at first resented hugely, he bore animosity toward his stepfather for the rest of his life. This story requires examination because nothing in George's many years suggests that he was anything other than a quiet, decent, large-hearted man. The only contradiction to this perception occurs in Joe Noble's one-sided, distorted recollections of his life with the McIntoshes, a life lived according to the normal expectations for a child growing up in a nineteenth-century rural setting, but a situation he viewed as abusive. His growing resentments manifested themselves in rebellious behavior that disrupted the small household in a way that echoes the "disorder" in John Mackintosh's house in seventeenth-century Dedham.

Joe seems to have been innately unable to comport himself with any grace. He nursed grudges and in adulthood sometimes acted violently, as when a neighbor altered fencing to encompass a water source that lay on Joe's property. It was a serious offense, but so was Joe's reaction to it. He assaulted the man with his fists and *then* took him to court. Joe achieved a legal victory, but it was at the expense of his wife's "humbled spirits and sense of shame." [455] Enna's reaction to the event suggests just how disproportionate she felt her husband's response was.

Joe seemed wired to react negatively in almost every instance. A new irritant entered his life when George and Amanda's first child, Mark Lee McIntosh (the infant received his uncle Richard's middle name and his mother's maiden name), was born on April 23, 1873. In Joe's young mind this arrival represented true displacement. It was shortly after Mark's birth that Amanda decided to remove Joe from the cabin, placing him first with a mountain rancher named Allen and then with a volatile man called Barney who did not tolerate the boy's sassiness. Joe stubbornly refused to make things easier for himself. He and Barney were at odds from the very beginning. He pushed the man too far one day when he watched a ram toss Barney's son into the creek and had the temerity to laugh at the scene. Barney, who beat Joe often, reacted by throwing a pine knot at Joe's head, knocking the boy out cold. When Amanda got word of the incident, her motherly instincts stirred. She jumped in a wagon and drove for three hours to retrieve her son. The irate Barney told her that, because he had bought Joe's clothes, the boy could not leave wearing them. Amanda did not hesitate to strip Joe then and there and, wrapping him in blankets, she drove him back to the McIntosh farm.[456]

As an adult Joe accused George of denying him the kind of education he was sure his learned father would have provided. Joe's fury over the way he felt he had been treated spilled over into a much later account given to his son, Leo, who wrote, "To his stepfather he was expendable. When his [George's] own children became ill with epidemic diseases, Joseph was assigned as nurse. They attended school – but not Joseph; he was kept at home at chores." [457] One has to wonder if Joe retained any of this vitriol for his mother who unquestionably had a say in his raising. The boy did attend the Pella school, in much the same way as George had gone to school; that is, he attended seasonally, as agricultural demands allowed. In Ohio George's family had functioned as a loving unit where everyone recognized that their work was for the benefit of the whole group and both George and Newell had been hired out occasionally to neighborhood farmers, so Joe's behavior must have puzzled, frustrated, and hurt George.

Certainly, both George and Amanda expected the boy to participate in doing chores. In Pella, just as in Mantua, everyone had to pitch in, putting in hours that we would find unacceptable – and illegal – today. Both boys and girls contributed to the family labor force. Even very young children could do simple jobs like collecting buffalo chips, also known as "dung coal", for fuel. [458] Sadly for Joe, his adoration of his recently deceased father made other people's demands especially difficult for him. William Noble had prized learning, passing along this goal to a son whose new circumstances precluded its complete realization. It is hard not to feel some empathy for Joe at this point. But even if George had intuited his stepson's hopes, he could not have fulfilled them then.

The household went on for about two more years without recorded conflict between Joe and George. Amanda gave birth to Walter Ralph on March 31, 1875. Then Joe faced a completely new chore, one that removed him from the cabin for the summers between 1875 and 1878 when he was thirteen to sixteen years old. Maybe George did have a deaf ear in regard to this difficult boy, but what he asked Joe to do was again in no way unusual for the time. The teenager was responsible for tending the family's herds of dairy cows and cattle that were pasturing in mountain meadows where the summer grass was especially abundant. There, he was the sole herder, milker and butter-maker, accompanied only by his horse and a dog. Usually, butter churning fell to the woman of the house, but Joe must have demonstrated that he had strong hands and a good technique to have been given this responsibility because the butter had to be of high enough quality to sell.

He lived a lonely and sometimes dangerous existence in a tiny cabin up there. His only human contact occurred when either George or Amanda drove a wagon up every week to retrieve the butter from a small cave where Joe stored it for marketing to the "colonists" in Longmont. [459] At the same time they checked up on him and took him supplies for his meals. Joe always had to be on the lookout for rattlesnakes and said later that he once "watched two mad bulls fight till one drove the other off a cliff." [460] It was a hard life for the young teenager who felt even more rejected. He desired separation from his stepfather and stepsiblings, but not from his mother. These mountain "furloughs" relieved the cabin of teenage tensions and generated extra income, but they can't have been a truly happy solution for anyone. A few years later, when he was eighteen, Joe broke away, "bringing to an end the free labor" and "follow[ed] the roundups in Idaho and Washington Territories and Oregon, though by that time, the stepfather owned several good farms and profitable beef herds."

George's relationship with Joe was a trial, but he and the rest of Amanda's family seem to have gotten along well. Malinda, loved by all around her, liked nothing better than to smoke her corncob pipe, a habit that would not have endeared her to the upwardly mobile Catherine. She was a literate woman whose only surviving book bears her neat signature on the title page. The book's topic might have inspired conversations with George. *Why Do I Live?* is a curious, scholarly volume first published in 1850 by the Reverend Thomas Smyth who argued that human beings should come together, no matter what their race. It attracted a positive review by none other than David McIntosh's childhood "passenger", Leonard Bacon, who by 1850 was an influential Connecticut minister known for his anti-slavery views.

Malinda became the family nucleus, with her sons Richard, John and Simpson settled on various sections of land all around the Pella area from about 1869 through the1880s when some of them moved on to other northeastern Colorado locales. George found probably found Malinda's motherly presence a comfort, especially after hearing that Jerusha had died on June 27, 1874. Amanda and George accepted help from Amanda's close relatives and reciprocated in kind, helping with tasks such as harvesting and threshing. While they toiled on the land, Longmont became increasingly urbanized, a process sped up by the railroad.

The Colorado Central Railroad added a stop in Longmont in 1873, bringing more and more people to the town, just as the construction of tracks throughout the country helped to shift populations westward. Although most of the colonists were farmers at first, the town they created quickly developed businesses to support a more diverse populace. By 1875 a bank (that had no offices at first, so it did business out on the street), blacksmiths, a drugstore, furniture store, shoe shops, a barber, two weekly newspapers, a hotel, churches, organizations such as the Masons, a school and even a lyceum had appeared on the scene. As the town grew, a division arose, just as in Mantua, between "townies" (or, Neil used to call them sardonically, "the aristocrats") and the farmers in outlying communities.

Sometimes people crossed the gap that separated them, (as when Amanda attended the Methodist Episcopal Church in town), but it became increasingly apparent that two different strata of society now existed side by side. Even though George opened a bank account at Longmont's Emerson and Buckingham bank and remained loyal to them for the rest of his life and his daughter would sell her butter to Longmont's Tyler Keeler Wadsworth Mercantile Company (known as TKW) and produce to the Empson Canning factory founded in the late 1880s, the McIntosh family remained far more comfortable with people who shared their way of life. The McIntoshes and their friends tended to socialize with other farm families at the St. Vrain Grange.[461] This local branch of the national grange organization was founded on December 26, 1873. It gave members a place to enjoy organized picnics on the banks of the St. Vrain, to attend dances known locally as "balls", and to hear talks on agricultural topics. Families also mingled at one another's homes and in church without feeling that they had to put on airs or pretend an interest in subjects that may have seemed superficial in the face of the serious business of agriculture.

Organizations such as churches, the grange, and lyceums added a polished veneer to life in Hygiene and Longmont in the 1870s. There were some bumps in the road to "civilized" living, though, when law and order had to be achieved in a rough sort of way. Some local incidents, enlarged and multiplied, helped bolster myths about life in the "Wild" West. Only too real, though, was the event that marred Longmont's February 22, 1870 celebration of George Washington's birthday. When Will DuBois shot Ed Kinney four times that day, Sheriff William Dickens (he became a prominent Longmont farmer and businessman) and a posse set off in pursuit of DuBois. Confronted eventually by the men, DuBois fired his weapon at Dickens and the posse opened fire, killing the culprit. [462] In 1915 Dickens himself was shot and killed under mysterious circumstances as he sat in his Longmont home.[463]

Although agricultural labor made for long, wearying workdays, most farmers and their families loved the land and the lifestyle that gave them the freedom to be their own bosses. George enjoyed that feeling so much that he began to increase his land holdings with the same careful deliberation with which he'd found his quarter-sections in Pella. In the decade between 1870 and 1880 he pursued a vigorous practice of buying and selling land, amassing close to 1000 acres. By the fall of 1877 he had attained some fame in Boulder County for his real estate dealings. When the *Boulder County News* asked about the rumored extent of his land holdings on October 19, 1877, he deflected the attention in his typical self-deprecating, slyly humorous manner:

> Here we come across many prominent farmers, among others Mr. G. R. McIntosh, who in answer to our interrogative statement that his farm consisted of a thousand acres, hastily corrected us, protesting that he had but NINE HUNDRED AND FIFTEEN and as we do not wish to do him injustice, we cheerfully credit him with the eighty-five acres. He has recently purchased the adjoining piece of S. P. Davis, which is a valuable piece of property.

George conducted the majority of the transactions in his name alone; just one real estate document during this decade, the sale of a quarter-section from Ebenezer Birdsill to George and Amanda for $500, executed four months into their marriage on November 18, 1872, bears Amanda's name in tandem with her husband's. It seems that Amanda had brought some money to their marriage and George wasted no time in putting it to use. The notary of the public was punctilious about assuring that Amanda's husband was not taking advantage of his possibly less worldly-wise bride:

And the said Amanda Jane McIntosh wife of the said George R. McIntosh having been by me examined separate and apart and out of hearing of her husband and the contracts and meaning of said instrument of writing having been by me made known, and fully explained to her she acknowledged that she had freely and voluntarily executed the same, and *relinquished her dower* [my italics] to the lands and tenements therein mentioned, without compulsion of her husband and that she does not wish to retract the same.

It wasn't just land that Amanda helped George to acquire early in their marriage. She was a mature, efficient woman who had already helped one husband run a farm. Even though George already had a good start on proving up his homestead claim when he married Amanda, she undoubtedly helped him speed up the process. They could have filed their proving-up claim immediately after the required five years had elapsed in 1873. Many homesteaders felt proud when they made their claims official, especially because there were so many who had been unable to achieve the government's requirements. But it was not always to the homesteader's benefit to apply for the final patent document immediately after fulfilling all the obligations. Until the homestead claim was officially registered, the homesteaders owed no taxes on the land for up to seven years. [464] Thrifty George and Amanda avoided the tax by delaying their filing of the proving up papers. Their Homestead Patent (#417) certificate bears the date May 1, 1875, seven years after George's first claim on the acres. No matter when their papers were filed, George and Amanda had accomplished much more than establishing a foothold in Boulder County. They owned a flourishing farm and ranch that was only to increase in size and productivity. So, when Colorado became a state a year later on August 1st, 1876, George and Amanda and their fellow homesteaders could congratulate themselves on the parts they had played in making the region a viable candidate for statehood.

By the mid-1870s George had begun to specialize in cultivating feed crops, setting an example for other farmers when he raised a spectacular crop of hay on the higher reaches of some of his land in 1875. It was so notable that on January 1, 1876 the *Colorado Springs Gazette* recognized his accomplishment: "George McIntosh sold ninety tons of hay this year and retained forty tons for his own use. One hundred and thirty tons is pretty good yield from one bluff farm. Our bluff farmers who are buying hay should make note of this. Six years ago there was no [more] hay on Mr. McIntosh's farm than there is on the cactus ridges on the prairie." [465] He would have realized approximately $1000 for such an abundant crop. [466] That kind of money was soon to come in very handy.

Taking a break with the threshing team in the field behind the 1878 house, circa 1885. George McIntosh stands second from the right and his children George Jr. and Walter are on his left. Courtesy of Cindy McIntosh.

The McIntoshes' only daughter, Minnie Gertrude, was born in May 1877. The change made by her arrival in the male-dominated household was a precursor to the major turnabouts that occurred in the family in the following year. There was something about 1878 that made it one of those years a family looks back on, wondering how they ever made it through twelve months that could easily be described as a rollercoaster ride. The McIntoshes' ride began when ex-Governor Evans, as a trustee of the Denver Pacific Railway and Telegraph Company (DPRTC), crossed paths with George once again, if only on paper. The railroad planned to lay tracks from Longmont, past George's property, to Lyons, approximately three miles from Pella. Railroads like the DPRTC received "millions of acres" of land grants from the federal government in order

The same field today shows that the appearance of the landscape remains much as it was in the mid-1880s. Photo by the author.

to lay their tracks. They could also sell the land they had received [467] and George was ever watchful for opportunities to buy. The DPRTC sold him a forty-acre parcel in Section Nineteen of Township Three on February 1, 1878, reserving a right of way on that property. George's obligations included fencing and maintaining the land along the road. Eight days later George obtained in the same manner a further one hundred-twenty acres in Section Nineteen. Evans' name appears on each of the deeds as a representative of the company.

A different use for a small piece of George's land cropped up late in 1878 when Pella's need for a community cemetery became apparent. George came to the rescue. On December 2, 1878 he deeded an acre of his land (for the nominal sum of $4) to the Pella Cemetery Association. The cemetery, lying on the south side of the present-day Hygiene Road across from the former United Brethren Church, contains the graves of a number of early area pioneers, including Malinda Lee's.

It was in the pivotal year of 1878, too, that George spent approximately $1000 [468] to construct a two-story house on land that he had begun buying piece by piece in 1875. The newly-acquired acres lay across the Ute Highway from the McIntosh cabin. With its circular gingerbread trim, large windows adorned with faux shutters, and a generous path made from flagstone quarried in nearby Lyons, the two-story frame home made a statement about the McIntoshes' prosperity to the rest of the community, although it is unlikely that that was the primary reason for building it.

The house, whether built from a specific published design or according to a plan George and Amanda drew up on their own, [469] fulfilled many of the requirements spelled out by the few nineteenth-century architects who even gave a thought to rural dwellings. It faced the road, a main arterial necessary for the transport of produce and livestock and for easy access to the farm itself. For Amanda the proximity to the road meant that she needn't feel isolated as so many farm wives did – she could watch the comings and goings of neighbors and farm workers from her kitchen windows. It is easy to picture young Mark and Walter walking down the driveway, across a small bridge that traversed the Longmont Supply Ditch (decreed in 1865) and over the road to visit Malinda on the original homestead. Another ditch curved northwards on the south side of the property. Both canals continue to be full of rushing water today.

Guests entered the house through the front door that opened into a parlor where the McIntoshes received company and where the family socialized in the evening. Red pine flooring warmed the interior. Close to the parlor lay the main floor bedroom. In many homes this was the bedroom offered to guests or used, because of its convenient location, for childbirth. [470] There were two bedrooms upstairs in the attic, accessed by a narrow, low-ceilinged staircase. Wood stoves heated some of the downstairs rooms. During harvesting and threshing, Amanda fed the crews of men on the front porch (now enclosed). Her kitchen was large enough to accommodate a table that seated eight. At the rear of the kitchen stood a sizable pantry with shelves arranged to take advantage of every possible space. Outside were two root cellars, the kitchen garden, a brick smokehouse, and several other outbuildings.

In George's day the house, with its generous proportions, multiple porches and tall windows would have been a prominent sight along the dusty Ute Highway. When Isabella Bird traveled through Longmont in 1873, she was not impressed with homes similar to the McIntosh house. Like her fellow countrywoman, Frances Trollope, who had sniffed her nose at the citizens of early Ohio, Isabella disdained much of what she saw around the young colony. Although delighted with the climate and scenery, Isabella found the town "altogether revolting, entirely utilitarian, given up to talk of dollars as well as to making them, with coarse speech, coarse food, coarse everything…" [471] It seems that Isabella expected this infant town to spring, fully formed as Venus from the ocean, with beautiful buildings, cultural institutions, and the citified manners that such an environment nurtured. George and Amanda, however, could be justifiably proud of the home they had created. It was to be in front of that house that they would array themselves in their best clothes for an 1895 photo of the family.

The frame home just bore out what George's neighbors already knew in the last quarter of the nineteenth century: his homesteading gamble had paid off and he was a success. In a single decade he had achieved most of his dreams. He would not have built the house to throw in his less fortunate neighbors' faces (he was not the only self-made man in the area or the only one with a substantial home). Most did not resent his success, but viewed George as a role model for what they might also achieve. [472] Just as George's childhood home had signaled John McIntosh's willingness to stay permanently in Mantua, so had George's new house showed how he and Amanda had rooted themselves to Boulder County's developing agricultural region. For Amanda the significance of the house was twofold: it offered spacious comfort *and* gave her bragging rights, an implicit declaration to Catherine that the Littleton rancher's wife was not the only one who prospered. [473] Leaving behind the humble log cabin for a beautiful new home elevated Amanda and her children. So, with the exception of Joe's rages, happiness reigned, at least for a while.

But a near tragedy occurred in that same event-filled year when George suffered a life-threatening accident. Although a cautious man, he was not immune to the kinds of mishaps that plagued farm families. Agricultural life was and continues to be fraught with manifold dangers. Among them were those carefully constructed ditches. The very lifeblood of the farm, they provided ideal spots for swimming, an activity George loved and indulged in on an almost daily basis, [474] but they also created drowning hazards for his children when they were toddlers. Livestock, possessed of enormous and unpredictable brute strength and flying hoofs, could become instant killers. Farming tools often had sharp edges; poisons used to eliminate pests posed their own dangers.

Mother Nature, too, killed without discrimination. Catherine's husband, Levi Palmer, was felled by a sudden change in the weather twenty years later in

Minnie McIntosh, circa 1878-1879. Unlike her two older brothers, Minnie would grow up knowing only the comfort of the home George and Amanda built the year after she was born. Courtesy of Cindy McIntosh.

May of 1898. He was at work in his field when a sudden thunderstorm arose.
A bolt of lightning hit Levi. He did not survive the strike, dying a week after the
accident. This was not the only farm accident that had befallen Levi or his livestock. In May of 1891 a bolt of lightning had killed his mare outright and three
years later he was injured by falling from a haystack.

George's worst accident occurred, probably while en route to or from taking supplies to Joe, in late July of 1878. [475] The contemporary newspaper
account in the *Boulder County News* on August 2 provides the best description of
the frightening event: "On last Thursday George McIntosh while driving a
spirited team between his home place and one of his upper places on the St.
Vrain, was seriously injured by the team running away. Mr. McIntosh was
thrown out of the wagon , his skull fractured, cut on one of the hips and one
shoulder badly hurt. He still remains unconscious and there is little hope of his
recovering."

But George, unlike his brother-in-law, did survive. Although he suffered
from headaches for the rest of his life and bore scars from the accident on his

hip and head, he eventually overcame the worst effects of the concussion and his other injuries to live for another forty-six years. Richard Lee must have been one of the first to find his friend. He waited until the "Physician had dressed [George's] head" and then took him home to Amanda. It was a good thing that the McIntoshes had built their new, more spacious home because Richard remained with his sister's family off and on for "three months." [476] So George lived, but the family lost Malinda four years later when she died of dropsy (congestive heart failure) on Colorado's sixth birthday, August 1st, 1882. She was seventy-two years old. George paid $12 in burial costs and they laid Malinda to rest in the cemetery for which George had deeded the land.[477]

In 1881 George built a large barn across the road on his homesteaded land. The roomy, multi-purpose structure served as a stable with feeding troughs and a grain threshing-storage area. It also contained spaces in which to milk cows and for the cows to give birth. An attached lean-to built into the side of a small hill created a cool enclosure for storing milk. Because of the powerful winds that often sweep down on northeastern Colorado, George designed his barn to withstand those forces. He allowed for spaces between the wall boards so that the walls could bend in the wind, but not collapse. And he used mortise and tenon construction, fitting wooden pegs into holes to provide additional structural flexibility. The barn, now almost one hundred-thirty years old, remains a feature of the Hygiene agricultural landscape to this day.

Despite the outward signs of progress, not all years were equally good for the McIntosh family and they couldn't always count on realizing large profits. Just two years after being singled out by the press for the abundant hay crop, their fortunes had changed. If George read the following item from the *Denver Daily Tribune* on August 25, 1878, the year he had expended so much money on his new house, he would not have been heartened: "A gentleman from the upper St. Vrain reported that the crop in his section would fall below that of last season. It even went lower than the farmers had expected. He instanced the McIntosh farm, which last year had yielded 40 bushels to the acre, and which this year would not exceed twenty." However, like all good farmers, George recognized that careful plans could counterbalance the occasional unlucky period.

Practicality determined George's decision to focus on livestock and feed crops as the backbones of his agricultural business. But he was sentimental in one respect when deciding what to raise. He loved apples, especially those that recalled the Mantua fruit grown by his father and uncles, so he had sent for young trees from that area as starts for his orchard. Eight apple trees of eight different varieties still grow on the land around the 1878 house. A small reminder today of the fifteen acres of orchard he planted, the trees hardly suggest the large profits generated during the height of George's apple-growing years, in the 1880s and 1890s when he shipped much of his crop to Denver. He was one of five Boulder County farmers exhibiting apples at the first state horticultural show in Denver in 1889. [478] While northeastern Colorado would never seriously rival the fruit growers of Colorado's Western Slope region, beautiful orchards like George's attracted the attention of travelers passing through the area and by 1922 varieties "such as Jonathan, McIntosh, [479] Northwestern Greening, Wealthy, Transparent, Sheriff, Gano, and Ben Davis [were] grown successfully all over the whole district [northeastern Colorado]." [480]

But it was cattle that formed the basis of his ranching operation. Cattle required little upkeep, fattening nicely on that natural hay that grew so abundantly in the area. There was demand for their meat. After the Civil War miners returned to the hills of Gilpin and Boulder Counties and they craved beef, so there was a ready local market for the product. In the early 1880s the Denver, Utah and Pacific Railroad extended its line to Lyons. "An assortment of freight was hauled on this route, including agricultural products, livestock, passengers, and quarry rock. In 1882, a horse could be shipped to Denver on this line for forty cents…" [481] The railroad opened new sales outlets for Boulder County cattlemen and the number of herds increased until the 1880s when the Texas open range system gave way to smaller ranches, leased grazing lands, and the "use of more productive irrigated pastures." [482]

George chose to raise Shorthorn cattle, a variety often raised in Ohio and the one raised by David Lykins. Shorthorns, a common breed both in the United States and in the United Kingdom, were hardy, versatile animals. Not overly fussy about their surroundings and feed, they possessed the quality of being both good beef *and* dairy cows, thus increasing the farmer's ability to diversify his product. But the beasts could be irritable.

George's grandson, Vandaver, looking back on his life on his father Mark's farm in Nunn, Colorado just north of Greeley, commented colorfully about Shorthorns, "Most folks when thinking milch cow think Holstein, Guernsey,

Jersey or maybe Swiss. Not us, we milked Shorthorns…I think they are a cross between a buffalo and a wildebeest, they can kick just as good as a mule at the most unexpected times." [483] Just as soon as they were old enough, Mark and the other McIntosh children learned to milk those ornery cows on George's farm. They had to milk them twice a day so the cow wouldn't go dry. "Milking cows is a hard way to serve the Lord," noted Mark [484] and the procedure was especially tricky if the cow were nervous or spooked by something. Once, when a city child asked Mark if the cows gave milk, the rancher responded, "Son, a cow don't give nothing. You got to take it away from them at the risk of life and limb." [485]

George's decision to raise cattle that produced both beef and dairy products was a smart one that agreed with this assessment made by a writer from the *Greeley Tribune* on December 2, 1874: "It seems not profitable to have cows that naturally excel as milkers, because Colorado grass is too dry and has a tendency to develop fat and muscle; and therefore it is most profitable to combine dairying with stock growing." [486] Having invested hard-earned money in their stock, the McIntoshes took good care of it, but displayed no sentimental feelings when it came time to send the beasts to slaughter. Mark, who had inherited not just his father's farming talent, but also his wry sense of humor, once said of slaughtering that "it is sort of like getting even for all the misery they have dealt us." [487]

The only extant chattel mortgage surviving from George's life as a farmer dates from June 24, 1878 when he paid $575 to a Samuel Davis (from whom he had bought some land in 1877) for a herd of "neat cattle [that is, oxen] consisting of cows, steers, calves, and one bull, about twenty nine in number and all branded 'SD' on left hip…" Included in this transaction were two mares, seven and ten years old. His acreage that year amounted to more than enough to support this herd of twenty-nine, probably added to other cattle he already owned, when the standard rule of thumb was that three hundred-twenty acres could feed "twenty-five head of stock, [with] sufficient land for a kitchen garden and plenty to cultivate fodder crops for the winter feeding." [488]

George seems to have been someone who learned most by experience, but he probably turned to other resources, too. As people realized in the late 1870s that Colorado's agricultural potential might equal the revenues produced by mining, they established a State Board of Agriculture. The Board met for the

first time on November 28, 1879. One of their acts was to establish Farmers'
Institutes. The groups tried to address issues of interest to farmers and, unlike
the granges, mostly avoided involvement in politics. The Longmont Farmers'
Institute met for the first time in the town's Congregational Church in the winter of 1879. Some of the McIntoshes' neighbors delivered lectures on such topics as keeping bees and "Reclaiming Alkali Lands" [489] at these meetings.
George's name never appeared as a speaker, although he certainly possessed
expert knowledge. It was more like him to share his expertise on a one-to-one
basis than in front of an audience.

He almost certainly kept abreast of current farming methods by consult-
ing specialized journals, such as the *Colorado Farmer* that began publication in
1872 or *Field and Farm* from 1886. The local newspaper, *The Longmont Ledger*,
carried many pertinent articles for its large audience of agriculturists. But
George needed neither Farmers' Institute meetings nor journal articles to conduct his business. Farming know-how was bred in his bones. Sometimes,
though the hurdles were just too high for even the most valiant and shrewd
rancher, although George's ability to make adjustments in his methods gave him
an advantage during hard years.

Tough as they were, cattle were vulnerable to eating poisonous plants,
drinking bad water, and frigid temperatures; it wasn't always possible to protect
the animals or the investment they represented. On October 19, 1877 the *Boulder County News* contained a sad little item related to this issue: "We noticed a
number of dead cattle on the road between Longmont and Boulder, and on
inquiring, found that they were cattle that had come down from the mountains
on account of the feed getting short, and not being salted as they should have
been, were killed by the quantities of alkali they imbibed in the water." A sudden blizzard could destroy large numbers of livestock when the animals might
wander blindly, eventually perishing from the cold and wind. But George recognized many of the dangers that imperiled his herds and he did something
about it.

Between 1884 and 1887 droughts and hard winters did more than create
extra worries for the McIntoshes and their neighbors. The price of beef
began to drop in those weather-battered years, too. George managed to
avert some of the effects of the economic downturn by employing new tac-
tics. He relied less and less on the mountain meadows to feed his herds and

planted alfalfa for fodder nearer the farm. Unlike many of area's other cattle, George's animals grazed on land enclosed behind fences rather than being allowed to roam freely on the range where he could not control their breeding. In this way he was able to produce highly marketable, prime quality beef. George's practice also did away with the need for ranch hands to sweep the range more than once rounding up all strays. [490] His cattle-raising techniques, like his horticultural ones, became renowned in the area.

But some disasters were of such magnitude that they defied prevention and could only be mitigated. The despair in Boulder County agrarian circles was high in the early-to mid-1870s because of a plague of Biblical proportions. The Rocky Mountain Locust (*Melanoplus spretus*) migrated across states in enormous black clouds hundreds of miles large, so large, in fact, that farmers at first mistook them for brewing storms. People dubbed them "hateful grasshoppers" because of their ruthless destructiveness. [491] The epithet hardly seems adequate to convey the dread people felt of them. The voracious winged insects swarmed great distances, alighting when a food source like a crop of wheat appeared. After gobbling it to the ground, they flew collectively to the next field. The grasshoppers were sometimes so thick that trains derailed, sliding off the tracks made slick by the gooey bodies of crushed insects. The odor of the dead creatures was appalling. The grasshoppers even forced their way into houses, devouring anything made of fabric, from curtains to carpets.

Farmers tried all kinds of ingenious methods for eradicating them: dousing them with kerosene, plowing up the areas where the grasshoppers laid their eggs, encouraging their poultry (known as "the chicken battalion", according to a creative report in the *Boulder County News* in 1876) to devour the crunchy tidbits, and so on. They tried drowning them, but, as the same newspaper reported with some Paul Bunyanesque hyperbole six months later, in September of 1876, "Confine one under water three or four hours and when released he'll kick the brown dust in your eyes and stride majestically away to the wheat field."

The inventiveness of most farmers was born out of necessity (and still is). Jacob Hetzel (1833-1897), who lived not too far from the McIntoshes, created an ingenious mechanical device called a "'hopper 'dozer", one of many such contrivances. He fashioned a twelve-foot long, two and a half foot-wide iron box that could be pulled by a team of horses. A fire fueled by pitch wood burned inside the box. As the horses hauled the metal sled through the fields, grasshoppers that leapt or flew into the box were incinerated. [492] (Similar devices relied on coal oil in the pan to destroy the unlucky insects that landed in it). Ultimately, the machine was not terribly efficient and farmers' hopes diminished as they realized they had to resort once again to natural predators or poisons.

The worst years for Colorado agriculture in terms of grasshoppers were 1866, 1874, 1875 and 1876, so George had to face this threat to his crops several times. And then a miracle seemed to occur. Each year the grasshoppers arrived in Boulder County a week or two later than in the year before. By late August 1877 the *Boulder County News* stated that there had been no sign of the insects. And then they disappeared from Colorado, never to appear in such numbers again. Those farmers like George who had enough in reserve to be able to weather such setbacks could re-seed their fields after the locusts had flown off to another locale and then assist their less fortunate neighbors in doing the same.

George and Amanda survived the grasshopper infestation, accidents and illnesses, births and deaths, blizzards, droughts and economic depressions. They prospered and changed alongside their community. Transitions affected the McIntosh family, too. Joe moved out in 1880. His departure produced a new era of calm within the household and early in the 1880s another child was born to George and Amanda. As if they sensed that this would be the last one, they named him for his father. George Robin McIntosh Jr. arrived in February of 1883. He was Amanda's seventh son and her eighth child. He may have borne George's name, but he would not choose his father's occupation. The younger George would be the child who embraced modernity wholeheartedly, a child who would be far more a part of the twentieth- than the nineteenth century. There were more huge surprises on the horizon for George McIntosh and his family as they advanced into the waning years of the eighteen-hundreds. Unexpectedly beckoning to them would be a land of sunshine where George's propensity for the acquisition of property assumed an entirely different dimension and where he would grow a crop he had never heard of as a child in Mantua.

CHAPTER SEVEN

Sowing Wild Oats

By the early 1880s George and Amanda's settled life in Pella was on the brink of a major unimagined detour from its familiar routines. Little did they suspect how events in the next decade would alter the whole family, but the transformation of Pella into a new place with a new name signaled that their familiar world and habitual activities might not be immutable.

When the post office was relocated from Pella to the newly constructed (1882) Hygienic Sanitarium, the residents nearby, including the McIntoshes, began to refer to their community as Hygiene. Then the Burlington Railroad built its line through Hygiene, establishing a depot there that helped the village evolve into a small, but viable "supply town for the farmers of the neighborhood." [493] Pella held on as a separate entity until 1916 when its school district was combined with Hygiene's — Pella then died away as a separate town – all of its other institutions and property became officially part of the town of Hygiene. [494]

The McIntosh family's personal landscape was to alter, too. On September 11, 1888 Joe Noble, who had returned to Longmont after his cowboy days in the West, became the first of Amanda's children to marry. The twenty-six-year old wed twenty-one-year old Enna Archie Adams in Longmont. In a rather astounding loop of connecting personalities, Pennsylvania-born Enna claimed descent from none other than Ebenezer McIntosh's manipulating mentor, Samuel Adams. [495] Amanda and her children by George and presumably

Joe's older brother, William, attended the ceremony – Joe and Enna must also have included George among their guests even though Joe's relationship with his stepfather never really improved.

With their wives, Enna and Minnie, standing behind them, Joe Noble, on the left, and George Lohr, on the right, pose for the camera, circa late 1940s. Although Joe seems never to have reconciled with his stepfather, he did socialize with the Lohrs. Courtesy of the Agricultural Heritage Center.

Although some of their Hygiene contemporaries went off to study at college, none of George and Amanda's offspring seems to have wanted a higher education. With the exception of George Jr., they found farming to be deeply satisfying work and they were good at it. But their parents did make an effort to provide Mark and Walter with opportunities in other areas. They first apprenticed seventeen-year old Mark to the Longmont harness-maker, Henry Roeder. That George felt he could release his eldest son from work on the family farm to acquire a new skill is noteworthy. Of course, by this point George could afford to hire extra help. Reporting on Mark's apprenticeship on July 25,

1890, the *Longmont Ledger* voiced the expectation that some day he would open his own harness-making establishment. The paper's prediction did not come true. Mark returned to farming and ranching for the rest of his life, but his talent for creating both useful and decorative harnesses and other such gear became legendary in the Nunn-Purcell-Prairie View dry land farming region of northeastern Colorado.

As their three eldest children grew into adulthood in the 1890s, George and Amanda entered a new phase of their own. George began to conceive of the unthinkable: relinquishing some control of his farming enterprises to his sons. His health worsened. Asthma had not released its hold on his lungs. He no longer turned to opiates as he had in his youth, but spent many nights inhaling a mentholated concoction heated over an ornate little spirit lamp. Rheumatism caused by those Nevadaville days when placer mining required him to stand for hours in cold water and the perpetual headaches that were a residual effect of the 1878 wagon accident caught up with him. In July 1893 he filed for a disability pension because, as his brother-in-law Richard Lee swore in the accompanying affidavit, George was "incapacitate[ed] for manual labor." The government rejected that initial claim, so George re-applied six years later, on November 14, 1899 when he was sixty-two years old. He added a number of ailments to his application, declaring that he was "unable to earn a support by manual labor by reason of disease of kidneys, asthma, rheumatism, and gravel in the bladder", all of which combined to make him not only unfit for physical work but also caused him continuing pain.

Having decided that work would no longer dominate their lives, George and Amanda yielded to the notion of taking a vacation, thus joining the ranks of ordinary American people for whom the new idea of leisure time was becoming a reality. [496] Making easier the decision to care for their ailing bodies while enjoying a change of scene was the knowledge that their children all shared the pair's agricultural vision — or at least showed no inclination to take up other occupations until well after turn of the century. George had taught them well and trusted in their management of his lands as he slowly gave up the reins. A new westward journey was in his immediate future.

It was during the 1880s that southern California, experiencing a period of good fortune, attracted the McIntoshes' attention. California's bubble burst in about 1888, but during the state's late-nineteenth-century boom it offered what

George wanted. There was land to satisfy all kinds of desires: acres for farming, property rich in minerals, and land valued for its picturesque qualities. [497]

Drought had reduced the prospects of many of the large California ranches in the 1860s, so small-scale farming became an attractive alternative to those who wanted to work the land. [498] Even more appealing than the claims for agriculture were those for the area's health benefits, often advertised in decidedly purple prose. One writer, typical of many, extolled the region, speaking of "…contact with the healthful, invigorating, sun-laden air of 'God's great out-of-doors', surrounded by flowers, trees, plants of every kind exhaling their balmy and soothing odors, what wonder that the children are beautiful, healthy and happy." [499] And it wasn't just children who might thrive there, but those with respiratory ailments could be assured of finding renewed vigor in the sunny, clean climes of bucolic southern California – or so the advertisements and even some doctors maintained.

People responded to the sale of these magical acres as if a second gold rush of sorts were taking place. "Men stood excitedly in line for days at a time in order to get first choice of lots in a new subdivision. Flag-draped trains hauled flatcars jammed with enthusiastic prospects to undeveloped tracts far from centers of development." [500] Joining the ranks of railroad boosters, such as representatives of the Southern Pacific Railway, were realtors and developers. Their pitches were hard to resist, although the claims they made were not always honest.

Even though southern California offered the two powerful inducements of property and better health to hook George, his initial impulse to sample southern California life grew out of a seemingly insignificant act by Amanda. On April 12, 1894 she asked for and received the following handwritten document from the Reverend Charles H. Koyl, the minister of her church in Longmont: "This certifies that Mrs. A. J. McIntosh the bearer has been an acceptable Member of the Methodist Church in Longmont. And is herewith dismissed at her own request to unite with the United Brethren Church. [501]

Amanda's decision to leave the brick church in Longmont was spurred partially by the fact that Koyl, who had replaced a popular minister, was not entirely to her liking. But it was certainly more convenient and more enjoyable socially for Amanda to attend the Brethren Church in Hygiene where so many of her friends were members. She remained with that congregation for the rest of her life and it was in that church that her funeral service would take place. The children seem to have attended the Brethren Church for a while, but Minnie later transferred her allegiance to the Hygiene Methodist Church (built circa 1904) and became a leader in its Ladies' Aid Society.

The Church of the Brethren, also known as the German Baptist Church, originated in Schwarzenau, Westphalia, Germany in 1708. At that time Germany recognized only three official religions — Catholicism, Lutheranism and Presbyterianism — so the Brethren had to flee to escape persecution, an act recalling that of the Metcalfs, George's Puritan ancestors. In 1729 a small group of the Brethren made their way across the Atlantic to Germantown, Pennsylvania where they founded their mother church in America. The members remaining in Germany were unable to withstand the forces against them and the sect eventually withered away there.[502]

On this side of the Atlantic the group became known as the "Dunkards" (sometimes "Dunkers" or "Tunkers") because of their practice of immersing new members three times in water. In 1874 the St. Vrain Church of the Brethren, the first of its kind in Colorado, gathered together initially in the Pella schoolhouse and then in 1880 built a small structure dedicated to worship.[503] The structure that later became a community hall for Hygiene is clearly visible from Hygiene Road today. In about 1877-78 (church records disappeared in a fire, so exact dating is impossible) the Reverend Jacob S. Flory (1836-1911) officially established the St. Vrain Brethren Church. Were it not for the charismatic Flory, Amanda and George might never have been lured from their Boulder County surroundings.

He was an enterprising church member who had spent his adult life attempting to support his wife, Eliza, and nine children by a patchwork of various endeavors. Elected to the ministry in Virginia in 1859, he became an ordained Elder in 1866. Because Brethren ministers were not customarily paid for their services, he still had to turn to many different kinds of employment, uprooting his family on multiple occasions to pursue these jobs.

By about 1874 the Florys had moved from Iowa to Weld County where they helped found a colony called Buffalo. Flory served as Buffalo's postmaster. Two years later the Florys headed for Greeley, ostensibly because Indians near Buffalo were threatening non-native families and because there were few good educational opportunities for his children there. While in Greeley he sold patent medicines and buffalo robes until 1877 or 1878 when the Florys settled on a small, eighty-acre farm five miles west of Longmont, thus becoming a neighbor of the McIntoshes. He grew fruit, became an expert beekeeper, and assumed leadership of the St. Vrain Brethren congregation. [504]

Flory was just a year older than George. Although contemporaries, the two men could not have been more different temperamentally, so their eventual link can be understood only with Amanda as the intermediary. An indefatigable self-promoter, Flory greatly enjoyed seeing self-referencing items in print and he seems to have created many opportunities to do just that. In 1873, with one of his sons, Flory published a monthly magazine, *The Home Mirror*, which was "devoted to the interests of health, home, and general news." [505] He later published an account of his travels in Colorado from twenty years before, called *Thrilling Echoes from the Wild Frontier: Interesting Personal Reminiscences of the Author*. In the book Flory voiced his appreciation of the intricate irrigation systems that marked the farmlands near George's acres, "Our drive soon brought us to the mouth of the St. Vrain canon, where on either side of the stream may be seen large irrigating canals one after another to the number of eight or ten verging out farther and farther into the broad rolling plains, like so many arteries to give life and vigor to the farms that lie stretched out as far as the eye can see." [506] Ever alert to the opportunities presented by the printed word, Flory used the last few pages at the back of his book to promote medicine of a dubious sort as he told readers that he had "gathered the secrets of Spaniards and old Trappers and Hunters of the Far West" in order to produce an "elixir of life!" derived from an herb found in the Rocky Mountain region. He claimed that his elixir could cure everything from "rheumatism to asthma." [507] There is no evidence to show that George ever fell for Flory's elixir, although he suffered from several of the ailments it swore would disappear if only one were to try it.

In 1882, as a "thorough student of the science of vital magnetism and suggestive therapeutics", Flory founded the sanitarium in Pella known as the "Hygiene Home" or "Hygienic Sanatorium". [508] The three-story building featured a deck enclosed by blue glass walls where the sun gently filtered through onto patients who rested as they drank mineral water that came from a nearby spring at Rabbit Mountain. When he told patients at his sanitarium that the light breaking though the sunroom's tinted windows could remedy just about

anything that ailed a person,[509] Flory subtly and perhaps unknowingly transformed the medieval idea that light streaming through a church's stained glass
had a holy origin into a notion that suited his own purposes.   Ultimately, the
sanitarium failed and, by the early 20th century it had become the Walnut
Grove Hotel, run by George's former boarders, James and Grace Cochran. In
1926 the building was demolished.

It was the Brethren church under Flory's leadership that fundamentally
changed the McIntoshes' lives. The church's membership numbered many in
their community, including friends and neighbors such as the Bashors, Secors
and Zwecks. Even more important for McIntosh family history was the fact that
J. W. McCory was a member – it was his daughter, Mary May, who would marry
Mark McIntosh in 1895. The congregation grew steadily under Flory, the
membership only dissolving in about 1907 when generational differences
caused insurmountable divides. But, even though the Dunkards flourished in
Hygiene in the last quarter of the nineteenth century, Flory already had his
sights set on a new venture that offered him another center stage role. This one
would take him to Covina, California and it would eventually, for many years
running, take the McIntosh family away from Colorado for a few months each
winter.

Covina, situated at the southern end of the San Gabriel Valley, became the
nucleus of a town in 1882 when Joseph Swift Phillips (1840-?) bought and then
advertised for sale 2000 acres of land. With his eye on development Phillips
had subdivided the fertile land into ten-acre lots that he claimed falsely would
remain moist "all the year round." A purchaser could own one of these lots for
between $65 and $100. In the middle of the tract lay the nascent town of Covina. Phillips promised buyers beautiful scenery, a healthy climate and "an abundance of pure, soft mountain water." The description overstated matters, but
Phillips seems at heart to have been an honorable man who later, at much personal expense and effort, brought water to his tract. [510]

In 1883 Covina had attracted the notice of a small group of Dunkards that
included Flory and another United Brethren minister named A. F. Deater.
They wanted to build a "Pilgrims' Home" there for church members. Phillips
had hoped that the group would buy his entire tract. They purchased substantial acreage from him, but were understandably apprehensive about the lack of
adequate water. [511] Many abandoned ship and went on to nearby La Verne

where they established their hoped-for community. They left behind in Covina eighteen Brethren who had decided to take a chance and establish their homes in the Phillips Tract. Flory and Deater remained with them for a time before joining the others in La Verne.[512]

The glorious scenes around him captivated Reverend Flory and he began transmitting descriptions of them in private letters to his former flock in Hygiene. More public puffery of the kind he relished appeared in the *Longmont Ledger* on October 31, 1884: "Rev. J. S. Flory and family have started for California where he has located a colony of Dunkards not very far from Los Angeles, of which we suppose he is to have charge of. [sic] He went to Kansas City a few days ago to secure a special car to the use of the colonists with excursion rates through to California." Eight years before, the Southern Pacific Railroad had established service along tracks that ran from San Francisco to Los Angeles allowing people to arrive "within twenty-five miles of their destination in the [San Gabriel] valley". [513] Flory could not contain himself when praising the region in a letter to the *Ledger* on December 26, 1884: "...it is hard to conceive how [such] beautiful homes may be fashioned in the land of perpetual summer and a continual growth of semi-tropical plants." The town was "...as near an ideal of what we wanted as a place to go to work and carve out a fruit farm and pleasant home, as could be expected."

Flory was not alone in his enchantment with the San Gabriel Valley and its environs. As early as 1870 the area was described oddly, but compellingly as "The Great Orange Belt and Sanitarium". [514] John Codman, writing in *The Round Trip* (1879), summarized the appeal, finding that citrus growing was a perfect occupation for asthmatics, "eminently adapted to their condition and circumstances. They can sit on the verandas of their pretty cottages...inhaling the pure air." [515]

Although asthma had not loosened its hold on George's weakened lungs, he would not have relished the idea of playing the part of an inactive invalid sitting on the veranda. However, he must have attended to Flory's words that appeared in the *Ledger* on that cold December day when the minister continued with his vivid depictions of the balmy climate in Covina "where fogs seldom reach...and where frosts and chilly winds are much less frequent than at Los Angeles..." [516] Might there be hope for some genuine relief, if not a cure? George's interest was not completely self-centered — he had passed along those asthma genes to his son Walter. There was a possibility that both men would benefit from a change of scene, especially because Colorado's winter months could not compare with southern California's where its celebrated interior lands remained generally warm and dry.

George was by now a well-established rancher-farmer who could have afforded to take some risks, but he resisted at first the allure of this West coast state. Once adventurous, he was now a married father, owner of a satisfying amount of property in both Boulder and Larimer counties to occupy his attention. [517] Unlike Flory, the perpetual chaser of rainbows, George's contentment with his adult life made him far less likely to pursue uncertain dreams as he had done in his youth. But as the minister's glowing reports of opportunities for renewed health *and* the acquisition of agricultural property appeared regularly in the Longmont press and passed from family to family among the many Dunkards of George's acquaintance, he felt some temptation. He was not to be the only one in the Hygiene community lured by Flory to California. In 1885 Martin Bashor and his family relocated to Covina, remaining there until they moved back to Longmont in 1898. In fact, it was in Bashor's Covina cottage that the Dunkards met to organize the Brethren Church of Covina on June 20, 1885. [518] Other Hygiene and Longmont families followed, some to stay for good. Having achieved his ambitions in Colorado, George, too, now turned his attention toward southern California.

He didn't view the prospect through rose-tinted glasses. He would never have removed his family from the home they loved, even temporarily, without good reason. Unlike many of the consumptives and would-be farmers who flocked to southern California in the 1880s, he bided his time before venturing westward again. No longer the callow young man who had set off on his own in search of gold in the mountains, George looked carefully into the pros and cons of growing citrus fruit before committing himself to a new agricultural project. Here really was a case of distinguishing between apples and oranges!

Catholic missions had imported the first oranges to the California area, but only by cross-breeding with Hawaiian and Central American seedlings did the resulting fruit become even halfway edible. [519] Luther and Eliza Tibbets of Riverside, California procured a navel orange variety from the United States Department of Agriculture in 1873 that thrived in Covina and other inland areas like the San Gabriel Valley. [520] The fruit stood up to transportation, eventually finding its way to United States' markets via refrigerated train cars. [521] Besides learning about the fruit itself, George discovered that he would not have pay a lot for land (a fact that appealed to the thrifty farmer) to get in on citrus-growing because so many orange trees could grow on each acre. Also appealing was the fact that a mature tree might bear fruit for hundreds of years. So there was potential over time for a serious grower to achieve some success with the fruit, especially in the fertile San Gabriel Valley. Growing oranges would not lead to instant wealth. If a farmer began with seedlings instead of already-established young trees, a decade would pass before a single orange appeared. [522] Even an already-planted grove would not yield immediate results. But farming had taught him patience and perseverance and he now had the financial wherewithal and presumably the years with which to begin such an endeavor.

Irrigation of citrus trees was essential, but there were sometimes problems in getting water to them. George was accustomed to Boulder County's fairly advanced water rights laws. Covina's less refined canon with regard to the scarce commodity held the potential for misunderstandings and violence as men tended to arm themselves when they approached head-gates of the San Gabriel River. Several inflamed disputes over water occurred as late as 1886 including the Duarte-Azusa Water War, prompting the formation of a committee like those that governed Hygiene's many irrigation ditches. [523]

It was Walter's asthma that finally tipped the balance in favor of taking a chance on an orange grove in Covina. George's matter-of-fact approach to life might have enabled him to disregard Flory's airy suggestions that southern California really was the land of milk and honey. Amanda's fondness for her minister might not have been enough to entice the McIntoshes from their settled existence in Hygiene. Even the welcome challenge of growing a new kind of crop might have been insufficient reason for George to head west again. But their son's poor health was another matter. The young man's family and friends were pessimistic about the outlook for him. As concerned contemporary Fred McLeod wrote to their mutual friend Percy Goss on February 24, 1897, "...I think Walter will never be a well man eney [sic] more for he is lingering so long."

George bided his time until 1894 when he reconnoitered the area with nineteen-year old Walter whose future was also at stake. Covina seems to have entranced both of them. Walter's zest for the town would turn out to be based on attractions other than sunshine and oranges. But George's eyes saw that, not only were Flory's claims generally true, but here was a place that might afford his second son better health — and perhaps some maturity. Walter, unlike his older brother Mark who seemed steady and sure of himself, worried his parents greatly because he showed no signs of settling down to anything serious in life. The young man himself had expressed a desire for employment of some sort, confiding on February 14, 1896 to his Hygiene confidant, Percy Goss, "I think I am going to be able to work next summer if I don't have sickness [asthma]." But wanting to work and finding a suitable job were two different matters. Walter lacked direction, but his father was about to remedy that state of affairs.

After looking around Covina, George bought lot number twenty, a ten-acre parcel in the Griswold Tract, part of Phillips' original land purchase. He paid between $150 and $200 for the land. [524] Whether through sentiment or because he thought he could turn a profit later, George held onto the lot until 1923. [525] Although usually a proponent of farming on a much larger scale than a mere ten acres, George might have been convinced by the *Covina Argus'* claim in about 1900 that "…ten acres in Covina carefully cared for will secure a man a larger income over and above expenses than two hundred acres of grain land in the East or Middle states." Managing a small orange grove might be just the ticket for Walter and its acquisition meant that Walter and his whole family were about to expand their horizons considerably beyond Hygiene, at least for a while.

By the mid-1890s Hygiene had become a "thriving farming village" that featured a "main avenue…lined with large and elegant shade trees". Its citizens were proud of their farms, but also wanted the outside world to know that, even though they made their livings by tilling the ground, they were people of "taste and refinement." Although overshadowed by Longmont with its greater assortment of amenities, Hygiene boasted its own creamery and cheese factory, a feed mill, two stores, the United Brethren Church and a public school. [526]

Just as in Mantua seasonal events measured Hygiene's days. Among the many and varied farming activities marking the town's calendar were cutting ice from Lake McIntosh in January and February, doing the spring plowing in February, monitoring blooming fruit trees in the spring, planting corn and getting ready to harvest the first alfalfa crop in May, irrigating certain crops in June, harvesting barley in July, preparing to thresh at the end of that month, picking apples from the end of the summer through fall, and pruning fruit trees in the winter. When not working, Hygiene residents entertained themselves with box socials and "balls" at the Grange, they went on picnics and fishing and hunting expeditions, and gossiped at quilting bees. Church gatherings formed another social outlet. The close-knit community celebrated when children were born and couples married and sustained one another when death snatched one of them from their midst. For many of these people, especially those of George and Amanda's generation, this predictable regularity was comforting, but its young people were not always so content with the status quo. Some of Hygiene's young women, like Mary May McCory, ventured to Longmont or other nearby towns to become teachers or seamstresses; Walter's male pals left for college or to work in mines or on the railroad, or volunteered to serve in the Spanish-American War of 1898. Walter experienced a similar sort of restlessness, especially after he had seen Covina – it was time to see what he was really made of.

While Walter was about to find *himself*, Mark had found a bride. On February 15, 1895 he wed Mary May McCory in Boulder. Two years older than her groom, May, as she was known to the family, had a sweet face, a lively personality, an inquiring intelligence, and a determined nature that sometimes caused friction when it encountered Amanda's equally forceful will. May worked as a schoolteacher at the second Bader schoolhouse in District 13, located west of Niwot. 527 She would always remain active in educational matters, but was equally at home in an agricultural setting. The young couple joined the rest of the McIntoshes in making Hygiene their home.

By late November of 1895 Walter was back on the train bound for Covina by himself, making the most of this liberating journey. His description of the trip in a letter to Percy Goss reveals a great deal about the kind of young man George was trying to form – or *reform*! Walter wrote on November 18, "I wish you could have been on the train with me — we would have had a lot of fun — there was 8 or nine girls on the train and they was full of fun – I had a grate time with them you can bet." Girls and what a young man could do with them became a perpetual refrain in Walter's correspondence. Outwardly he was an unlikely Lothario. Both Mark and Walter were attractive young men, but Mark possessed a sturdy build while Walter resembled a meek scholar with his reedy frame and eyeglasses. But his appearance belied a hot-blooded temperament.

In 1895 the family poses rather stiffly, but proudly, in front of the 1878 home that announced their success to their community and beyond. George and Amanda are seated; Minnie, whose fashionable mutton-chop sleeves are just slightly less voluminous than her mother's, stands behind George. Walter is to Minnie's right, then come Mark's new bride, Mary May, Mark, and George Jr. Courtesy of Cindy McIntosh.

The McIntosh family's 1878 home today. Like the field behind the house, the front facade has changed little since the 1895 family portrait. Photo by the author.

He boarded at Fred Ackerman's house (the Ackermans were another Hygiene family that had relocated to Covina) where, he explained in the same letter as noted above "they board me cheeper (sic) than I can get at other places." Walter was very much his father's son in this regard, but not in the amusement he sought out. He doesn't seem to have spent a lot of time in the house, but rather went out frequently to explore the small town in search of young women, vying with the Ackerman's son Harry for their attention and enjoying his ability to make Harry jealous. Covina was not large, but by the early years of the twentieth century it had become notable for its social organizations. Orange groves defined the local landscape, perfuming the town with its flowers. George James noted in his *Traveler's Handbook* (1904) that, "The possibilities of Covina are many, and it impresses one like a wide, boundless garden, with all its blossoms in the bud." [528] Walter was like a new Adam in this garden of earthly delights where the budding flowers were young women rather than floral specimens. He was more than ready to give in to temptation.

Asthma certainly did not hinder his attempts to make love to any girl with whom he came in contact. He became increasingly frank and sometimes downright coarse, even by today's standards, about such matters in his letters to Percy. Walter's epistles have a spontaneous quality, but they are barely literate and his language descends to describing some of his encounters with the opposite sex as if they were the rutting of farm animals. Perhaps Walter felt some competition with his "old Pard" Percy when he indulged in youthful boasting about his conquests. The earthy expressions flowing from the pen of this young man whose libido had developed in a family of church-going Victorians shocks at first. But as Peter Gay has amply demonstrated in his examination of 19th-century bourgeois sexuality, we twenty-first-century observers of the past are often deceived by our ancestors' aura of prudishness regarding sexual matters. Gay speculates that "the century of Victoria was at heart more profoundly erotic than ages more casual about the carnal desires and consummations." [529] In any case, Walter hesitated not one whit in writing about his elemental physical desires to his friend. If his words are to be believed, he found many willing females in both Hygiene and Covina, so it seems that there was plenty of premarital experimenting going on by both genders.

Young females seem to have occupied his every waking thought; at least that is the impression conveyed by the words he wrote to his friend and contemporary.

His letters to the McIntosh household would have been far more circumspect and businesslike. Had his parents known of all of his extracurricular activities they would have summoned him home immediately. Despite the number of willing girls in Covina, it was that home that he surprisingly longed for. Walter returned to Hygiene in April, remaining there for the summer. His parents were gratified to see that he had put on weight and that he appeared to be much healthier than when he had left home the winter before even if he was still at sea career-wise – the orange grove did not seem to require much of his attention.

They repeated the experiment the following November when, for the first time, Walter mentioned oranges in a November 24th letter to Percy and apologized for doing some proselytizing for the citrus- growing profession, although he noted that "the Orange crop is light here this yere." But he was not dedicated to the art of citrus culture and remained very much a pleasure-seeker, discovering every way he could to get girls alone with him. Walter could not afford the horse and buggy he craved for much more latitude in courting, but he did buy a "cheap wheel" (a bicycle). Bicycles were extremely popular in Covina in the 1890s, as they were in Hygiene and Longmont, too. In 1894 Covina formed a bicycle club and it was common for people to cycle to seaside places like Long Beach for a day of recreation. [530]

Even though he spent many hours on his wheel, Walter continued to gain weight, achieving one hundred-thirty pounds by February of 1897. Six months later he would tell Percy, "You never saw me as well in your life. I have lost my Asthma Medicine…I am in hopes I will never need it again." He returned to Hygiene that spring, only to be back in Covina at the end of November 1897 when his free-wheeling lifestyle would become severely cramped. Accompanying him for this particular winter visit was the entire McIntosh family, (minus Mark and May who had had their first child, Phygenia Gertrude, on October 3, 1897). Poor Walter! They intended to stay in Covina for the winter.

The family settled happily into the journey out. Amanda, Minnie and George, Jr. enjoyed the beautiful scenery viewed through the train windows while Walter, as usual, only had eyes for the girls aboard the train. Even George was able to relax because winter was a far less hectic season for farmers, but he obviously could not have left the farm and livestock without careful supervision. The fact that Mark and May were living on the McIntosh farm at this time, with Mark, assisted by a live-in farm laborer, in charge of the entire operation, made the winter hiatus possible for George. The arrangements seem to have been satisfactory because the family repeated the trip to Covina the following two Novembers.

There is no doubt that Walter had mixed feelings about having his family in the town where his liberated lifestyle as a rake now had to be curtailed. If the tone of his letters is any indication, he was a singularly irrepressible young man whose outsized enjoyment of life's lusty pleasures lacked George's moderation. Even if he had had no inkling about Walter's amours – and that seems unlikely — George undoubtedly viewed his second oldest child with some dismay. He had made allowances for Walter's asthma. But as the young man approached his twenty-third year, by which time George had worked as a store clerk, school teacher, and miner, Walter still had no real occupation. With the family reunited in Covina that winter, George decided to place Walter in a business that would not tax his respiratory system too heavily, yet would force responsibilities upon him.

George entered into a partnership with J. W. McBride, a former Covina blacksmith who had bought the hardware stock of a Joseph Amon in 1894 in order to open his own store. [531] Thus was born the McBride and McIntosh Hardware store, a one-story structure located at the corner of Citrus Avenue and College Street in the center of Covina. It was in that building that Walter worked for the next three years. The store's letterhead advertised "Hardware, Stoves, Tinware, Graniteware, Implements" and in smaller letters, "Tools and Bicycle Repairs". It is George's name that appears with McBride's at the top of the letterhead. Although Walter was a partner's son, he took his place in the shop as an employee. The hardware store was one of a number of small businesses that catered to a wide variety of Covina's citizens' needs as the town grew. As so many of his ancestors had done, George had provided his son with the opportunity to earn his living.

At the same time he had opened a whole new world to his family. George and Amanda liked southern California so much that their neighbors thought that they were considering a permanent move there. Percy's mother Nellie Goss even reported their inclinations to the *Longmont Ledger* on December 23, 1897, "…if they are suited with California's climate they will likely make that their future home." In the long run they never left Colorado for more than a few months at a time. Their familiar Hygiene life was just too strong a pull.

Deciding against moving to California, (all of the McIntoshes felt unhappy when they were away from Hygiene for too long) George, Amanda, and young George went back to Hygiene at the beginning of March 1898. [532] When they boarded the eastward-bound train in March, they left twenty-one-year old Minnie "to batch", as Walter described it in a letter to Percy on March 2, 1898, with Walter, perhaps hoping that the earnest young woman might curb Walter's excesses. He and Minnie seem to have been poorly matched companions. She was a strait-laced, exceptionally self-controlled young woman who curried and won her parents' favor and he was in so many ways the opposite. Was Walter putting a good face on the situation when he wrote to Percy on July 29, 1898 that "Minnie and I are both feeling fine and having a good time."? Whatever their relationship at that point, her presence did nothing to inhibit her brother.

Although Walter "like[d] the business allright" and reported on March 16, 1898 that the hardware store occupied his time six days a week from 6:30 a.m. until 9 p.m., there were many hours between nine and daybreak. Walter used them fully for his own pleasure. He had a girlfriend named Maude, wrested away from Harry Ackerman, who was not a very prepossessing fellow, according to Walter. But by July 29 Maude had disappeared from the picture because, as he so salaciously puts the matter, "she stopped me slidding on her seller doors." Minnie left no record of her reactions to her brother's evening absences, but we do know that she was unhappy in Covina. Walter's behavior and the probable gossip that followed made her discontent worse. She stuck it out until September when she, too, returned to Hygiene. The *Longmont Ledger* reported on September 23rd that Minnie "thinks there is no place like a 'home in Hygiene, Colorado.'"

Minnie must have felt displaced by Walter's amours. Cherished and cosseted as the only daughter in the family, Minnie was used to commanding her family's attention. Their favoritism turned her into an indomitable young woman; as she grew older her steely will and possessiveness caused pain for her own two sons, Neil and Harry, long after they were grown men.[533] But in the late 1890s she was still somewhat tractable and there was a young man in Hygiene who had begun to pay her some attention.

George McLelland Lohr (1864-1953) had arrived in Hygiene in about 1895, coming west from Chambersburg, Pennsylvania. He worked as a carpenter and a brick-layer (as did his younger brother, Andrew). [534] Providing

A formal portrait of the McIntosh family, 1899. Standing, from the right: Mark, Walter, Minnie, and George. George and Amanda are seated. Courtesy of Cindy McIntosh.

some insight into this quiet man who was soon to enter the McIntosh family is his small leather ledger whose entries begin on January 1, 1895. His neat handwriting, miniaturized to fit the 3 ½" by 6" pages, records not daily events, but his wages and purchases. From these brief notations it is easy to deduce a few things about the thirty-one-year old's character. He attended church regularly, donating 15 to 20 cents each Sunday to the collection plate and kept up on the daily events by subscribing to a newspaper. The bachelor bought thread and buttons with which to mend his own clothes and a washboard on which to launder them. He indulged in sweets, cheese, crackers and oysters and whiskey (perhaps he altered his drinking habits after marrying George's daughter). He enjoyed treats like a cigar on election eve of November 1896 and occasional theater outings and dances, turkey shoots and trips to the mountains for hunting, but he was also a practical man who was, like George, careful with his money.

George Lohr often put in more than nine hours a day doing carpentry or masonry. Sometimes he worked on the Highland Ditch. He also hired himself out to do farm labor for Hygiene families like the Gosses, Bashors, Laycooks, and Nelsons. In 1896 George McIntosh employed him at least once to help out on the farm and the following year he paid Lohr the rather large sum of $110 for similar work. In 1898 the young man installed a ceiling in the community's grange building and in March of that same year he assumed the duties (serving in that post until 1901) of the Hygiene postmaster, with the *Longmont Ledger* noting on April 4 that "George is 'one of the faithful' after the McKinley stripe." In other words, George was, like his future father-in-law, a staunch Republican.

Family tradition maintains that it was on his mail route that George first encountered Minnie, but it is likelier, if less romantic, that they first met one another while he was doing tasks on her father's farm. The extra salary from the post office allowed him to spend almost $50 on a horse and buggy – useful for delivering the mail, but also handy for courting (as Walter's desire for such a conveyance suggested). According to entries in his notebook for 1898-1899, Lohr had some teeth filled and bought quite a few new clothes during that period. Was it because Minnie had entered his life?

Whatever he did, it worked because the couple became engaged. Before George McIntosh gave his blessing to the upcoming union between his only daughter and this man, he had a serious discussion with George Lohr. The postmaster's answers proved satisfactory and George's bachelor life ended "at high noon" on September 26, 1899 when he and Minnie were married in the front parlor of the McIntosh home. Mark and May served as the official witnesses. Three days later the *Longmont Ledger* satisfied the curiosity of those not in attendance, noting that Amanda had prepared a "sumptuous wedding feast" and George gave the couple "a fine organ" as a wedding gift.

Walter became a husband just a few months later. His reputation as a small-town roué apparently did nothing to harm his chances to form a happy union of his own. The young woman who agreed to marry him was Nellie Raymond, the youngest daughter of Mr. and Mrs. J. B. Raymond of Covina. In Walter's slightly confused, but heartfelt words written three months after they were wed, she was "the best girl on earth in California…She is the best looking but by gosh ge[e] whiz."

Throwing a damper on the pre-nuptial celebrations was the attempted theft of Walter's beloved Crescent bicycle just a month before his wedding. There was considerable excitement in Covina when gunfire stopped the thief in his tracks. When the *Longmont Ledger* learned of the incident, it reported on

George and Minnie Lohr as a newly married couple in 1899. Minnie already wears the domineering expression that her family grew all too used to seeing – and fearing. Courtesy of Cindy McIntosh.

Walter, and Nellie, the young woman who tamed his wild heart and became his wife. Circa 1900. Courtesy of Cindy McIntosh.

November 17, 1899 that, "The thief was captured with the wheel in his posses-sion, but it took three shots from a revolver to make him give up; two in the ground and one close to him." The newspaper item's passive construction leaves the shooter's identity up in the air. Was it the passionate young Walter who fired the weapon?

The wedding went ahead as planned, taking place at Nellie's parents' home on East College Street (not that far from the hardware store) just before Christmas 1899. Holly and roses decorated the interior for the occasion. Years later, when the Raymonds were both deceased, Walter and Nellie moved into that house, making it their residence. Officiating at the small ceremony was the Reverend Enyeart of the Covina Methodist Church where both the bride and groom were members of the congregation. The *Covina Argus* reported in early January that "the immediate relatives of the contracting parties" were present. The wedding had probably been planned to coincide with the elder McIntosh-es' annual stay. In a fitting gesture, Walter gave his fun-loving bride one of those popular Crescent bicycles for a wedding gift.

Walter sold his interest in the hardware store in September of 1901 (per-haps George had given the couple his interest in the store as a wedding gift). Two years later the *Covina* Argus reported that Walter and Nellie had returned to Colorado to "tend his father's ranch... in Hygiene". There is no record of what occupied Walter's time between giving up his work at the hardware store and moving back to Hygiene. The young couple arrived in a small town whose landscape was undergoing an exciting transformation that plunked it right in the middle of early 20th-century technological developments. No longer were silos the only structures to rise high above the fields of Hygiene. Walter brought Nellie to a landscape increasingly punctuated by oil derricks.

CHAPTER EIGHT

Snowbirds

Was George McIntosh about to add oil baron to his list of professions? In the late 1890s that possibility certainly seemed to exist. About forty years after the discovery of gold in Boulder and Gilpin counties, some people found "gold" of a different color beneath their Boulder County land – black gold. Fed by the intoxicating prospect of productive oil wells, over a hundred companies arose locally to deal in the commodity. Normally level-headed farmers under whose land the petroleum was thought to lie were enthralled by the possibility of almost risk-free easy money. As George watched oil pumps springing up all around him, he diverged from his normally cautious nature and leapt at the opportunity to see what might be percolating below his own acres.

As early as January 31, 1902 the *Boulder Tribune* commented on the new industry with a slightly disapproving tone that recalled the moral concerns about the Colorado gold rush, "Longmont, according to all reports, has the oil fever in a most malignant form. Derricks are being projected all around that town with a scattering of odd ones off toward Hygiene." Perhaps the newspaper was also lamenting the mechanical intrusions into the agricultural landscape. Longmonters, who often felt they were the country cousins of Boulder's somewhat more urbane citizens, naturally viewed the prospect somewhat differently when the *Longmont Ledger* predicted that Longmont and Hygiene could be the "centre of the greatest producing wells in the district." In the end the prediction proved to be disappointingly false, but in the midst of the initial frenzy few anticipated failure.

On September 16, 1901 George made his move, entering into two agreements with an H. E. Rowland. In each case Rowland paid George one dollar to lease part of the original McIntosh homestead land and portions of some of his other holdings. According to their contract, Rowland leased the land "for the sole purpose of drilling for and removing oil, gas, or other valuables which may be found under the ground." In return for the use of his property George would receive 10 per cent of "the said oil or its equivalent in cash at the market price". Any oil derricks were to stand well away from farm buildings so that they would in no way endanger those structures from fire (the derricks were powered by a boiler similar to that used in a locomotive engine, set at some distance from the actual well so that they could not ignite the fuel pumping to the surface).[535] George retained the right to use the rest of his land for his own purposes. It was a five-year lease, remaining in effect "as long as oil is found in paying quantities…" If, after thirty days of drilling, there was no tangible result, the contract would be nullified.

Rowland wasted no time in bringing in the components of a derrick. The McIntoshes could see the pieces lying on the ground across the road from their house until framework was assembled early in the following year. On February 8, 1902 the *Longmont Ledger* reported that there was a "force of men at work putting up a derrick on the McIntosh place preparatory to putting down a well. It begins to [look] like business." Amanda surely informed Catherine that the McIntoshes might be sitting on land that had the potential to make them very wealthy, but she would not have divulged the following comments that appeared in the *Longmont Ledger* on January 24, 1902: "The oil excitement in Hygiene is great at present. Some of the hayseeds can smell oil on their farms." The item's condescending tone further emphasized the fundamental difference between farm families like the McIntoshes and the "townies". There was some envy too because most Longmonters did not own land that could be turned into an oil field. But Hygiene farmers did not pay attention to such attitudes. Joining the McIntoshes in similar speculative oil ventures were likewise respectable families such as the Gosses and Webbers. So, whatever the judgment of Longmonters about their rural neighbors, derricks began to dominate Hygiene's quiet farmlands and another crack appeared in the Jeffersonian agricultural ideal.

Drilling began at the McIntoshes' farm in March and on the 21st of the month a corny community spirit infected the newspaper accounts written by Hygiene reporters: "…they expect to strike oil and don't you get it. Hurrah! For Hygiene, she will be oil right." Seven days later the drill had gone down 300 feet on George's property — W. Dan Sheppard, the foreman, planned to go as deep as 2800 feet, if necessary.

As the year progressed so did the drilling. Elation seized the McIntosh household on August 1st when the derrick struck oil. That day the *Ledger* told its readers that the drillers claimed that they had the "best well in the district so far." [536] The euphoria continued off and on through late autumn of that year, but the *Ledger* sounded an ominous note on January 30, 1903 when it reported that all of the oil-drilling equipment at the McIntosh place was moved to another Hygiene ranch. A month later on February 20th the newspaper noted that many oil companies had completely given up all hope of making any lucrative finds and had begun to remove their equipment from the Hygiene area for good. George's hopes for easy wealth evaporated with their departure.

But his land did hold a valuable resource lying below its surface, one that was more easily accessed than petroleum. There was that water that had attracted him to the land in the first place. The crude irrigation ditches that carried the water vital to the early St. Vrain Valley farms had by the 1880s evolved into a complex system of waterways. With complexity came the organization of ditch companies and regulations to help resolve conflicts over water rights, the kinds of regulations that Covina had so badly needed. Land sales almost always included shares in ditch companies. In 1891 George McIntosh and John Dawson, co-owners of the small lake that crossed both of their properties, had sold to the Highland Ditch Company those portions of their land on which the bulk of the lake lay.

When the Great Western Sugar Company was established in Longmont in 1903, many farmers began to grow sugar beets for sale to the factory (George and Minnie Lohr included sugar beets among the crops that they grew). Suddenly, there was an increased need for water for these vegetables and the Highland Ditch directors were in a position to fulfill that need. They intended to use Lake McIntosh as a reservoir with a pipeline to transport the water to the Highland Ditch that ran roughly north-south on land north of George's original homestead.

To create a reservoir of a useful size the company had to enlarge the lake considerably. Replacing the derrick as a topic of conversation in the *Longmont Ledger* on December 11, 1903 was the "big piece of work going on at the McIntosh lake." It was a massive project that, when complete, would make the body of water "one of the largest lakes in this part of the state." Under the direction of an E. C. Phillips, one hundred-forty men and eighty teams labored to raise the banks of the lake by nine feet.

By allowing drilling on his property and selling his portion of the lake George McIntosh sagely nurtured his own interests, but he also had an innate sense of social responsibility. The example of his uncle David's civic-mindedness accounted for part of the feeling that one should give back to the community. However, unlike David, George rarely joined an association. He did belong to Longmont's Grand Army of the Republic (G.A.R.), McPherson Post #6. The national organization, founded in 1866 for veterans of the Civil War, wielded considerable political clout and for many years it consistently backed Republican presidents. On December 16, 1921 the *Longmont Ledger* observed that George was, at eighty-five, the second oldest member of the Longmont post. He remained aloof from the largely social groups that arose in the 1890s when the concept of the American "joiner" took hold. 537 His son-in-law became a longstanding member of the Odd Fellows – for George McIntosh there seems to have been no attraction.

In the main George chose to share his precious extra hours with Hygiene organizations where his common sense might directly affect community and farming issues. (He also did his civic duty, serving on at least once occasion as a local election judge and attesting before a judge for fellow farmer David Bestle when the German native became a naturalized United States citizen in 1873). As the years passed and Hygiene developed more of its own businesses, George assumed an active role in the governance of some of them. He was an elected Trustee of the Oligarchy Ditch Company. He had good reasons to help supervise usage of the old ditch that ran right through his original homestead. His advice was particularly valuable when the Oligarchy members negotiated with the Highland Ditch Company for exchanges of water after the lake was enlarged.

The Hygiene Dairy Company also required a board to oversee its operations. It had been established in 1895 for the use of Hygiene farmers like

George. The company was, according to the *Longmont Ledger* on May 17, 1895, capable of processing each day 5000 pounds of milk from the farmers' dairy herds into cream, butter and cheese. In 1896 George was elected as a board member, serving in that capacity for several years. By the following year the *Ledger* could laud their stewardship, observing that, "With these gentlemen in the lead, the factory will be safe for the next year." Joining him in 1899 on the board that included James Cochran (his former boarder), prominent Hygiene rancher, Matt McCaslin, and J. D. Bashor, was his then soon-to-be son-in-law, George Lohr. [538]

The hours devoted to ranching and community service ran by quickly in the last decade of the nineteenth century and began to race in the early years of the twentieth. By 1905 when George was sixty-eight and Amanda just a few years younger, they felt a heightened sense of days gone by as they could see that death was no longer such a far-off event. Their nostalgia also affected someone else in the family in that year. George's eighty-year old brother Hen took the train out from Ohio early that September with his son Carl (1872-1941) and daughter Adelaide, (whose sister had reported Addie's fall into a mud puddle to her "Unkle" George in 1864) along with her husband Theodore Taylor, for a week-long stay with George and Amanda. Other than the brief September 8, 1905 notice about the visitors in the *Longmont Ledger*, nothing remains to mark what occurred when the two brothers reunited after a span of fifty-three long years, [539] but it must have been a touching reunion filled with reminiscing about Mantua days. There would also have been mourning of siblings who had died (Jo in 1873 and Eb in 1896) leaving Hen and George the only remaining children of John and Jerusha McIntosh. And, as George's own retirement from farming appeared imminent, he must have discussed this transition with his older brother.

The McIntoshes had to say farewell to more than family members that autumn. Thirteen years before, George had reduced his Boulder County land holdings to 528 acres around the 1878 farmhouse. [540] George and Amanda readied themselves to leave farming and ranching for good. Walter was about to help them further lessen the McIntosh hold in the area. On September 25th the *Ledger* advertised an auction to take place four days later. Walter McIntosh and Joe Bashor, "having sold and rented our farms", offered livestock and equipment to the highest bidders. Although he is listed in the ad as a co-owner of the items for sale, much of what was up for sale must have come from George's own chattel.

At ten a.m. on September 29, 1905 a crowd of people attended the big sale held at "the old George McIntosh ranch 5 miles northwest of Longmont." The location of George's land right on the Ute Highway made it an ideal spot for the event that probably took place at the barn where farmers could examine such animals as a three-year old sorrel filly, a shorthorn cow described as being "fresh and extra fine", 50 hogs, and 24 "Stands of bees." If a farmer needed machinery, he could choose from a large array of harrows, cultivators, rakes, wagons, and drills, among other items. Fruit from George's famous orchards ensured that there were "apples according to demand." In case buyers became thirsty, there was also cider on tap. Were George and Amanda there, observing the downsizing from the farmhouse porch? If so, they must have witnessed the event with decidedly mixed feelings.

But the couple had prepared for the moment when they did what would have been almost unthinkable a decade before — they would leave the farm that he loved and the house that she so prized. On January 22, 1903 they had bought a standard-size city lot in the 700 block of Kimbark Street of Longmont, paying Jessie Bashor $325 for the property. The lot was part of the original planned town site of the Chicago-Colorado Colony and was large enough to accommodate a small house. On June 21, 1904 George applied for and received a government pension that would help supply extra funds for their life beyond farming, so in about 1905 they felt secure enough to begin to building a home in what became "Longmont's oldest core residential neighborhood". [541]

They were part of the town's growth spurt in those first years of the twentieth century, an increase caused in part by a minor exodus of retiring farmers from Hygiene. The *Ledger* reported proudly on March 4, 1904 that "Former residents of Longmont would be surprised if they could see how the empty lots all over Longmont have filled up with attractive houses." Kimbark Street was no exception. Some commercial establishments anchored the ends of the neighborhood, but families, retired couples, and single women who supported themselves by taking in sewing or giving music lessons were building the homes that dominated the road.

The McIntoshes' boxy little hipped-roof house (it still stands today) provided a cozy dwelling with enough room in the small yard for a vegetable garden. The informal snapshots taken of George and Amanda after the move show a much more relaxed couple than the one that appears in the portrait of

George and two unidentified figures in front of the 714 Kimbark house in Longmont. That is probably Neil Lohr's bicycle leaning against the house and it is likely he who snapped the picture. Circa early 1910s. Courtesy of Cindy McIntosh.

After putting in years of hard work on their farm and ranch, Amanda and George seem at their ease on the front porch of their Longmont home. Courtesy of the Agricultural Heritage Center.

the entire family posing stiffly in front of their home in Hygiene in 1895. Relieving the pair of many worries was their knowledge that Minnie and George Lohr now occupied the 1878 farmhouse and had taken over farming duties on some of the remaining land. Minnie's father had implicit trust in their ability to manage things capably, but he couldn't stop himself from interfering occasionally in small matters. Even though he was no longer an active part of the Hygiene agricultural sphere, George never lost interest in what was happening on the land he had nurtured for so many years. Since 1900 it wasn't just the land that had occupied his and Amanda's interest. Although they had other grandchildren, perhaps it is no surprise that it was Minnie's sons, Neil (1900-1991) and Harry (1906-1976) who seem to have become the nearest and dearest to their hearts. Several times a week "Grandpa Mack" put a hat on his now bald head and ambled the approximately five miles from Longmont out to the farm, just to chat, offer a bit of advice, and to be with his grandsons. Young Harry was weak and ailing as a child, but acknowledged to be the "brainy" one. Although George loved both of the Lohr boys (and, indeed, all of his grandchildren), it was with Neil that he truly bonded.

Despite the fact that they had no grandchildren right there in Longmont, town life offered diversions for George and Amanda, too. Most important to them was the fact that more and more of their longtime friends from Hygiene were also moving into Longmont. George's former boarders, the Cochrans, were among them and George enjoyed "swapping jokes" with James Cochran, but one of his closest friends was still Amanda's brother Richard. Richard and his wife had left their farm sometime before 1906 and settled into a small home at 728 Gay Street, just about six blocks from Kimbark. The couples liked dropping in on one another; sometimes George strolled over for a visit on his own. The McIntoshes and Lees had shared the trials and tribulations of a life devoted to agricultural pursuits, and now they looked forward to spending their golden years in one another's company. But their dreams of mutual conviviality were sadly not to come true.

Where George appeared satisfied with his new way of life, Richard, in his mid-sixties, did not entirely take to full-time retirement in town. Even before the McIntoshes were comfortably ensconced in the Kimbark house, Richard had taken up gold mining at Eldora, a Boulder County area a few miles west of the foothills community of Nederland. It was at his "Delaware" mine on

Spencer Mountain at about five p.m. on Wednesday, April 18, 1906 that disaster struck. The horrible incident was set in motion when dynamite he had set failed to explode. According to the *Boulder Tribune* two days later, in an ill-advised attempt to retrieve the "missed charge" Richard jostled it, causing the dynamite to blow up. The miner's body took the full force of the blast. When he didn't arrive back at their home in Longmont at the expected time, Jane rushed to the mine site, finding him two hours later "with his left arm mashed to a pulp, his left side a mass of bruises, full of small pieces of rock and powder burns," according to the *Ledger* on April 20th. In shock and suffering from massive loss of blood, Richard never made it back to Longmont, but died at the Sugar Loaf train station en route. The tragedy shook George and Amanda badly – once again she had lost a beloved family member to violence and George had lost a dear friend.

The family's grief was mitigated the following year in a rather unexpected way. Once again, as in so many instances in this family, it was poor health that started events rolling. George Jr. was the one who was ailing this time. The nature of his illness is not known, but it very likely had to do with respiratory issues. The Hygiene sanitarium was by then the Walnut Grove Hotel, so the closest residential nursing facility, the Place Sanitarium, lay about fifteen miles away in the university town of Boulder. It was there that George went to receive medical treatment. Conveniently located in downtown Boulder at Twelfth and Spruce Streets, the sanitarium offered Boulder County residents up-to-date care in a pleasant, interesting setting.

The director, Dr. Olney Galen Place (1860-1926), subscribed to the Battle Creek, Michigan health care ideals established in 1866 by Dr. John Harvey Kellogg and influenced by principles of the Seventh Day Adventist Church. The Battle Creek system advocated a restful environment accompanied by vegetarian meals, hydrotherapy and electrical treatments, massage, and light exercise. [542] Dr. Place specialized in women's health issues (Minnie, too, was his patient at various times) and surgery, but the sanitarium treated all kinds of illnesses.

The doctor employed a staff of well-trained nurses. One of them was a smiling, bespectacled young woman named Nettie Brown who came from Winthrop, Iowa. Besides performing more standard medical procedures, Nettie administered hydrotherapy and provided massages, [543] intimate treatments that gave the right two people the chance for conversations that could lead to a romantic relationship. It was at the Place Sanitarium that George Jr. and Nettie met and fell in love. On April 23, 1907, without notifying their families, twenty-four year old George Jr. married Nettie in Boulder in front of V. G. Holliday, Justice of the Peace. Dr. Place and Ida Dineson, the woman who was to become Place's second wife (the first Mrs. Place had died in 1905), were the only witnesses. The young couple honeymooned in Colorado Springs and Manitou Springs, enjoying the former so much that they moved there with their only child, Paul (1914-?), sometime before 1920. It was in Colorado Springs that George Jr. would most emphatically turn his back on farming. But for the time being the young couple made their home in Hygiene, farming on land purchased from George and Amanda.

1907 turned out to be a pivotal year for all of the young men in the McIntosh family. It was then that Mark, and Walter and George Jr. all began to show signs of detaching themselves from their parents' sphere of influence. They wanted their own farms and also wanted to practice agriculture in their own ways. Almost simultaneously in 1907 the three young men declared acts of independence. Of the three brothers Mark freed himself in the most dramatic way. George's eldest infuriated his usually mild-mannered father by moving his family to near the tiny Colorado town of Nunn, about twenty miles slightly northwest of Greeley. Mark had discovered the region a few years before when running cattle there.[544] He intended to homestead, employing dry land farming methods to work the land.

In a nutshell, dry land farming eschewed irrigation in favor of techniques like rotating crops, planting drought-resistant crops, and trying to save moisture in the soil. George, a fervent believer in irrigation, was disgusted by his oldest son's stubborn determination to go against proven farming techniques in favor of ways that had foiled many a farmer. There may have been some humor intended when, as reported by the *Nunn News* in about 1910, he referred to Mark's homestead as the "desert", but it was also an uncharacteristically derisive comment.

Mark and May, however, were not swayed by George's comments and remained convinced by the correctness of their decision. In fact, they even tempted Minnie and George Lohr to take up some land near theirs. George's anger toward Mark intensified when he confronted the prospect of losing his only daughter to the really formidable struggle of turning unirrigated acreage into productive farmland. But he need not have fumed. Once Minnie "took a look around and built one buffalo chip fire", she rebelled. According to Mark's son Van, she said, "'I'm going back where they wear silk hose and have green perfume and the fire don't smell like s***, and Mark, I'll sell you my interest and whatever there is real reasonable and take as long as you like to pay for it." [545] Whether her husband still wanted to farm in the area or not, headstrong Minnie took him back to Hygiene with her and turned her back on the arid land. (The quiet George Lohr wasn't entirely cowed by his wife. He kept some of that land for several years after returning to Hygiene for good.)

On January 22, 1907 George and Amanda sold Walter and George Jr. a considerable portion of the land surrounding the farmhouse for $16,000, to be paid at intervals of five and ten years at 6 per cent annual interest. Their intent to farm there, however, weakened within a few years. Minnie and George Lohr continued to live in the 1878 farmhouse, until just about when Minnie's brothers bought the land around the house. Then, in about 1909, they decided to use mail order plans to build their own place right across the road on the site of George McIntosh's original log cabin. The house that rose between 1909 and 1911 was a modest two-story frame home – George and Minnie lived there for the rest of their lives and it was Neil's home until almost the end of *his* life. No official paperwork exists to show that the Lohrs bought the property from the McIntoshes, although most people believed that George Lohr had made the purchase when he married Minnie. [546] George and Amanda continued to pay taxes on the house and land until at least 1913. There were undercurrents of resentment among Minnie's brothers and their wives about matters surrounding the McIntosh real estate. It may have been that Minnie conveyed a presumptive attitude about the property to her brothers that was just a little bit too much to take. In any case, Walter and Nellie returned to Covina in about 1910 and George Jr. took an entirely different path: he became an automobile dealer in Denver and then in Colorado Springs.

With most of their offspring established in one way or another, George and Amanda had come to a point in their lives when they could spent the winter months in southern California, just the two of them, without compunction. Both older people suffered from many of the standard complaints of aging, like stiff joints and decreasing physical capabilities. But each also had more serious

George Jr., who gave up farming for selling automobiles, fills a Maxwell Touring Car with members of his family, circa 1908-1909. In the back seat are Amanda on the left and Minnie (?) on the right; in the front seat sit George's wife, Nellie, and George McIntosh. George Lohr lolls against the front fender, keeping a watchful eye on his sons, Harry, on the left, and Neil, on the right. Courtesy of the Agricultural Heritage Center.

The Lohr family circa 1916-17. From the left: George Lohr, Harry, Minnie. Neil stands behind his family. Harry's body language may be significant, even at this early date, as he leans slightly away from his mother. He was the most insistent of the Lohrs' two sons on maintaining his independence from her. Courtesy of Cindy McIntosh.

health issues. George's asthma had never really abated. By 1906 Colorado doctors were beginning to question just how beneficial Colorado air was for the
asthmatic. Dr. James Arneill, a Denver physician, confessed that, "Most of us
have grown body weary, heart sore and mind distraught in our efforts to relieve
and cure many of our stubborn cases of asthma." [547] Despite the plethora of
touted asthma remedies (usually advertised as "cures"), ranging from the Nixon
Depurator Company's "inhaling cabinet", to various elixirs like Flory's and
assorted unpleasant diets,[548] to the mentholated fumes emitted by George's little spirit lamp, nothing really helped. George also continued to experience
severe headaches that stemmed from the 1878 wagon accident, in addition to
the rheumatism and other problems listed on his application for a disability
pension.

Amanda's condition involved chronic pain in her neck and spine, pain
seemingly caused by a growth in her neck. No one was able to give her a definite diagnosis or even to her offer much relief from her continual and increasing torment. The elderly pair needed to find a place that offered both a warm,
dry climate and a competent, modern medical facility. Covina had introduced
them to California, but it was to the state's southern coast that they headed in
the winter of 1905 for the first of their six winter stays in Long Beach, California.

The resort town with its famous stretch of sandy beach and long pier, was
located about twenty-five miles southwest of Covina and nineteen miles from
the center of Los Angeles. Many Longmonters had already blazed this particular trail, so George and Amanda could not claim to be pioneers in this
instance. In fact, by the time the McIntoshes began to winter there, people
from all over the United States, many of them suffering from some kind of illness, had discovered the charming coastal town. Some southern California residents felt as if an influx of invalids were invading their region. Kevin Starr, the
author of several histories of California, notes that, "At one time it seemed as if
the region would become one vast sanitarium." [549] A large number of elderly
candidates for medical attention flocked to the area, but not all of them fell into
that category. In fact, "…the average southern California health seeker was typ-
ically American – middle class, middle-aged, and middle western." [550]

One can easily imagine an exhausted, cold Midwestern farmer bundling up
his family to board a train, perhaps for the second western exodus in their lives,

after reading this paragraph from a guide to the area: "And between mountains and sea are miles and miles on either hand, of orange orchards, lemon groves, avenues of palms, great mesas dotted over with poppies, lupines, and mustard, the groves of stately eucalyptus, and all where the odors of a million times a million flowers and blossoms unite with the salty tang of the sea air and the pine tree and balsam breezes from the water." [551]   Southern California became known as the "Switzerland-Italy of America"[552] – no longer did health-seekers have to take an expensive ship to Europe. Overblown prose aside, even today when southern California highways clog with sluggish streams of cars, smog can occlude the scenery, and development has consumed so much of the land, the climate and vegetation can still seduce a person weary of winter.

Longmonters, especially those with respiratory diseases, who found Colorado winters too difficult had paved the way to Long Beach as early as the 1880s.   The advance guard of those from Longmont who ventured to the beach town enticed many more of their fellow citizens out after the turn of the century. Morse Coffin's son, George, wrote to the *Longmont Ledger* on December 8, 1905 that the "land of fruit and flowers", although in danger of being overrun by real estate agents and their ubiquitous "For Sale" signs, was indeed "a fine place to winter in" and "Long Beach in particular is a nice place to live." He liked the number of churches and good schools and the fact that Long Beach was a "dry" city. (Both Hygiene and Longmont were dry towns with active Woman's Christian Temperance Societies.)

Long Beach had the potential to be an incomparable recuperative site. It offered an artesian water supply, saltwater bathing for those who cared for such things, a temperate climate, clean air, "strict municipal rules for sanitation", and well-respected medical facilities. [553] Amanda had great hopes that the town's new (it had opened in 1906) sanitarium's reputation for healing would help her, too.   Like the Place Sanitarium in Boulder, it based its healing principles on those established by the Battle Creek Sanitarium and offered "baths of every description" and "electricity in every form." [554] It was to those electrical treatments that Amanda would turn in some desperation toward the end of their final stay in the town.

Through the years from 1905 to 1911 George and Amanda spent the winter months residing in a variety of modest Long Beach boarding houses. George, if not the stereotypically tight Scot, was as careful with his money as so many other self-made men who respected the value of the hard-won dollar. Mark, having absorbed his father's teachings thoroughly, used to say, "Your hand is the best one to put a dollar in" and "It takes no special knowledge to spend money, any fool will do just fine." [555] This time, however, there was a reason for his budgetary concerns. Long Beach and the surrounding areas were not cheap. "… coal, wood, gas, water, ice, and all manufactured articles cost about 40 per cent more than in the East." [556] Even during the winter of 1911-1912 when they were comfortably well off, George and Amanda chose respectable, but less-than-luxurious abodes. The retired farm couple who had rarely mingled socially with Longmont's town families would have felt uncomfortable in Long Beach's Hotel Virginia, although they eventually found a place just half a block away from the fashionable and expensive resort. But there were plenty of smaller places close to the ocean where the presence of this unassuming couple would not have been remarkable.

They were fortunate to find lodgings in which to live on a temporary basis. Long Beach's mushrooming growth between 1900 and 1910 made it "the fastest growing city in the United States." [557] So, although small apartment buildings sprang up rapidly, many specifically in order to accommodate invalids, [558] the flood of health- and pleasure seekers almost exceeded the number of available dwellings. For those on a budget the choice was even more limited.

George and Amanda, accompanied by Nettie's younger sister, Ula Brown (c. 1889-?), arrived in Long Beach in mid-December for the 1911-1912 sojourn. Ula, a nurse like her sister, had come out with them to begin a new job, probably at the sanitarium. She soon got her own place, but checked in on the older couple from time to time. It was to Minnie, though, that Amanda directed her most personal thoughts. From their arrival until the end of February, 1912 letters flowed to Minnie from Amanda, with occasional postscripts written by George. [559] Although Minnie's replies are no longer extant, we know from Amanda's responses that Minnie corresponded regularly with her mother. Filtered through Amanda's complaining, querulous, but also frequently humorous words, the letters convey a sense of what life in Long Beach was like for this relatively unsophisticated couple during their seventh winter in the town. Finding rooms was always their first and most troublesome priority and Amanda detailed the process for her daughter.

Long Beach widows and other single women were among those who cap-
italized on the city's allure. The McIntoshes sampled several small relatively inexpensive apartments/boarding houses run by such women, but they seemed unable
to settle down during that winter just over two years before the outbreak of World
War I. First they tried the Alpha Flats at 234-236 Pacific Avenue located at a
seemingly ideal site near the heart of downtown Long Beach and just a few blocks
from the ocean. But the Alpha fell short of their simple expectations. Amanda
complained to Minnie on December 19 that it was permeated with "the Perfumes
of Gass and Coaloil [and] gave Papa the Asthma." These were common odors in
Long Beach and not specific to the Alpha. [560] But it was also chilly because the
thrifty landlady, Mrs. B. Lambert, perhaps relying on promoters' claims of temperate winters, did not light the fires in her guests' fireplaces. Unfortunately,
southern California experienced a cooler than usual winter in 1911 and both
George and Amanda caught colds. So they moved to the Yale apartments at 143
West First Street where it was at least warm, but they had to climb three stories to
reach their rooms and that was just too much for them. Money worries kept them
from selecting higher priced, more comfortable quarters for a while.

Perhaps George held the monetary reins a bit too tightly. At least that is
what Amanda's December 19th lament about prices suggested: "...we have to
pay so mutch rent. If we had Paid the Price and got a good place when we first
cam we would have been all right." She even had to delay treatments on her
neck because "Money is to scarce." While Amanda vented her frustrations
about housing and finances in letters to Minnie, George sunbathed outside and
strolled the ocean promenade, perhaps hoping to escape his wife's fault-finding
as much as to dry out his ravaged lungs.

It was fortunate that they had few needs and therefore did not run up
expenses. They spent Christmas at the Yale, dining out at a nearby eatery
(probably the Park View Cafeteria located at 130 ½ Pacific Ave.) where they ate
a meager meal of soup, bread and butter, tomatoes, cheese, tea and pumpkin
pie. The oldest cafeteria in Long Beach, the Park View was just a short walk
from the Yale. On Christmas afternoon they attended an unnamed play.

Even though they were not extravagant people, George and Amanda had
certain standards that the Yale did not meet. On January 6, 1912 Amanda told
Minnie that she hated its "awful little kitchen" with its "gass plate with two
burners and the tufest looking things to cock in you ever saw." She spent some

of their precious pennies on a teakettle and a pot in which she could boil potatoes, but little else. It was potatoes day in and day out for them — the lodging
had rules against cooking any vegetables other than potatoes because of the
odors that wafted into other people's rooms Although they appreciated the
place's toasty temperature, the wretched cooking facilities and top-floor rooms
combined to make yet another move imperative.

Finally, in January of 1912 the pair transferred to more upscale digs at The
Panama. It was a brand new building that had just opened in October of 1911.
Run by Mrs. Susie Hills, The Panama stood at 41 Chestnut Avenue. [561] It featured fireproof brick construction and a rooftop view "well worth the visit,"
advised the *Long Beach Daily Telegraph* on October 7, 1911. More important to
the McIntoshes than the view were the ground floor furnished rooms they
rented from Mrs. Hills – no more exhausting steps to climb. Their apartment,
one of twenty-five in the building, contained a bedroom, kitchen and nicely
tiled private bathroom that was the site of a nasty accident for Amanda not too
long after they moved in. The Panama must have represented a significant
improvement over the previous two places for them to pay $35 a month. Like
both the Alpha and the Yale, it was close to the ocean. Even though neither one
of these original Midwesterners took pleasure splashing in the salt water
bathing as so many other visitors did, George certainly enjoyed the proximity to
the waterfront where he walked, "one of his greatest pleasures", [562] daily.

Their arrival at the Panama was duly noted in the *Long Beach Daily Telegraph's* weekly column delightfully titled "'Guests and Gossip in Hotels and
Apartments' Interesting Items about the Strangers within Our Gates" on January 17, 1912: "Mr. and Mrs. G. R. McIntosh, a [sic] retired fruit grower of
Longmont, Colo., and Miss Ula Brown of Denver are new arrivals. This is the
seventh winter spent here by the McIntoshes." For George to identify himself to the reporter as a fruit grower rather than as a rancher shows just how
important those orchards were to him.

Amanda found much to admire in the Panama, but her pleasure was seldom unalloyed. She noted wryly in a letter written on January 24th, a week after
their arrival there that, "This winter we have a Nice Place – we pay a nice
Price." In Amanda's opinion, "it had Aught to bee good." A photo of the pair
in front of the Panama that winter shows sunlit smiles on their faces, so the
change seems to have been beneficial for them.

Amanda and George enjoying the Long Beach sunshine in front of the Panama apartment house where they finally found suitable rooms in January, 1912. Courtesy of the Agricultural Heritage Center.

The older couple's frugal habits restricted them to mostly free entertainment like walks through Pacific Park where they could enjoy the "palms and other tropical vegetation, ...lawns...at all seasons gay with roses and blossoms" and the "mounted skeleton of an enormous whale..." [563] There were certainly more Long Beach amusements that George and Amanda could have reached by the town's efficient street cars, but their letters describe none of the exciting events seizing the imaginations of the town's residents. In December 1911 Long Beach hosted its "second annual international aviation meet". George and Amanda made no mention of the event, but they could hardly have been unaware of the report of "champion altitude flyer" Archie Hoxsey's spectacular death when his plane flipped over in mid-air and plummeted to the ground." [564] That same month an aviator named Calbraith Perry Rodgers (1879-1912) landed his aircraft at the east end of the beach after successfully making "the first transcontinental airplane flight in history." [565]

What *did* pique George's interest were the small things he noticed on his waterfront strolls. He shared his observations with his Lohr grandsons in postscripts added to letters Amanda sent Minnie. On December 19, 1911 he confirmed again his feelings about unnecessary expenditure, saying to the boys that, "a boat haz been laying off the pier with two big fish one 14 the other 17 feet long it cost 25cts to go and see them so I did not go." The next month he wrote, "...I will tell you I was on the pier this morning and Seen a Seadog [a seal] eight feet long he came nea[r] to get stuff thron from whare they dress fish." He didn't hesitate to praise Neil and Harry for pictures they had drawn and enjoyed hearing that Neil was doing well at school. He wanted to know how Phygenia fared at school, but noted wistfully that "she does not write." He also remained concerned with the Lohrs' farm, giving his son-in-law advice on February 22nd about paying ditch taxes and reassuring him that he would "come home as soon as I can or dare." George also shared his worries about the orange crop that winter, stating resignedly that, "frost & drouth make them look blue – such is the life of a farmer."

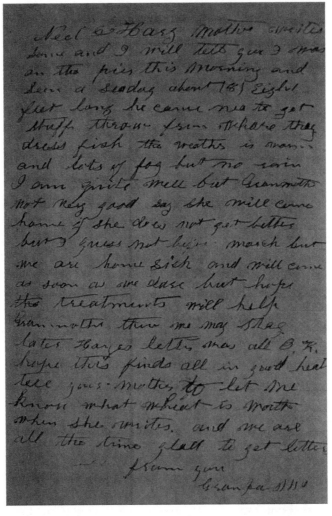

George writes to his grandsons, Neil and Harry, in this one-page postscript to one of his wife's letters to Minnie from Long Beach, California. Courtesy of Cindy McIntosh.

The correspondence tells us much more about Amanda than can be gleaned from documents and George's character also opens more fully in his addenda to his wife's notes. Amanda's large, emphatic, painstakingly formed handwriting, neatly contained by lined paper, contrasts with George's lighter, spidery script – and his lighter spirit. Misspellings, grammatical errors and lack of punctuation emphasize the directness of feeling expressed. Their words throw light on complex family relationships and offer succinct commentary on more ordinary events. In addition to their concerns about their family, both of them clearly felt an almost biological connection with the Hygiene farming community.

Amanda mixed the description of mundane occurrences with spontaneous outpourings of rancor about family spats. With little transition between the thoughts, there is a stream-of-consciousness immediacy about them. Holidays, as in so many families, stirred hostilities within the house of McIntosh. Amanda had sent small Christmas gifts to Hygiene that winter (a tie for George, Jr., bead necklaces for Minnie and Nettie) and she made sure that Minnie knew on January 12th that she had spent two dollars on the beads, so "they aught to bee pretty nice" , her words echoing what she had said about the pricey Panama. Minnie was not one to mollify matters. She reported to her mother that May had voiced her hurt when she realized that Amanda had sent nothing to that branch of the family. Amanda responded, "May['s] Featheres were a little ruffeled …I did not send them any thing [for] Xmas…I thought they would bee so mad they would not want it." George added a postscript: "I am sorry May and the folks are cross but will go up when I get home and will try to get them better natured and perhaps sell out in that place." George sounds like the kind man his neighbors described, anxious to restore peace to his much-loved family, but he had also obviously not given up his residual resentment about the dry land farm place to which Mark and May successfully dedicated their lives.

The disagreement seems to have been about Phygenia, Mark and May's daughter, who had begun attending Longmont High School in September 1911 and boarded with the Lohrs. Did Amanda engineer this situation to provide Phygenia with a better education than she might have had in the "desert"? Did her parents agree reluctantly to the plan? It may be that they feared Minnie's influence over their daughter. Even though she was a big believer in education, May undoubtedly resented this well-meant, but probably heavy-handed interference, especially when it meant that her only daughter was to live at Minnie's house. Whatever the facts, the situation caused huge family tension for a while.

The tension had worsened by the next week, pulling Minnie right into the "falling out". Amanda did not repress her reaction. She accepted her part in the quarrel, but then went on in a furious flow voicing emotions that lay deeper than resentment over unsent Christmas gifts: "i guess she came over there full and had to emty out on som[e] person —if i had ben their i would have caut it instead of you — i am to blame for the hole thing...May does not Care whether or not i was well Enough or not just so i did it—where i fel[l] down was when i had her come down to go to School—Papa says May will go for him when he goes up there next Summer."

Just when the conflict with May seemed to have simmered down a bit, a new one arose, this time with Amanda's sisterly nemesis, Catherine. The dispute centered on George Jr.'s sale of a car to his cousin Frank, Catherine's only surviving son. Amanda avidly shared the controversy with Minnie on January 12 when she wrote, "She met him [George, Jr.] on the street and went for him...She wanted him to stay a way from Frank and let him alone. George toled him to go to Hell." Catherine's concern was with her apparently spend-thrift son. According to Amanda's interpretation, Catherine worried that if he went through his money, "she would have him to keep." Amanda could not let the topic go, reminding Minnie that her aunt never thought Amanda's children would achieve success in anything and going on to say that, "Her children are shoing for themselves – she is making People think Frank does not know Enough to come in when it rains."

Minnie's responses to this cascade of hurt and resentment do not survive, but she seems to have done little to shield her mother from the strife at home. On the other hand, Minnie fully satisfied her parents' need to hear all about the Lohr family, farming conditions, and Hygiene neighbors. Amanda fretted about five-year old Harry's health, advising Minnie not to let him go to school that winter and worried that Minnie would get headaches after she broke her glasses. Minnie seems to have been dutiful in answering Amanda's questions, reporting that butter was selling for 40 cents a pound and assuaging Amanda's worries about how freezing Colorado temperatures that winter would affect produce left in the cellar.

Minnie also kept them apprised of Hygiene events. Her report of the death of the forty-one year old widower, Samuel Wagner, who had succumbed to pneumonia after riding a handrail to an Odd Fellows' meeting in Longmont in mid-January's frigid temperatures stirred Amanda. She added Wagner's six orphaned children to her list of worries on January 24th, saying, "It is pretty bad for them to loas boath their Parrents." It was George who voiced concern on February 11th when he responded to news of a fire near the Lohr place. Wrote Amanda, "Papa said if the wind had been in the north your House would have had a Pretty close call."

The news from home just intensified the McIntoshes' yearning for Colorado, even while they enjoyed the change of scene in Long Beach. Both were therefore eager to connect with people from Hygiene and Longmont who also vacationed or resided in Long Beach. They received some visits from friends who were in the area, but a more formal annual social occasion also helped them stay in touch with home.

Because so many people from so many states flocked to the area, groups formed to provide social gatherings for like-minded people.[566] Strictly limited in membership to those who originated from a particular state, these organizations were especially popular in the early years of the twentieth century. Iowa had the strongest contingent in Long Beach, a fact that bolstered the town's nickname of "Iowa by the Sea", [567] but residents and former residents of the Longmont area constituted a significant enough group to call for reunions of their own that were unconnected to more general Colorado gatherings. Organized initially by Morse Coffin's brother, Reuben, the annual meeting was described by the *Ledger* on February 24, 1911 as an opportunity for "old friends and neighbors, sojourning at different points on the west coast [to] come together to renew acquaintances and revive happy recollections of good old times back in the shadow of Long's Peak." They called their celebration "Longmont Day". For as long as they wintered in Long Beach the McIntoshes made sure they attended this event.

The famous long pier that extended out into the water from the end of Pine Street formed the venue for this assembly of Longmonters. By the time George and Amanda began coming to the town the pier was already in its third incarnation, the earlier versions having succumbed to the depredations of ship worm and violent waves. It was a two-storied affair, the upper level reserved for pedestrians and the lower for freight. Red, white and green paint brightened the pier, but it was its 1000-foot length that made it famous. [568] A large "sun parlor" embellished the ocean end of the structure, creating a shaded area from which to view the water or to enjoy the music played by a variety of bands. [569]

A 1911 postcard depicting the Long Beach Pier and the ocean. Although George did not indulge in swimming in the waters off Long Beach, he very much enjoyed strolling along the promenade by the beach and observing the sights from the pier. Courtesy of Cindy McIntosh.

In their previous year's stay in Long Beach, George and Amanda enjoyed the "Longmont Day" celebration in that sun parlor on February 13. Seventy-three people attended, each wearing a badge colored the Columbine-blue of the Colorado state flower. Heavy rains prevented greater participation, but George and Amanda braved the wet weather to be there. Members of the group read letters from those unable to attend; talks followed that reminisced happily about the good old days in Longmont and about its equally sunny prospects for the future. George was one of several men who gave short speeches. A thematic thread ran through the informal addresses: while they enjoyed their stays in southern California, "at heart" each speaker "must always be a Longmont man."

(One presumes that the women felt the same way.) A. K. Wright even embellished his memories with a poem he had composed called "The Irrigating Ditch"
whose sentimental third verse ran as follows:

> I heard the sweet voice of my sisters,
> As under the willows we played,
> Where the headgate divided the waters
> At the turn of the ditch in the shade. [570]

The words, however conventionally written, must have conjured up fond
memories for George and other early settlers.

The organizers had arranged for the group to take a boat tour of the inner
harbor, but the drippy weather scuttled their plans, so George, Amanda, and
their friends engaged in "social converse" instead. Back home the *Longmont
Ledger* praised the town's far-flung citizens for turning adverse conditions into
a positively successful experience. The reporter went on to celebrate their
virtues in general:

> There is something about the Longmont atmosphere that
> develops an abounding patriotism, the love for the place naturally
> inducing a strong brotherhood of feeling that seems but the stronger
> with distance. And so it is that however black the clouds may be over-
> head, there will always be sunshine in the hearts of the people who
> gather at Long Beach or otherwhere to extend the glad hand and
> revive old memories of Longmont Day. [571]

It is worth reflecting on these sentiments that included everyone in attendance. The Longmont Day gatherings blurred Longmont's normal social
strata: Hygiene farmers and ranchers mingled with the town's "aristocrats" in
ways that would not have occurred so easily at home. It was their love for that
particular segment of northeastern Colorado that for that one day at least
bound them together and allowed them to proclaim their superiority over those
from other states. This strongly-held allegiance to place extended to daily life
in Long Beach where Coloradoans tended to mix with fellow Coloradoans,
even though visitors from all over the United States lived in apartments like the
Panama.

George and Amanda enjoyed social occasions like "Longmont Day", but their primary reason for wintering in Long Beach in 1911-12 was to improve their health. He certainly did not feel completely well, noting in an understated aside to Minnie on December 19th that he was "a little off and may to go back in the hills [Covina?]." But George was accustomed to his problems. Both of them felt that diagnosing and healing Amanda was of paramount importance and the more quickly that was done, the better — then they could return home again. The unrelenting throb of pain in her neck and spine definitely made Amanda's day-to-day life a misery and her torment increased after she slipped on the bathroom's slick tiles, hitting the side of the bathtub and badly wrenching her back.

But before trying the Sanitarium, Amanda seems first to have placed her faith in a probably unscientific course of some kind of daily therapy offered by a woman who charged a dollar a day, even though George was more than willing to loosen the purse strings so Amanda could have treatments at the more rigorously supervised hospital. Finally, Amanda, having achieved no relief whatsoever for her dollar a day, decided to undertake a series of electrical treatments at the Sanitarium. Others, unscrupulous and unqualified, offered electrical "cures" to the invalids flocking to the area in the early 1900s. Amanda's decision to patronize the Sanitarium was the safer, if still slightly dangerous, choice.

"Therapeutic Electricity" was a healing technique promoted by many legitimate doctors in the last part of the nineteenth century and the early years of the twentieth. They represented it as a miraculous medical tool, capable of effecting both relief from and cures for a huge variety of ailments. "To-day [1891] there is hardly an educated member of the profession who will deny its virtue if intelligently applied...[But]...very few diseases... can be cured by electricity, galvanism, or electro-magnetism alone...Recourse must be had to mild medication. [572] Some practitioners of therapeutic electricity were quacks, but others sincerely believed in its curative powers. A portion of the medical community exhibited more caution about electricity's efficacy, taking a wait and see attitude.

Brave was the patient who endured these sessions. Instruments that looked like and, in the hands of an inexperienced operator, *felt* like tools of torture, introduced electricity by alternating current into the patient's body in order to stimulate damaged nerves and/or muscles with the hope of achieving some regeneration. The standard "local application" lasted anywhere from two to five minutes. [573] Sometimes burns and blisters occurred at the application site – deaths by electrocution were rare, but did happen. "Some pain is involved," cautioned Dr. George Jacoby in his 1919 treatise on the subject. [574] Jacoby elaborated, "It is often very difficult to prevent a spark from jumping from an electrode to the skin of a patient. The spark is always the cause of greater or less pain and in consequence startles and distracts the patient often to such an extent that it becomes impossible properly to apply the current." [575]

But Amanda, who was so attuned her bodily aches and pains, never mentioned in her letters to Minnie any negative experience during an electrical treatment, so she must have been in the hands of competent practitioners. She also underwent x-ray therapy, hoping that the doctors' claims that radiation could exterminate tumors were correct. The sight of the x-ray operator in his lead apron, mitts, and weird rectangular mask intensified the frightening strangeness of the procedure. She took three x-ray treatments in February, after which the doctors assured her that the condition in her neck was slightly improved. By February 11th Amanda could not tell "whether it is any better or not – the Dr thought i would have to take about six before their would bee mutch change – if it is not better when i take the 6 six (sic) treatments we are Coming Home." And yet, however practiced their ministration, the Sanitarium physicians were unable to alleviate much of her neck pain. The elderly couple, still sick and longing for home, left Long Beach that March. They never spent another winter there.

Amanda continued to suffer from what was almost certainly a cancerous growth on her neck. In April she underwent an operation at St. Luke's hospital in Denver. By November her condition was far worse and, with Mark by her side, she traveled to Denver for some kind of treatment. The very fact that Mark left his farm work to accompany his mother shows how serious the matter was. A pathologist examined a sample of her neck glands, but again no definite diagnosis emerged. Amanda lingered in pain with the quality of her life greatly diminished. She returned to St. Luke's again in June of 1913. But it was all of no avail.

On the morning of October 28, 1913 Amanda died at the age of seventy-two. At the time of her death her children were scattered: William lived in

Cheyenne Wells, Colorado and Joe was in Billings, Montana; Mark had settled for good near Nunn while Walter had drifted to Avondale, Arizona where he seems to have taken up winter residence for quite a few years. George, Jr. lived in Denver. Only Minnie remained in Hygiene. The burial took place, not in the Dunkard graveyard, but in Longmont's Mountain View Cemetery. [576] Mark remained with his father for about a week after Amanda's death, helping him pack for the first of many winters George would spend with Walter and his family in Arizona. [577]

George would not have wanted his wife of forty-one years to live on in pain, but he found it lonely in the Kimbark house without her. But "Grandpa Mack" had affectionate children and grandchildren who distracted him from his grief by including him in their lives. He continued the walks out to the old homestead where Minnie's holiday gatherings always included him and was also a fairly frequent visitor to Mark's place where he had the good grace to admire what his eldest had achieved on his "desert" ranch. In 1922, two years before George's death, the family celebrated his 85th birthday. It was the occasion for a four-generation photograph of George, Mark, Phygenia and her little daughter, Violet, who would die of peritonitis by the next year.

George's last years were peaceful ones. He had survived a sickly childhood, his walk out to Colorado's gold fields, war, heavy-duty freighting and the rigors and hazards of farming to arrive at a fairly comfortable old age. He had witnessed his offspring become the kinds of adults most parents wish for: happy, thriving, productive members of society. He had numerous grandchildren and great-grandchildren. It had been a good life and when, toward the end of that life, George appeared in a photograph taken with another early Boulder County settler, Alex Montgomery, he appears contented.

In the end it was George's eighty-seven-year old lungs that finally gave out. On October 22, 1924 an oxygen tank was delivered to his home where Minnie was helping to care for him, but it arrived too late to be of any use. He died of pneumonia that day. The small, supposedly weak man had outlived his wife and all of his siblings. His family buried George next to Amanda where his stone notes his membership in the First Colorado Cavalry and the G. A. R. Touching additions to his marker and Amanda's are the words "Father" and "Mother".

Four generations of McIntoshes in 1922. In the front row are, left to right, George McIntosh, Phygenia McIntosh Newkirk and her little daughter, Violet. Mark McIntosh, Phygenia's father, stands behind the group. Courtesy of Cindy McIntosh.

George McIntosh with fellow early Boulder County settler, Alex Montgomery, circa early 1920s. Courtesy of the Agricultural Heritage Center.

George's obituary from the *Longmont Ledger* on October 24th went beyond the usual platitudes that had revealed so little of Rind's personality when she died. The anonymous writer made some effort to capture the nature of the man who had for so long been a respected and even beloved part of the Hygiene-Longmont community,

> Geo. R. McIntosh was a man of very unusual character, full of optimistic vision, benevolent, philanthropic in every way. His largness (sic) of heart, and broad- mindedness made friends for him wherever he went, and one went out of his presence feeling he was better for having come in touch with a man of his noble character. In his home and among his children he could not be excelled. As some one expressed it, 'he was a Prince'."

Just a year before his death, George had received a letter from Cora McIntosh Cook, Eb's youngest daughter. Cora lived in Hiram, Ohio, but she had just returned from a road trip that had taken her and her family from Ohio to California and back again. The group had planned to return by way of Colorado to see George, but decided they could not prolong their journey any further and so missed the chance to see him one last time. As if she realized that her uncle would appreciate knowing both the distance – and the cost – of the drive, Cora wrote, "We came 4, 066 miles on $40.03 worth of gasoline." George, too, had come great distances on foot, by wagon, and by train. He had extended his Scottish ancestor's tenuous foothold in America to include the ownership of many acres of productive land in western states unimaginable in John Mackintosh's era. His intelligent, early vision recognized northeastern Colorado's agricultural potential and he combined agrarian and financial canniness to help make it a viable, attractive place for other settlers. The seed that had come from Scottish shores so many centuries before had taken firm hold in the soil of the western United States. George McIntosh made sure that it was, indeed, one that "would grow".

EPILOGUE

When Neil Lohr looked out over his grandfather's former land for the last time, he could take comfort from the knowledge that he had taken steps to preserve that land for future generations. The Boulder County fields that so bewitched George in 1868 no longer stretched out in all directions. By 1984 the remaining property was threatened with complete annihilation as housing developments encroached. Neil, who never had much use for city dwellers, knew that if he didn't do something before his death to halt the borders of the expansion, the original homestead and everything it represented would be swallowed up and lost forever.

In the years between George's death and his grandson's provisions for the land farming had become increasingly mechanized, scientific, and expensive. Huge agribusinesses supplanted independent family farms. As individual farmers capitulated in the face of these new demands, large swathes of agricultural lands vanished, consumed by roads, houses, shopping developments and the like because where agribusiness left off, real estate developers often stepped in. Neil was especially concerned that the construction of new homes would greatly reduce the local farmer's ability to produce foodstuffs and that people would lose all connection to the production of the food they ate.

Neil, who had never married, continued to live in his parents' home until just before he died in 1991. Harry's death in 1976 had left Neil the sole heir to his parents' estate, so he was not a poor man. He also possessed both foresight and George McIntosh's knack for making critical decisions about property. He had a plan that came to fruition in early 1985 when he was eighty-five years old — he sold over 200 acres to Boulder County to create an island of land that would retain its focus on agriculture. He sold the property for a sum below market value, less than half of the $15,000 per acre that was the going rate for such acreage at the time. Equally important, he established a trust fund in the amount of $250,000 specifically for the purpose of creating some kind of entity dedicated to his goal of preserving the area's (and his family's) agricultural history and educating the public about local farming practices.

Neil Lohr in 1984 in front of the house his parents built where George McIntosh's cabin once stood.   Courtesy of Cindy McIntosh.

In May of 2001 the doors of the Agricultural Heritage Center at the Lohr-McIntosh Farm, managed by Boulder County Parks and Open Space, opened to the public. Several descendants of George and Amanda McIntosh and of Rind and Clark Reed attended the opening ceremony, a circumstance George could never have foreseen when took up the land one hundred thirty-three years before. George would have been pleased to see how his grandson, the one who most shared his great affection for the area, had saved it for future generations. Today thousands of visitors — city families, school groups, former farmers, people from other countries and more — pass through the swinging wooden gate entrance each year to tour the Center. Once inside that gate they can visit the first floor of the farmhouse George and Minnie Lohr built and view the outbuildings, including the barn that George constructed in 1881.

A view from the entrance to the Agricultural Heritage Center located on part of George McIntosh's original Boulder County homestead. The farmhouse constructed circa 1909-1911 by George and Minnie Lohr sits just inside the main gate and behind it can be seen part of the barn George McIntosh built in 1881. The barn standing in the left background belonged to William Dickens of Longmont and was moved to the AHC where it now serves as space for permanent AHC displays related to farming in the county. Courtesy of Jim Drew.

The large, dark structure in the center is the weather-beaten barn that George McIntosh built in 1881. Ute Highway, now known as Highway 66, parallels the fence in the background — across the road is the house (not visible in this photograph) George and Amanda built in 1878. Courtesy of Jim Drew.

On their way to interactive exhibits that demonstrate various aspects of farming in the county visitors to the site pass those all-important water ditches. At certain times of the year they can also observe livestock on the farm and learn how to make butter or shoe a horse, among many other ages-old crafts. And they get to hear the story of how this particular farm, now representative of so many others, chosen and nurtured by a particular early settler, came to be. George's story now belongs to those people.

ENDNOTES

[1] Woolf, *A Room of One's Own*, 94.

[2] Tocqueville, *Democracy in America.*, 495.

[3] In the early history of the McIntosh family the women often remain shadowy characters known to us only through their relationships to husbands, fathers, or brothers.

[4] *Encyclopedia Britannica*, 11th ed., s.v. "Inverness".

[5] Anderson, *Ebenezer Mackintosh*, 15.

[6] Grant, *Scottish Clans and Tartans*, 180.

[7] Anderson, *Ebenezer Mackintosh*, 16.

[8] *Encyclopedia Britannica*, 11th ed., s.v. "Scotland, Church of".

[9] Atkin, *Cromwell's Crowning Mercy*, 7.

[10] Magnusson, *Scotland* , 433.

[11] *Encyclopedia Britannica*, 11th ed., s.v. "Cromwell, Oliver".

[12] Magnusson, *Scotland*, 456.

[13] Ibid.

[14] Ibid., 458.

[15] Atkin, 14.

[16] Ibid., 32.

[17] Ibid., 30.

[18] *Encyclopedia Britannica*, 11th ed., s.v. "Charles II". Only in 1660, after Cromwell's death, was Charles restored to the throne.

[19] Smith, Abbot, *Colonists in Bondage*, 152.

[20] Hartley, E. N. *Ironworks on the Saugus*, 198-199. The English were not enthusiastic about the cost of keeping the prisoners of war, but returning these potentially rebellious men to Scotland seemed like a foolhardy prospect.

[21] Atkin, *Cromwell's*, 126; Hartley, 200.

[22] McManis, *Colonial New England*, 54.

[23] Hartley, *Ironworks*, 3.

[24] Anderson, *Ebenezer Mackintosh*, 16-17.

[25] Smith, *Colonists*, 157.

[26] Polk, *The Birth of America*, 36.

[27] Anderson, *Ebenezer Mackintosh*, 17.

[28] Hartley, *Ironworks*, 3.

[29] Federal Writers' Project, *Massachusetts*, 413.

[30] Hartley, *Ironworks*, 123.

[31] Taylor, *American Colonies*, 169.

[32] Hartley, *Ironworks*, 201.

[33] Atkin, *Cromwell's*, 132; Hartley, *Ironworks*, 202.

[34] Banks, C. E. "Accounts of Lynn Iron Works", 23.

[35] Parrington, *Colonial Mind*, 28-29.

[36] *Hutchinson Papers* (Prince Society) I, 264-265. Quoted in Anderson, *Ebenezer Mackintosh*, 16-17.

[37] Anderson, *Ebenezer Mackintosh*, note 2, 18.

[38] Hawke, *Everyday Life*, 143

[39] Polk, *Birth of America*, 130.

[40] Hartley, *Ironworks*, 4. John Mackintosh's great-great-great grandson George would also experience the discomfort of being the object of public observation while drilling as a Union soldier in Denver over two hundred years later.

[41] Ibid., 7.

[42] Smith, *Colonists*, 240.

[43] Coldham, *Emigrants in Chains*, 5.

[44] Games, *Migration*, 164.

[45] Lockridge, *A New England Town*, 5.

[46] Hill, ed., *The Early Records of the Town of Dedham, Massachusetts 1659-1673*, vol. 2, 11.

[47] Lockridge, *A New England Town*, 9.

[48] Brown, "Puritan Democracy", 393.

[49] Hanson, *Dedham, Massachusetts, 1635-1890*; Hotten, *The Original Lists*, 289.

[50] Hill, *Early Records*, vol. 2, 44.

[51] Ibid., 88.

[52] Ibid., 200.

[53] Lockridge, *A New England Town*, 67.

[54] Ibid., 69.

[55] Ibid.

[56] Butler, *Becoming American*, 143.

[57] Hurt, *American Agriculture*, 39. Hurt suggests that land that did not belong specifically to a family was understood to be available for common use to supply wood for fuel or grass for livestock, but that does not seem to have been the case in Dedham.

[58] Hill, *Early Records*, vol. 2, 79.

[59] Ibid.

[60] McIntosh, *Genealogical Record*, 5.

[61] *Dedham Historical Register*, vol. 4, 1894, 43.

[62] Quoted in Lockridge, *A New England Town*, 15-16.

[63] Dwight, *History of the Descendants* , 102.

[64] *New England Historical and Genealogical Register*, vol. 99, October, 1945, 312. The entry for John Mackintosh Jr. queries, "Does not this death entry for John Macintosh in the Dedham vital records, with the day lacking, indicate that he did not die at home?"

[65] Torrey, *New England Marriages*, 482; McIntosh, Walter H., *A Genealogical Record*, 5.

[66] Bailyn, *Peopling* , 93.

[67] St. John, *Letters*, 24-25.

[68] Wight, *The Wights*, 11.

[69] Henretta, "Economic Development and Social Structure in Colonial Boston", 83.

[70] Foppes, "Ebenezer Mackintosh", 5.

[71] Ibid.

[72] Ibid., 22.

[73] Butler, *Becoming American*, 85.

[74] Ebenezer's political connections at this point undoubtedly helped his father obtain the appointment.

[75] Boston Town Records, *A Report of the Record Commissioners of the City of Boston, 1758-1759*, 203.

[76] Anderson, *Ebenezer Mackintosh*, 21.

[77] Towner, *A Good Master Well Served*, 26.

[78] Anderson, *Ebenezer Mackintosh*, 28. Anderson suggests that in the significant year of 1765 Ebenezer may have opened a shoemaking shop with Benjamin Bass. He bases this supposition on information found in a lawsuit lodged against the pair by Samuel Adams.

[79] Towner, *A Good Master*, 29

[80] Anderson, *Ebenezer Mackintosh*, 22.

[81] Butler, *Revolution*, 111.

[82] Bourne, *Cradle*, 102.

[83] Kay, *Lost Boston*, 28-29.

[84] Henretta, "Economic Development," 81.

[85] Ibid.

[86] Cooper, *Pathfinder*, 220.

[87] Morison, Samuel Eliot, Commager and Leuchtenberg, *Growth*, 163-164.

[88] Foppes, "Ebenezer Mackintosh", 5.

[89] Bourne, *Cradle*, 120.

[90] Schwartz, *French and Indian War*, 60.

[91] Borneman, *French and Indian War*, 56-57.

[92] Leckie, *"A Few Acres of Snow"*, 236.

[93] Borneman, *French and Indian War*, 41.

[94] Foppes, "Ebenezer Mackintosh", 5.

[95] Anderson, *Ebenezer Mackintosh*, 24.

[96] Foppes, "Ebenezer Mackintosh", 6.

[97] Boston Town Records, *A Report of the Record Commissioners of the City of Boston 1754-1763*, 120.

[98] Henretta, "Economic Development", 35.

[99] Langguth, *Patriots*, 63.

[100] Rowe, *Letters*, November 5, 1764, 67-68.

[101] Foppes, "Ebenezer Mackintosh", 28.

[102] Rowe, *Letters*, February 7, 1765, 76.

[103] Zobel, *Boston Massacre*, 27.

[104] Foppes, "Ebenezer Mackintosh", 31, 32

[105] Miller, *Sam Adams*, 71; Zinn, *People's History*, 65.

[106] Foppes, "Ebenezer Mackintosh", 33, 34.

[107] Anderson, *Ebenezer Mackintosh*, 27.

[108] Zinn, *People's History*, 66.

[109] Miller, *Sam Adams*, 52.

[110] Foppes, "Ebenezer Mackintosh", 64-65.

[111] Miller, *Sam Adams*, 52.

[112] Langguth, *Patriots*, 60.

[113] Miller, *Sam Adams*, 63.

[114] Bourne, *Cradle*, 116, 134.

[115] Langguth, *Patriots*, 64; Foppes, "Ebenezer Mackintosh", 99.

[116] Hutchinson, *Diary and Letters*, vol. 1, 71.

[117] Anderson, *Ebenezer Mackintosh*, 25. The tree had become a rallying point for foes of the Stamp Act.

[118] Young, Alfred *Shoemaker*, 95.

[119] Foppes, "Ebenezer Mackintosh", 118-119.

[120] Shoemaker, *London Mob*, 116.

[121] Bourne, *Cradle*, 113.

[122] Young, Alfred, *Shoemaker*, 29.

[123] Foppes, "Ebenezer Mackintosh", 149.

[124] Anderson, *Ebenezer Mackintosh*, 44; Wyman, *The New North Church*, 81.

[125] Wyman, 81.

[126] Harvard Ms., Sparks, 10, quoted in Foppes, "Ebenezer Mackintosh", 158.

[127] Foppes, "Ebenezer Mackintosh", 152

[128] Young, Alfred, *Shoemaker*, 29.

[129] Zobel, *Boston Massacre*, 182.

[130] After Mehitable's death, Jotham married a Mary Williams in 1748. One of their children was Samuel Maverick. *New England Historical and Genealogical Register*, Vol. 97, 1943, 56.

[131] Zobel, *Boston Massacre*, 191; Bourne, *Cradle of Violence*, 157.

[132] *Boston Gazette and Country Journal*, March 12, 1770, 1.

133 Thomas, *Tea Party to Independence*, 44.

134 Foppes, "Ebenezer Mackintosh", 162.

135 Drake, *Tea Leaves*, cxxvii.

136 Thomas, *Tea Party to Independence*, 68.

137 Ibid., 122.

138 *Massachusetts Spy*, May 19, 1774. Quoted in Anderson, *Ebenezer Mackintosh*, 53-53.

139 Anderson, *Ebenezer Mackintosh*, 55.

140 Ibid, 58.

141 Hayward, *New England Gazetteer*, np.

142 Federal Writers' Project, *New Hampshire*, 53.

143 Ibid., 75.

144 Foppes, "Ebenezer Mackintosh", 174.

145 Ibid., 175.

146 Anderson, *Ebenezer Mackintosh*, 57.

147 Whitcher, *History of the Town of Haverhill*, 92.

148 Anderson, *Ebenezer Mackintosh*, 56.

149 Whitcher, *History*, n. 2, 579.

150 Hurt, *American Agriculture*, 96.

151 McIntosh, Paschal to Elizabeth McIntosh Bigelow. May 1, 1826. Quoted in Anderson, *Ebenezer Mackintosh*, 59-60.

152 Ferguson, *Ohio Land Grants*, 4.

153 Ibid., 8.

154 Howard, *New Encyclopedia of the American West*, 81.

155 DeRogatis, *Moral Geography*, 33, 32.

156 Hatcher, *Western Reserve*, 55. Hatcher notes that just a few decades after these surveyors led the way to the Western Reserve it would be possible for pioneers from New England to follow established "pack-train trails" over Pennsylvania's Appalachian Mountains to Pittsburgh and then into Youngstown, Ohio.

157 *Encyclopedia of Cleveland History*, "Cleaveland, Moses", http://ech.case.edu/echcgi/article.pl?id=CM10.

158 Hatcher, *Western Reserve*, 122.

159 Ohio History Central. "Moses Cleaveland", http://www.ohiohistorycentral.org/entry.php?rec=86.

160 Pfaff, *Rediscovering Mantua.*, 10,19.

161 Hatcher, *Western Reserve*, 52.

162 Ibid., 50.

163 Upton, *History*, vol. 1, 53.

164 Harmon, "Historical Recollections", 16.

165 Ibid.,

166 Harmon, "Historical Recollections", 14,

167 Upton , *History*, vol. 1, 639.

168 Nash, Emily. Diary. Quoted in Wheeler, Robert, ed. *Visions of the Western Reserve*, 135.

169 *New England Historical and Genealogical Register*, vol., 90, October 1936, 376.

170 Harmon, "Historical Recollections", 14. Jotham consoled himself at the altar with Laura Kellogg of Hudson on Paschal and Abi's first anniversary.

171 Pfaff, *Rediscovering Mantua*, 19.

172 Miller and Wells, *History of Ryegate*, unnumbered note, 289; Anderson, *Ebenezer Mackintosh*, 58.

173 McCormick, *Brimfield*, 21-22.

174 Bittinger, *History of Haverhill*, 372.

175 Ibid, 385.

176 Foppes, "Ebenezer Mackintosh", 176.

177 According to Whitcher, *History of the Town of Haverhill*, 579: "Some of his descendants recently sent to the Coosack Chapter of the D. A. R. [Daughters of the American Revolution] at North Haverhill funds for the erection of a monument to his memory."

178 New Hampshire State historical marker, Haverhill, New Hampshire.

179 Their children were: Laura, John W., Amanda, Hannah, William F., Mary, David S., Jerome, and Norman who died in 1820 at age three and a half. McIntosh, Paschal to Elizabeth McIntosh Bigelow, c. 1826. Quoted in Anderson, "Ebenezer McIntosh", 59.

180 Harmon, "Historical Facts", 1866, 24.

181 Pfaff, *Rediscovering Mantua*, 51.

182 *1874-1978 Bicentennial Atlas of Portage County*, Plough, Cyrus T., ed., " General David McIntosh".

183 "Mantua – 1798-1843"

184 Harmon, "Historical Facts", 14.

185 Wheeler, Robert, ed., *Visions of the Western Reserve*, 168-169; Troyer, Loris, *Portage Pathways* , 64.

186 Fowler, Henry, "Leonard Bacon, D. D." in *The American Pulpit*, 317. Fowler notes that at age ten Leonard left Hudson to attend school in Hartford, Connecticut. He went on to Yale and became a clergyman at the First Congregational Church there. Bacon became known as the "Congregational Pope of New England." *Encyclopedia Britannica*, 11th ed., s. v. "Bacon, Leonard". Perhaps David would have been more careful of his charge had he foreseen Bacon's future!

187 *1874-1978Bicentennial Atlas*, 26.

188 Troyer, *Portage Pathways*, 34, 77.

189 Weisenburger, *The Passing of the Frontier*, Vol. 3, 152.

190 *A History of Portage County, Ohio*, 484.

191 Roseboom, *The Civil War Era*, Vol. 4, 215.

192 Ogg, *The Old Northwest*, 127, 128.

193 Riddle, *Bart Ridgeley*, 87.

194 Harmon, "Historical Facts", 18.

195 McIntosh, Paschal to Elizabeth McIntosh Bigelow, c. 1826, quoted in Anderson, *Ebenezer Mackintosh*, 59-60.

196 Harmon, "Historical Facts", 8.

197 Greenblatt, Miriam, *War of 1812*, 63.

198 *History of Portage County*, 262.

199 *Roster of Ohio Soldiers in the War of 1812*, 56.

200 *History of Portage County*, 279.

201 Ogg, *Old Northwest*, 154.

202 Knauer, *Making of America*, 140.

203 Harmon, "Historical Facts", 6

204 McIntosh, Paschal to Elizabeth McIntosh Bigelow, c. 1826, quoted in Anderson, *Ebenezer Mackintosh*, 59.

205 Griffiths, *Two Years*, 51-52.

206 Harmon, "Historical Facts", 8.

207 McIntosh, Paschal to Elizabeth McIntosh Bigelow, c. 1826, quoted in Anderson, *Ebenezer Mackintosh*, 59.

208 The Lockwoods, like the McIntoshes, must have been readers because they named this son after the eponymous hero of Samuel Richardson's lengthy novel, *The History of Sir Charles Grandison*, 1753-1754. Clegg, *Portage County, Ohio Newspaper Obituary Abstracts 1825-1870*, Ohio Newspaper Abstracts Series, vol. 2, 1982, 58 records George's maternal uncle's sad and violent death in 1867. Grandison Ferris cut his throat shortly after his second wife died.

209 "Bombs and Bones: A Ferris Family Tree",www.ferristree.com.

210 Aldrich, *History of Henry and Fulton Counties*, 682.

211 Greenblatt, *War of 1812*, 43.

212 Jenkins, *Ohio Gazetteer*, 280.

213 Morison, *Growth*, 455; "Panic of 1857", Ohio History Central, http://www.ohiohistorycentral.org/entry.php?rec=537.

214 Buley, *Old Northwest: Pioneer Period 1815-1840*, vol. 2, 273.

215 Frary, *Early Homes*, 122.

216 Larkin, *Shaping of Everyday Life*, 117.

217 Wright, *Letters from the West*, 67.

218 Trollope, *Domestic Manners*, 99

219 Frary, *Early Homes*, 93.

220 Weisenburger, *Passing of the Frontier*, 120.

221 Pegram, *Battling Demon Rum*, 9-10.

222 Havighurst, *Ohio*, 111.

223 *1874-1978 Bicentennial Atlas*, 28 ¼.

224 Jefferson, Thomas, "Notes on Virginia", in *The Life and Selected Writings of Thomas Jefferson*, Koch, Adrienne and William Peden, eds., 259.

225 Hurt, *American Agriculture*, 73.

226 Hartzell, *Ohio Volunteer*, Charles I. Switzer, ed., 6.

227 Howells, *Years of My Youth*, 52

228 Jones, Mary Ellen, *Daily Life*, 120, 121.

229 Harmon, "Historical Facts", 8.

230 "Pioneer Gardens".

231 Friends of Hiram Gardens, 'Early Gardens and the Practice of Horticulture in the Western Reserve", http://hiram.edu/fhg/live/reservelandscape/orchards.html

232 Harmon, "Historical Facts", 8.

233 Riddle, *Portrait*, 135.

234 Harmon, "Historical Facts", 9.

235 Hatcher, Harlan. *The Western Reserve*, 101. Hatcher notes that within a few years Harvey, Royal and Royal's brother, Samuel, founded prosperous dairies where they made cheese and butter, selling their products as far south as New Orleans.

236 Maria's father was a Tilden, a prominent Hiram family. He served as a Hiram trustee. Maria was perhaps overly proud of her origins. Young, Clinton, "Hiram", in *Portage Heritage*, James B. Holm, ed., 377.

237 In the end Milton served a nine-month tour of duty in Company B, 184th Ohio Infantry in 1865.

238 Maddock, , *Practical Observations*, 2nd ed., 31.

239 Reece, *The Medical Guide*, 15th ed., 81.

240 Jones, *History of Agriculture*, 45.

241 Hartzell, *Ohio Volunteer*, 5.

242 Turner, *Frontier*, 271.

243 Buley, *Old Northwest*, 330, 354.

244 Rind accepted the job reluctantly, having witnessed how badly the children had treated her predecessor. She studied without enthusiasm for her teaching certificate. In the end she need not have studied at all because the authorities decided not to examine teaching candidates with previous experience, like Rind. All received their certificates.

245 Morgan, "Mantua School Buildings", no newspaper name, no date.

246 Lottich, Kenneth V. *New England Transplanted*, 142.

247 John Hartzell reported that he and his friends used to travel long distances to attend a spelling school, as did the McIntoshes. He evoked the atmosphere of such an event: "...the school houses were packed full...excitement ran high." Hartzell, *Ohio Volunteer*, 63.

248 Rind's visit to the Mormon service did not inspire her. She called the three local girls who were baptized into the Mormon church "fools". After reading Maria Ward's book about Mormon polygamy, Rind joined many Portage County people in considering the Mormons a bad religious influence.

249 Ling, Adelaide W. "Mantua Home Coming", June 26, 1909, 17.

[250] *A History of Portage County*, 197. Mantua's population remained fairly constant from 1850-1870, hovering at around 1500.

[251] Ibid., 751-752.

[252] Young, Clinton, "Hiram", in *Portage Heritage*, James B. Holm,ed, 371-380.

[253] Riddle, *The Portrait*. Much of Riddle's novel deals with Joseph Smith's experiences in Portage County. Riddle writes, "In the autumn of 1830, rumor had already reached the Mantua settlement of the new revelations that had been made to an obscure young man in…New York.", 64. He goes on to speak of Smith and his friends coming from Hiram for a "meeting at the School-house in Mantua." 65. Riddle used factual foundations for his novels, so it is safe to assume that this event, or one very like it, really did take place.

[254] Bushman, *Joseph Smith*, 178.

[255] *Encyclopedia Britannica*, 11th ed., s.v. "Mormons" , n. 2, 843.

[256] Rutkow, *James A. Garfield*, 6; Garfield, Introduction, *The Diary of James A. Garfield*. Vol. 1, Harry James Brown and Frederick D. Will, eds. xvii, xix. Jesse Grant, the father of another future President of the United States, Ulysses S. Grant, had a tannery in Ravenna (near Mantua) for a few years in the early nineteenth-century. Grant, Ulysses S. *Personal Memoirs*, 5.

[257] Garfield, *Diary*, April 30, 1853, 190.

[258] Ibid., April 18, 1853, 188.

[259] Ibid., May 29, 1853, 195.

[260] Roseboom, *Civil War Era*, 234.

[261] Ohio. Portage County. *Guardianship Prior to 12/1/1991*, #774, 117.

[262] Weisenburger, *Passing of the Frontier*, 58.

[263] "John McIntosh Estate. Final Settlement." August 26, 1853.

[264] Aldrich, ed. *History of Henry County*, 682.

[265] Moorman, Harriet Reed to Genie Davis, 1954.

[266] Ohio History Central, "Panic of 1857", http://ohiohistorycentral.org/entry.php?rec=537.

[267] Buley, *The Old Northwest*, vol. 2, 268.

[268] Moorman, Harriet Reed to Genie Davis, 1954.

[269] Roseboom, *Civil War Era*, vol. 4, 205.

[270] Upton, *History of the Western Reserve*, vol. 2, 1297-1298.

271 Riddle, *Bart Ridgeley*, 149.

272 "Naturalizations from Portage County Records 1816-1878 (Including Admissions to the Bar and Revolutionary War Pension Applications", William C. Johnson, comp., 1983, 5.

273 Roseboom, *The Civil War Era*, 6.

274 West, *Contested Plains*, 115.

275 *History of Clear Creek*, 662.

276 Gay, *Cultivation of Hatred*, 117.

277 Riddle, *The Portrait*, 375.

278 *A History of Portage County*, 766.

279 Ibid.

280 Hunt, *Wisconsin Gazetteer*, 204.

281 "Early History of Education in Wisconsin", *Collections of the State Historical Society of Wisconsin*, vol. 5, Goldthwaite, Reuben, Dir., 345.

282 It is unclear who this young boy was. George was known as "Grandpa Mack" or "Mr. Mack" to many people at this point in his life.

283 "McIntosh, George", Longmont Public Library Biography File.

284 *History of Clear Creek*, 662.

285 Taylor, Bayard, quoted in *Encyclopedia Britannica*, 11th ed., s. v. "Colorado".

286 Dorset, *The New Eldorado*, 166.

287 Quoted in Hafen, ed. *Pike's Peak*, 84, 85.

288 *New York Tribune*, January 29, 1859, quoted in West, *The Contested Plains*, 116.

289 West, *Contested Plains*, 125.

290 Quoted in Hafen, ed., *Pike's Peak*, 265-266.

291 Cushman, *Gold Mines*, 39; *History of Clear Creek*, 662.

292 *New York Tribune*, October 2, 1858, quoted in Hafen, *Colorado Gold Rush*, 73.

293 Goodwin, O.P. in the *Kansas Daily Herald*, March 19, 1859, quoted in Hafen, Ibid., 229.

294 Quoted in Hafen, *Colorado Gold Rush*, 73.

295 *History of Clear Creek*, 662.

296 Smith, Duane , *Rocky Mountain West*, 6.

297 "McIntosh, George", Longmont Public Library Biography File.

298 West, *Contested Plains*, 121.

[299] Jones, *Daily Life*, 127.

[300] Anonymous, quoted in Hafen, ed. *Pike's Peak*, 218. The author noted that the antidote required some kind of acid; lacking that, the pioneer was advised to shove "oil, lard or pieces of fat bacon" down the poor beast's gullet."

[301] Anonymous, quoted in Hafen, ed. *Pike's Peak*, 102.

[302] Smith, *Rocky Mountain West*, 11.

[303] *History of the City of Denver*, 196.

[304] Granruth, *Mining Gold*, 15.

[305] Lamar, Howard R., ed. *National Encyclopedia*, 436.

[306] Milner, et al, *Oxford History*, 202.

[307] Clark, "Across the Plains", *Colorado Magazine*, no. 6, January 1929, 138.

[308] Ibid.

[309] "Proceedings of the Miners' Meetings of Nevada District in Gilpin County, April 28, 1860", quoted in Mumey, *History and Laws*, 4.

[310] Milner, et al, *Oxford History*, 198.

[311] Granruth, Alan, comp., *.Index to Gilpin County*, 9, 13-14.

[312] Mumey, *History and Laws*, 1.

[313] Paul, *Mining Frontiers*, 122.; Cushman, *Gold Mines*, 9.

[314] Hollister, *Mines of Colorado*, 162.

[315] Dorset, *New Eldorado*, 166.

[316] Sagstetter, Beth and Bill, *Mining Camps*, 167.

[317] Fossett, *Colorado*, 324.

[318] Cushman, *Gold Mines*, 87.

[319] Limerick, *Legacy*, 102.

[320] Paul, *Mining Frontiers*, 118.

[321] Dorset, *New Eldorado*, 166.

[322] Smith, Duane and Ronald C.Brown, *No One Ailing*, 54.

[323] Limerick, *Legacy* , 99.

[324] Walker, *Wagonmaster*, 2.

[325] Steinel, *History of Agriculture*, 122.

[326] Accounts vary as to exactly when George acquired this property. I have placed the acquisition at this point in the narrative because it seems the likeliest time for it.

[327] *History of Clear Creek*, 391.

328 Ibid.

329 Neil Lohr, interview by Anne Dyni, 1987 (updated 2007), OH #363, Part II.

330 Ibid.

331 Scott, *Colorado Voters*, Book 1, District 1, Precinct 4 ½, I-27.

332 Ellis, Richard N. and Duane A. Smith, *Colorado*, 7.

333 Sanford, "Camp Weld, Colorado", *Colorado Magazine*, vol. 11, 1934, 46.

334 Charles Reed to Genie McIntosh Davis, nd.

335 Smith, Duane, *Rocky Mountain West*, 16; Colton, *Civil War*, 42.

336 Colton, *Civil War*, 141

337 Ibid., 44.

338 Hollister, *Boldly They Rode*, 12.

339 *Daily Colorado Republican and Rocky Mountain Herald*, November 1, 1861, 3.

340 *Rocky Mountain News*, September 5, 1861, 2.

341 Dorset, *New Eldorado*, 142.

342 Whitford, *Colorado Volunteers*, 49.

343 *Daily Colorado Republican*, October, 18, 1861, 3.

344 Josephy, *Civil War*, 76.

345 Reid, *Ohio in the War*, vol. 1, 933.

346 Josephy, *Civil War*, 77.

347 Sanford, "Camp Weld", 48

348 Dorset, *New Eldorado*, 142.

349 Ibid.

350 Hollister, *Boldly They Rode*, introduction, np.

351 Hollister, 49.

352 Ibid., 292. Hambleton was cashiered from the Colorado First in November 1861, but redeemed himself by enlisting in the Third Colorado Volunteers the following September. He became a Second Lieutenant in January, 1863.

353 Quoted in Dorset, 146

354 Scott, *Glory*, 119.

355 Ibid., 125.

356 Ibid., 124.

357 Eventually someone *did* shoot him. Slough's imperious path continued until the end of the Civil War and beyond. He was an extremely unpopular person wherever he worked. After the battles in New Mexico, he

became a despised Brigadier-General at Alexandria, Virginia. He
returned to Colorado as Chief Justice of the Territorial Supreme Court.
On December 17, 1867 W. L. Ryerson, a Territorial legislator who had
tried to censure Clough publicly, shot him to death in the La Fonda
Hotel at Santa Fe. Kennedy, ed., *Civil War Battlefield Guide*, 43. Ryerson's plea of self-defense was successful. Mumey, *Bloody Trails*, note 135,
96; Josephy, *The Civil War*, 77

358 Dorset, *New Eldorado*, 146.

359 Colton, *Civil War*, 47.

360 Whitford, *Colorado Volunteers*, 79.

361 Josephy, *Civil War*, 77.

362 United States. Dept. of War. *The War of the Rebellion*, vol. 9, 535.

363 Colton, *Civil War*, 48.

364 Josephy, *Civil War*, 48.

365 Chivington would lead the vicious slaughter known as the Sand Creek
[Colorado] Massacre on November 29, 1864, an act for which he was
later roundly condemned.

366 Josephy, *Civil War*, 81.

367 Some dispute that it was Chivington's cleverness that led to the ambush,
contending that he merely stumbled upon the Texans while ignoring
Slough's need for him elsewhere.

368 Brown, George M. to his wife, April 20, 1862, quoted in Hollister, *Boldly
They Rode*, 262.

369 Ward, *The West*, 187.

370 *Civil War Battlefield Guide*, 43.

371 Hollister, *Boldly They Rode*, 112, 113.

372 Scott, *Glory*, 134.

373 Josephy, *Civil War*, 85.

374 Scott, *Glory*, 186, *Civil War Battlefields Guide*, 43.

375 Scott, *Glory*, 187.

376 Ickis, *Bloody Trails*, 88, 96.

377 Scott, *Glory*, 201, Josephy, *The Civil War*, 87

378 Ickis, April 15, 1862, 97

379 Josephy, *The Civil War*, 91

380 Scott, *Glory*, 323

381 *Weekly Commonwealth Republican*, August 21, 1862, 1.

382 Hollister, *Boldly They Rode*, 331-332.

383 Scott, *Glory*, 226.

384 Hollister, *Boldly They Rode*, 235.

385 State of Colorado. Boulder County. "Physician's Affidavit, Proof of Physical Disability, Statement of George R. McIntosh, July, 1892.

386 Gray, *Cavalry and Coaches*, 36.

387 Ibid.

388 Hafen, *History of Colorado*, 485.

389 McKechen, *Life of Governor Evans*, 120.

390 Ibid., 121

391 Kelsey, *Frontier Capitalist*, 132.

392 Leonard, Stephen J. "John Nicolay in Colorado: A Summer Sojourn and the 1863 Ute Treaty", *Essays and Monographs in Colorado History*, no, 11, 1990, 43.

393 Downing, Finis E. "With the Ute Peace Delegation of 1863, Across the Plains and at Conejos", *Colorado Magazine*, vol. 22, 1945, 203.

394 Kelsey, 133; Weiser, "Legends of America", 2008: www.legendsof America/outlaw-espinosagang.html.

395 Stephen, 43. The story of the Espinosas' fates is prone to exaggeration and unclear information that even confuses the main players. Jose was killed at some point after the Evans trip. Eventually a frontier scout named Tom Tobin (1829-1940), who may have been a distant cousin of the Espinosas, tracked down and ambushed Felipe and Jose as they sat by their campfire. He shot and beheaded both of them ,taking the grisly relics in a sack back to Fort Garland to collect bounty on the men. Leonard, *Lynching in Colorado*, 152; McTighe, *Roadside History*, 340, 341.

396 Van Tassel, David and John Vacha, *"Beyond Bayonets"*, 13.

397 Cochran, William C., *The Western Reserve and The Fugitive Slave Law*, Publication #101, (Cleveland: Western Reserve Historical Society, 1920), 79.

398 Troyer, Loris, *Portage Pathways*, (Kent, Ohio: Kent State Univ. Press, 1998), 34.

399 Dee, Christine, *Ohio's War: The Civil War in Documents*, The Civil War in the Great Interior Series, (Athens, Ohio: Ohio Univ. Press, 2006), 94.

[400] Troyer, "Benefits Endure from Patriotism of Portage General". *Ravenna-Kent Record-Courier*. April 16, 1983, np.

[401] *A History of Portage County*, (Chicago: Warner, Beers, 1885), 765.

[402] Rutkow, *James A. Garfield*, 15.

[403] Van Tassell, "*Beyond Bayonets*", 52.

[404] Stevens, Larry, compiler. "177th Infantry" www.ohiocivilwar.com/cw177html

[405] Quoted in Dee, *Ohio's War*, 133.

[406] *Defiance Democrat*, April 3, 1864. Quoted in Dee, *Ohio's War*, 174.

[407] Waggoner, v. 1, 205

[408] Hendrickson, 472

[409] Neil Lohr, interview with Anne Dyni, 1987 (updated 2007), OH #363, Part II.

[410] Dale, "Otoe County Pioneers", 2109.

[411] Ibid.

[412] The National Bank Act of 1863, in response to the need for funds to finance the Civil War, authorized the creation of banks that could issue a nationally-recognized currency. "National Bank Act of 1863", www.nationalbankhistory.com, "National Bank Act of 1863".

[413] Ahlbrandt and Stieben, *Larimer*, vol. 2, 592.

[414] Walker, *Wagonmaster*, 276.

[415] Duncan, *Memories of Early Days*, 26.

[416] *Weld County*, vol. I, A21, A23.

[417] Neil Lohr, interview by Susan Allison-Smith, 1987. OH #363, Part I.

[418] "Church Family History"

[419] "Elephant Corral" www.lodo.org/walking_tour/elephant_corral.htm

[420] Walker, *Wagonmaster*, 193.

[421] Howard, Lamar, ed. *New Encyclopedia of the American West*, 910

[422] Gates, "Free Homesteads for All Americans", 3

[423] Ibid., 7.

[424] Ibid., 6-7

[425] Large, "Appropriation", 5.

[426] Coffin, Morse. "Pioneer Days – Reminiscences No. 4", *Boulder County Miner*, January 15, 1914, 2.

427 Neil Lohr, interview by Susan Allison-Smith, 1987, OH #363, Part I.

428 Coffin, "Pioneer Days", 2

429 Large, "Appropriation", 2.

430 Steinel, *History of Agriculture* , 109-110.

431 Limerick, *Legacy*, 125.

432 Boulder County, Colorado Territory, Warranty deed, August 10, 1867.

433 Parker married a woman named Phebe Ann Carter in 1863 and paid school taxes in the Pella area in 1866, but thereafter his name disappears from local records. Benedict, *Refuge*, 143.

434 Harris, *Long Vistas*, 58.

435 I wanted to give this man his rightful last name, but there is very little solid evidence to go by. He may have been the "J. Gerry" listed as a "non-white male" in the 1866 Weld County census that also includes George's name. Monk, comp.,*Index to A Weld County Census*, np. In 1910 an African-American couple named Wesley and Lucille Gary lived in Boulder at 1036 Water Street. (Corson, "The Black Community in Boulder, Colorado", np; *Boulder City Directory*, 1911, 68) But whether Wesley was the son of George's friend is impossible to know.

436 Van McIntosh, interview by the author, April 14, 2008.

437 Moore, Jesse T., "Seeking a New Life", 173.

438 Steinel, *History of Agriculture* , 50.

439 Hollister, *Mines of Colorado*, 272.

440 Ibid., 420.

441 Large, "Appropriation", 33.

442 Neil Lohr, interview with Anne Dyni, 1987, OH #363, Part II.

443 Steinel, *History of Agriculture*, 392-393.

444 Lee family Bible. The Bible is now owned by the Littleton (Colorado) Historical Museum, but the pages related to Joseph and Malinda's family were removed by a descendant. I have relied on photocopies of those pages.

445 Noble, Lois Flanders, *Noble Ancestors*, 2nd supplement and revisions, 1965, np. The Noble family history calls this man John G. Rogers, but John's name does not appear in the 1860 U. S. Census while Nutter's does. Also, Francis and Eliza Lee named their first child Nutter, suggesting that Eliza was the elder Nutter's daughter. Nutter Lee, the son of

Francis and Eliza, also settled somewhere near George McIntosh and achieved local fame from his expert knowledge of horses.

[446] "American Civil War Soldiers Record – William S. Noble", www.ancestry.com.

[447] "William S. Noble", www.ancestry.com

[448] Noble, *Noble*, np.

[449] Levi's story parallels George's in many ways. He was born in Ohio, but his family moved to Wisconsin fifteen years later, so they were living there when George arrived in Sheboygan. Just like George, Levi left Wisconsin in 1869 for the gold fields of Gilpin County. Noted as a "good businessman", he also shared that quality with George. *Littleton Independent*, June 10, 1898, 1.

[450] Noble, Lois., *Noble* , np.

[451] "Another Indian Attack", *Helena Herald*, May 18, 1871, 1.

[452] United States. Department of the Interior. Bureau of Pensions. The statement about his marriage was made by George McIntosh in his application for a pension on, April 9, 1915.

[453] William may have remained in the Palmer household for a time, but when he was eighteen he lived with George and Amanda and worked for them as a farmhand. Ten years later he appeared in the local census as a "boarder" with them. By 1910 William listed his occupation as "farmer" when he lived in a boarding house with about thirty other men. In 1913 he lived in Cheyenne Wells in eastern Colorado. He never married and died in a Denver hospital in 1918.

[454] Renks, R. White. "Eben White 1845-1922" in *They Came to Stay*, p. 259.

[455] Noble, "Noble Lineage", 3.

[456] Ibid., 3-4. Joe's memories of this incident's details were probably faulty, although the basic outline was undoubtedly true. It seems that he conflated Allen and Barney into one figure. The Territory of Colorado, St. Vrain District Census of 1870 shows a rancher named William Barney who owned a quarter-section not in the mountains, but near the McIntosh place. Barney had a son who would have been about six years old at the time of the accident with the ram.

[457] Ibid.

[458] Holt, *Children*, 108.

459 The dairy products obtained from cows feeding on the area's richly nutritious grasses were said to be of "unrivaled excellence", making them a distinct cut above the leek-flavored butter from Portage County. (Fossett, Colorado,170) .

460 Noble, "Noble Lineage", 4.

461 The National Grange of the Patrons of Husbandry arose in 1867. It was devoted to farming issues and advocating on the farmer's behalf. It subsequently became an active political lobby. Steinel, *History of Agriculture*, 36.

462 *So Long, Longmont*, 41,

463 Dickens' Longmont barn now stands on George's former property where it was moved to form part of the Agricultural Heritage Center at the Lohr-McIntosh Farm.

464 Harris, 122

465 *Colorado Springs Gazette*, January 1, 1876, 4.

466 Fossett, Colorado,173.

467 Library of Congress. "The Rise of Industrial America 1876-1900: Railroads in the Late 19th Century", memory.loc.gov/learn///features/timeline/riseind/railroad/rail.html.

468 I have deduced this amount from the averages attached to similar homes built in 1878.

469 Farm wives were frequently active participants in the design of their homes because that was their domain while their husbands labored outside. Some of their plans won prizes at state fairs. Berg, *American Country*, 65.

470 Berg, *American Country*, 11.

471 Bird, *Lady's Life*, 34-35.

472 Harris, 99.

473 Amanda's love of the house may have transcended her death. Bob and Rachel Koenigsberg, the home's owners since late 1996, related the following story to me: a man hired to do interior repairs fled the room where he had been working. The Koenigsbergs found him sitting outside, obviously shaken. He told them that while he was inside he noticed a woman at the window looking in at him. He was startled and then completely unnerved when he realized that she was wearing nineteenth-century clothing. When she suddenly and inexplicably disappeared, he

bolted to the patio. The Koenigsbergs showed him the photo of the McIntosh family sitting in front of the house in about 1895, whereupon he pointed immediately to Amanda as the voyeur. The spectral appearance did not entirely surprise the Koenigsbergs who had seen flickers of something in their peripheral vision as they worked on the interior of the house prior to moving in. They never felt afraid. Rachel believes that Amanda liked the fact that they were improving her house and that she sometimes tried to detain them when they were about to leave by causing a pipe to break or creating some other similar emergency. The house was Amanda's pride and joy, the place where her children grew up, the place where favored daughter Minnie was married and where Minnie's own family lived for a while. No one has seen or felt her presence since the Koenigsbergs moved in. They insist that the home always feels happy to them. Interview with Bob and Rachel Koenigsberg, 2008.

[474] McIntosh, Van, interview with author, April 14, 2008.

[475] Almost twenty years later Mark McIntosh "had the misfortune to have his team run away last week while hitched to a mowing machine." Unlike his father, Mark came away from the accident unscathed. *Longmont Ledger*, August 23, 1897.

[476] Barclay, Dr. J. B., affidavit, July 9, 1892.

[477] Benedict, *Hygiene Cemetery*, n.p.

[478] Steinel, *History of Agriculture*, 514-515.

[479] George McIntosh was unrelated to the Canadian man named John McIntosh who developed this variety in 1811.

[480] Sandsten, E. P. and C. M. Tompkins. "Orchard Survey", 3.

[481] Dyni, *Pioneer Voices*, 51.

[482] Wyckoff, *Creating Colorado*, 158, 160.

[483] McIntosh, Van W. "Where the Grass Grows" 121.

[484] Ibid., 122

[485] Ibid., 124.

[486] *Greeley Tribune*, December 2, 1874.

[487] McIntosh, Van W., "Where the Grass Grows" , 125.

[488] Clason, *Free Homestead*, 128.

[489] Steinel, *History of Agriculture*, 612.

[490] Fossett, *Colorado*, 177.

491 Steinel, *History of Agriculture*, 74; *Encyclopedia Britannica*, 11th ed., s. v. "Locusts" , 858.

492 Steinel, *History of Agriculture* , 78.

493 Benedict, *Refuge*, 59; *Longmont City Directory*, 1903-04.

494 Benedict, Ibid.,116.

495 Noble, *Noble Family*, 1.

496 Morison, Commager and Leuchtenberg, *Growth*, 785.

497 Dumke, *Boom*, 11.

498 Ibid., 5

499 James, *California Romantic*, 223.

500 Dumke, *Boom*, 4

501 The note suggests that George either did not join his wife in her decision to leave the Longmont church or that he was not a member to begin with.

502 *The Brethren Church*, np.

503 Ibid., np; *The Brethren Encyclopedia.*, Vol. 1, 641.

504 *History of Clear Creek*, 636.

505 Ibid., 637.

506 Flory, *Thrilling Echoes*, 39.

507 Flory, *Thrilling Echoes*, np.

508 Holsinger, *Holsinger's History*, 326.

509 Baucke, Robert, "History of Colorado" in *Hygiene Methodist Church*, 9.

510 Pflueger, *Covina*, 42.

511 Ibid., 29.

512 Ibid., 252.

513 Pflueger, *Covina*, 24.

514 Bauer, *Health Seekers*, 116.

515 Ibid.

516 *Longmont Ledger*, December 26, 1884.

517 In the early 1880s George had taken advantage of the 1873 Timber Culture Act to obtain a quarter-section of free land in Larimer County. His only obligation was to plant ten acres of the land in trees.

518 *The Brethren Encyclopedia*, s. v. "Bashor, Martin", 348.

519 Dumke, *Boom*, 15.

520 Starr, *Inventing* , 143.

521 Dumke, *Boom*, 14-15.

522 Baur, *Health Seekers*, 124.

523 Hall, *Covina*, 16.

524 Pflueger, *Covina*, 47.

525 In 1924 Covina built a new hospital nearby and today, with the exception of a few small cottages, the complex and its parking lot have erased the Griswold Tract.

526 *Boulder City Directory*, 1896, np.

527 "First Annual Commencement Program, Districts 7, 13, 20, 24, and 48", June 27, 1895; Dyni, *Back*, 42, 153.

528 James, *Traveler's Handbook*, 391. In reality Covina was not quite as beautiful as James maintained. Although blue gum and pepper trees relieved the scrubby landscape, the town Walter roamed had no sidewalks or paved streets. The roads turned to mud in wet winter weather.

529 Gay, *Tender Passion*, 422.

530 Hall, *Covina*, 29.

531 Lippman, Rosemarie to the author, e-mail, April 11, 2007.

532 *Covina Argus*, November 18, 1899, quoted in *Longmont Ledger*, December 1, 1899. The McIntoshes returned to Covina the following November to spend the winter months, staying in cottages on Badilla Street.

533 Minnie kept Neil at home almost all of his life, thwarting relationships with women whose company he enjoyed. Harry, who attended school with Rudy Brand, father of the astronaut Vance Brand, obtained a business degree from the University of Colorado at Boulder (working on the farm during the summer months). Then he married (Jeannette Lockwood), and eventually moved to Fort Collins where he was a banker at the First National Bank. According to family members, it wasn't far enough away; when Minnie felt aggrieved, she drove to Fort Collins and confronted him in his office.

534 Lohr, Delmar, e-mail to the author, July 14, 2004.

535 *Encyclopedia Britannica*, 11th ed., s. v. "Petroleum".

536 *Longmont Ledger*, August 1, 1902.

537 Morison, et al, *Growth*, 7th ed., vol. 1,787.

538 *Longmont Ledger*, March 24, 1899.

539 There is a hint in a letter from Jo to George written on December 27,

1870 that George might have returned to Mantua briefly in 1870 for a visit when Jo states, "I have not heared from Mother or hen since you left."

540 "Directory of Farmers of Boulder County", 12.

541 Colorado, Longmont, Cultural Resource Survey, OAHP 1403.

542 Clemons, Mrs. J. H., "History of the Boulder County Sanitarium", March 4, 1958, 1, 3.

543 Ibid., 5.

544 McIntosh, Vandaver, *Where the Grass Grows*, 8.

545 Ibid., 10.

546 "McIntosh, George R."   Longmont Public Library Biography file.

547 Arneill, James, quoted in Shikes, *Rocky Mountain Medicine*, 150.

548 Bauer, *Health Seekers*, 90.

549 Starr, *Americans*, 443.

550 Bauer, *Health Seekers*, 177.

551 James, *California Romantic*, 273.

552 James, *Travelers' Handbook*, 9.

553 Case, *History of Long Beach*, 655.

554 Ad on the reverse of a postcard depicting the Long Beach Sanitarium, c. 1911.

555 McIntosh, *Where the Grass Grows*, 79.

556 Bauer, *Health Seekers*, 23.

557 "Summary of Long Beach History"

558 Baur, *Health Seekers*, 36.

559 No letters from George and Amanda's previous stays in California are known to exist.

560 Bauer, *Health Seekers*, 23.

561 Today a towering luxury condominium complex has replaced the apartment house and its immediate neighbors.

562 "George R. McIntosh", Longmont Library Biography File.

563 James, *Travelers' Handbook*, 466.

564 Ibid., 648.

565 Rodgers died the following year in Long Beach after he flew into a flock of birds and crashed in the ocean.

566 James, *Travelers' Handbook*, 463.

[567] "Summary of Long Beach History".

[568] Case, *History of Long Beach*, 173, 178.

[569] Ibid., 184.

[570] *Longmont Ledger*, February 24, 1911.

[571] Ibid.

[572] Foote, Edward, quoted in Hechtlinger, *Great Patent Medicine Era*, 117.

[573] Ibid., 406.

[574] Jacoby, *Electricity*, 404.

[575] Ibid., 241.

[576] *Longmont Ledger*, October 31, 1913.

Nunn News, November, 14, 1913.

ACKNOWLEDGMENTS

The story of George McIntosh and his family could never have been told without the help of many other people. In the forefront of those people are the McIntosh descendants who willingly shared both time and original documents with me. Cindy McIntosh, George's great-great-granddaughter, gave me repeated access to all of her extensive genealogical files and, before she donated them to the Agricultural Heritage Center, family letters and objects associated with George McIntosh. Her father and mother, Wayne and Shirley McIntosh, were equally generous with family scrapbooks and George's Army papers. They also graciously submitted to hours of interviews. Rind's great-great-granddaughter, Judith Rice-Jones, kindly provided copies of Rind's diaries for 1855 and 1866 and other family papers. Van McIntosh, George's great-grandson, gave me a copy of *Where the Grass Grows*, his father's lively account of life on Mark McIntosh's dry land farm; he and his wife Josie conversed with me over a period of several hours, patiently answering all of my questions.

Thanks are also due to Larry Goss, Percy Goss's grandson, who sent copies of the letters Walter McIntosh wrote to Percy and Delmar Lohr provided George Lohr's genealogy and other background material.

It was Cole Early, Boulder Country's Agricultural Heritage Center's first Cultural History Interpretive Coordinator, who hired me as a volunteer historical researcher and assigned me the task of annotating the nineteenth-century McIntosh letters, thus setting me off on the path toward re-creating George

McIntosh's life. Cole's successor, Tom McMichen, opened AHC files to me and provided a critical and enthusiastic audience for my theories about George McIntosh's life. Jim Drew, the AHC Cultural Resource Technician, has been a huge help in sending many of the photographs from the AHC collection for use in this book and in providing his own pictures of the AHC itself. I also thank Pascale Fried, the Education and Outreach Coordinator for Boulder County Parks and Open Space, for her support for this project.

My research was supported in part by grants from Colorado Humanities and the Boulder County Commissioners. I am very grateful to the generosity of both groups.

Wendy Hall, Mary Jo Reitsma and Marti Anderson, librarians at the Boulder Branch Library for Local History, were unfailingly helpful, as was Erik Mason, Curator of Research for Longmont's Museum and Cultural Center. The staffs of the Longmont Public Library, Golden Public Library, Aurora Public Library (Ohio), Long Beach Public Library, Covina Public Library, and the Morton-James Public Library in Nebraska City, Nebraska all assisted me. Jennifer S. Morrow, of the Hiram College (Ohio) Archives and Peggy A. Ford of the Cultural Affairs Department, City of Greeley Museums also deserve my thanks, as do the staffs of the Archives of the Arthur Lakes Library at the Colorado School of Mines and the Colorado State Archives. The Boulder County Clerk and Recorder's Office looked up scores of George's deeds and other official documents for me. The Portage County Courthouse in Ravenna, Ohio located documents related to George's guardianship and other official matters.

A number of historical societies allowed me to look through their files and books. Thanks are due to the Portage County Historical Society in Ravenna, Ohio, the Western Reserve Historical Society in Cleveland, the Long Beach Historical Society, and the Covina Historical Society.

Two special families opened their homes to me, homes that were formerly part of George's life. Bob and Rachel Koenigsburg invited me to explore and photograph the 1878 farmhouse that they have so lovingly and faithfully restored. Janet and Steve Pancost allowed me to tour every floor of their home, the Mantua, Ohio house where George grew up, even as they were packing to move.

My thanks also go to the following individuals who assisted me at various points along the research trail: Darrell and Carol McIntosh, Anne Dyni, Diane

Karash, LaVerne Chalker, Marv Van Peursem, Diane Benedict, Marilane Spencer, Rosemarie Lippman, Ed Tregow, Sandra Haney, and Jeff Kugel.

Throughout this long process I used my family as a much-needed prop. They didn't always understand my passion for the subject, but they stood by me while I pursued it. Special gratitude goes to our son, Nicholas, who steered me through all kinds of technological dilemmas, while his wife, Pam, read my original manuscript with a careful eye. My mother, Donna, who first stimulated my curiosity in history by taking me and my sister on walks through cemeteries while she read the inscriptions on the markers to us, who taught me that reading and words were precious, and who relishes the telling of a good story, knows already how much I owe her.

To my husband, Grant, who encouraged me to go forward at those moments when I was ready to give up and who was always there when I needed his advice, goes my very loving appreciation.

SELECT BIBLIOGRAPHY

Books

Abbott, Carl, Stephen J. Leonard, Thomas J. Noel. *Colorado: A History of the Centennial State.* 4th ed. Boulder: University Press of Colorado, 2005.

Adam, Frank. *The Clans, Septs and Regiments of the Scottish Highlands.* 8th ed. Edinburgh: Johnston & Bacon, 1975.

Ahlbrandt, Arlene (Briggs) and Kathryn "Kate" Stieben. *Larimer County History.* Vol. 2. Fort Collins, Colo., 1987.

Aldrich, Henry Cass, ed. *History of Henry and Fulton Counties, Ohio.* Syracuse, New York: D. Mason and Co., 1888.

Anderson, Fred. *A People's Army: Massachusetts Soldiers and Society in the Seven Years' War.* Published for the Institute of Early American History and Culture. Williamsburg, Virginia. Chapel Hill, North Carolina: University of North Carolina Press, 1984.

Anderson, George Pomeroy. *Ebenezer Mackintosh: Stamp Act Rioter and Patriot.* Reprinted from *The Publications of the Colonial Society of Massachusetts,* Vol. 26, Cambridge, Mass.: John Wilson and Son, 1924.

Atkin, Malcolm. *Cromwell's Crowning Mercy: The Battle of Worcester 1651.* Thrupp, Shroud, Gloucestershire: Sutton Publishing, 1998.

Bailyn, Bernard. *The Peopling of British North America: An Introduction.* New York: Knopf, 1986.

Baur, John E. *The Health Seekers of Southern California, 1870-1900.* San Marino, California: Huntington Library, 1959.

Benedict, Diane. *Hygiene Cemetery 1865-2002: Hygiene, Boulder County.* Lyons, Colorado: Applications Plus, 2003.

_____. *Refuge in the Valley 1800s Pella, Colorado.* Lyons, Colo.: Applications Plus, 2004.

Berg, Donald J. *American Country Building Design.* New York: Sterling Publishing Co., 1997.

Billington, Ray Allen. *Westward Expansion: A History of the American Frontier.* 4th ed. New York: Macmillan, 1974.

Bird, Isabella. *A Lady's Life in the Rocky Mountains.* 1879. Norman, Oklahoma: University of Oklahoma Press, 1960.

Bittinger, Rev. J. Q. *History of Haverhill, New Hampshire.* Haverhill: Cohos Steam Press, 1888.

Boatner, Mark M., III. *Encyclopedia of the American Revolution.* 3rd ed. Mechanicsburg, Pennsylvania: Stackpole Books, 1994.

Borneman, Walter R. *The French and Indian War: Deciding the Fate of North America.* New York: HarperCollins, 2006.

Boston Town Records. *A Report of the Record Commissioners of the City of Boston, 1754-1763.* Boston: Rockwell and Churchill, 1887.

_____. *A Report of the Record Commissioners of the City of Boston, 1758-1759.* Boston: Rockwell and Churchill, 1886.

Bourne, Russell. *Cradle of Violence: How Boston's Waterfront Mobs Ignited the Ameri-can Revolution.* Hoboken, New Jersey: John Wiley and Sons, 2006.

Buley, R. Carlyle. *The Old Northwest: Pioneer Period 1815-1840.* Vol. 2. Bloomington, Indiana: Indiana University Press, 1951.

Burkett, Charles W. *History of Ohio Agriculture.* Concord, New Hampshire: The Rumford Press, 1900.

Bushman, Richard Lyman. *Joseph Smith: Rough Stone Rolling.* New York: Knopf, 2005.

Butler, John. *Becoming American: The Revolution before 1776.* Cambridge, Massa-chusetts: Harvard University Press, 2000.

Cackler, Christian. *Recollections of An Old Settler.* 1874. Reprint, Ravenna, Ohio: Record Publishing Co., 1964.

Case, Walter H. *History of Long Beach and Vicinity.* Vol. 1. 1927. Reprint, New York: Arno Press, 1974.

Clason, George S. *Free Homestead Lands of Colorado Described: A Handbook for Settlers.* Denver: Clason Map Co., 1915.

Clegg, Michael Barron, compiler. *Portage County, Ohio Newspaper Obituary Abstracts 1825-1870*. Ohio Newspaper Abstracts Series. Vol. 2. Fort Wayne, Indiana: Privately printed, 1982.

Cochran, William C. *The Western Reserve and the Fugitive Slave Law*. Publication # 101. Cleveland: Western Reserve Historical Society, 1920.

Coldham, Peter Wilson. *Emigrants in Chains: A Social History of Forced Emigration to the Americas 1607-1776*. Baltimore: Genealogical Publishing Co., 1992.

Colorado Territory Civil War Volunteer Records. Records extracted by Columbine Genealogical and Historical Society, Inc. Littleton, Colorado: 1994.

Colton, Ray C. *The Civil War in the Western Territories: Arizona, Colorado, New Mexico, and Utah*. Norman: Univ. of Oklahoma Press, 1959.

Cooper, James Fenimore. *The Pathfinder: or, The Inland Sea*. New York: The Library of America, 1985.

Cross, Coy F. *Go West Young Man! Horace Greeley's Vision for America*. Albuquerque: Univ. of New Mexico Press, 1995.

Cushman, Samuel. *The Gold Mines in Gilpin County, Colorado*. Central City, Colorado: Register Steam Printing House, 1876.

Dale, Raymond. "Otoe County Pioneers: A Biographical Directory" in *History of the State of Nebraska*. Chicago: The Western Historical Co., 1882.

Davis, Hugh. *Leonard Bacon: New England Reformer and Antislavery Moderate*. Baton Rouge: Louisiana State University Press, 1998.

Dee, Christine, ed. *Ohio's War: The Civil War in Documents*. The Civil War in the Great Interior Series. Athens, Ohio: Ohio University Press, 2006.

De Rogatis, Amy. *Moral Geography: Maps, Missionaries, and the American Frontier*. Religion and American Culture Series. New York: Columbia University Press, 2003.

The Diary of James A. Garfield. Vol. 1. 1848-1871. Brown, Harry James and Frederick A. Williams, eds. Lansing: Michigan State Univ. Press, 1967.

Dorset, Phyllis Flanders. *The New Eldorado: The Story of Colorado's Gold and Silver Rushes*. New York: Macmillan, 1970.

Drake, Francis S. *Tea Leaves, Being a Collection of Letters and Documents Relating to the Shipment of Tea to the American Colonies in the Year 1773, By the East India Company*. Boston: A. O. Crane, 1884.

Dumke, Glenn S. *The Boom of the Eighties in Southern California*. San Marino, California: Huntington Library, 1944.

Durnbaugh, Donald F., ed. *The Brethren Encyclopedia*. Vol. 1. Philadelphia: Brethren Encyclopedia, Inc., 1983.

Dyni, Anne Quinby. *Back to the Basics: The Frontier Schools of Boulder County, Colorado, 1860-1960*. Boulder: Book Lode, 1991.

Eberhart, Perry. *Guide to the Colorado Ghost Towns and Mining Camps*. 4th rev. ed. Athens, Ohio: Swallow Press, 1969.

Ellis, Richard N. and Duane A. Smith. *Colorado: A History in Photographs*. Rev. ed. Boulder: University Press of Colorado, 2005.

Federal Writers' Project. Works Progress Administration. *Massachusetts: A Guide to Its Places and People*. Boston: Houghton Mifflin, 1937.

_____. *New Hampshire: A Guide to the Granite State*. Boston: Houghton Mifflin, 1938.

Fite, Gilbert C. *The Farmers' Frontier 1865-1900.* Histories of the American Frontier Series. New York: Holt, Rinehart, Winston, 1966.

Flory, Jacob S. *Thrilling Echoes from the Wild Frontier: Interesting Personal Reminiscences of the Author.* Chicago: Rhodes and McClure, 1893.

Fossett, Frank. *Colorado: Its Gold and Silver Mines.* 1879. Reprint, The Far Western Frontier Series. New York: Arno Press, 1973.

Fowler, Henry. *The American Pulpit: Sketches, Biographical and Descriptive, of Living American Preachers.* New York: J. M. Fairchild and Co., 1856.

Frary, I. T. *Early Homes of Ohio.* New York: Dover, 1970.

Games, Alison. *Migration and the Origins of the English Atlantic World.* Cambridge: Massachusetts: Harvard University Press, 1999.

Gay, Peter. *The Cultivation of Hatred.* Vol. 3. *The Bourgeois Experience Victoria to Freud.* New York: Oxford Univ. Press, 1986.

_____. *The Tender Passion.* Vol. 2. *The Bourgeois Experience Victoria to Freud.* New York: W. W. Norton, 1993.

Gladden, Sanford Charles. *The Early Days of Boulder County 1859-1900.* Vol. 2. Boulder: Boulder Genealogical Society, 1982.

Glavinick, Jacquelyn Gee, extractor and comp. *U. S. Patent Records from Weld County.* Weld County Genealogical Society, 1966.

Goldthwaite, Reuben. *Collections of the State Historical Society of Wisconsin.* Vol. 5. Madison, Wisconsin: State Historical Society, 1907.

Granruth, Alan. *Index to Gilpin County, Colorado, 1860 Census: Extracted from the 1860 . U. S. Census of Arapahoe County, Kansas Territory.* Lakewood, Colo.: Foothills Genealogical Society of Colorado, 1995.

_____. *Mining Gold to Mining Wallets: Central City, Colorado 1859-1999.* N.p: Gilpin County Historical Society, 1999.

Grant, Neil. *Scottish Clans and Tartans: A Fully Illustrated Guide to over 140 Clans.* New York: Lyons Press, 2000.

Greenblatt, Miriam. *War of 1812.* "Updated edition". America at War Series. New York: Facts on File, Inc., 2003.

Greenly-Hastings, Frances. *So Long, Longmont: A Critical Look at Longmont As It Was And As It Is.* Longmont: CQG Ltd., Publishing, 1996.

Griffiths D., Jr. *Two Years in the New Settlements of Ohio.* Ann Arbor, Michigan: University Microfilms, [1966].

Hafen, Le Roy. *Colorado and Its People: A Narrative and Topical History of the Centennial State.* Vol. 1. New York: Lewis Historical Publishing Co., Inc., 1948.

_____, ed. *Colorado Gold Rush: Contemporary Letters and Reports 1858-1859.* Reprint of 1941 ed. The Southwest Historical Series, 10. Philadelphia: Porcupine Press, 1974.

_____, ed. *Pike's Peak Gold Rush Guidebooks of 1859.* Reprint of 1941 ed. The Southwest Historical Series, 9. Philadelphia: Porcupine Press, 1974.

Hall, Barbara Ann. *Covina.* Charleston, South Carolina: Arcadia, 2007.

Hansen, Robert Brand, ed. *Dedham, Massachusetts 1635-1845.* Camden, Maine: Picton Press, 1997.

Harris, Katherine. *Long Vistas: Women and Families on Colorado Homesteads.* Niwot, Colorado: University Press of Colorado, 1993.

Hartley, E. N. *Ironworks on the Saugus: The Lynn and Braintree Ventures of the Company of Undertakers of the Ironworks in New England.* Norman: University of Oklahoma Press, 1957.

Hartzell, John Calvin. *Ohio Volunteer: The Childhood and Civil War Memories of Captain John Calvin Hartzell, OVI.* Edited by Charles I. Switzer. Athens, Ohio: Ohio University Press, 2005.

Hatcher, Harlan. *The Western Reserve: The Story of New Connecticut in Ohio.* Cleveland: World Publishing Company, 1949, 1966.

Havighurst, Walter. *Ohio: A Bicentennial History.* New York: W. W. Norton, 1976.

Hawke, David Freeman. *Everyday Life in Early America.* New York: Harper and Row, 1988.

Hayward, John. *New England Gazetteer.* 6th ed. Boston: John Hayward, 1839.

Heads of Families at the First Census. Baltimore: Genealogical Publishing Company, 1966.

Heads of Families at the Second Census of the United States Taken in the Year 1800. Madison, Wisconsin: Privately published by John Brooks Threlfeld, 1973.

Hechtlinger, Adelaide. *The Great Patent Medicine Era: Or, Without Benefit of Doctor.* New York: Grosset and Dunlap, 1970.

Hendrickson, Robert. *The Henry Holt Encyclopedia of Word and Phrase Origins.* New York: Henry Holt and Company, 1987.

Hickey, Donald R. *The War of 1812: A Forgotten Conflict.* Urbana, Illinois: University of Illinois Press, 1989.

Hill, Don Gleason, comp. *The Early Records of the Town of Dedham, Massachusetts, 1659-1673.* Vol. 4. Dedham: Dedham Transcript, 1894.

_____, comp. *The Record of Births, Marriages and Deaths in the Town of Dedham 1635-1845.* Vol. 1. Dedham: Dedham Transcript, 1886.

Hine, Robert V. and John Mack Faragher. *Frontiers: A Short History of the American West.* Abridged edition of *The American West: A New Interpretive History.* New Haven: Yale University Press, 2007.

History of Clear Creek and Boulder Valleys, Colorado. Reprint of c. 1880 ed. Evansville, Indiana: Unigraphic, Inc., 1971.

History of Portage County, Ohio. Chicago: Warner, Beers, 1885.

History of Trumbull and Mahoning Counties. Vol. 1. Cleveland: H. Z. Williams and Bro., 1882.

Hollister, Ovando. *Boldly They Rode: A History of the First Colorado Regiment of Volunteers.* 1863. Reprint, Lakewood, Colo.: The Golden Press, 1949.

_____. *The Mines of Colorado.* Springfield, Massachusetts: Samuel Bowles and Co., 1867.

Holsinger, H. R. *Holsinger's History of the Tunkers and the Brethren Church.* Lathrop, California: Pacific Press Publishers, 1901.

Holt, Marilyn Irvin. *Children of the Western Plains: The Nineteenth-Century Experience.* Chicago: Ivan R. Dee, 2003.

Horton, John. J. *The Johnathan Hale Farm: A Chronicle of the Cuyahoga Valley.* Publication # 116. Cleveland: The Western Reserve Historical Society, 1961.

Hotten, John Camden. *The Original Lists of Persons of Quality 1600-1700.* 1880. Reprint, Baltimore: Genealogical Publishing Company, 1962.

Howard, Robert West. *The Vanishing Land*. New York: Villard Books, 1985.

Howe, Henry. *Historical Collections of Ohio in Two Volumes*. Cincinnati, Ohio: C. J. Krehbiel and Company, 1902.

Howells, William Cooper. *Recollections of Life in Ohio from 1813 to 1840*. Cincinnati: The Robert Clarke Co., 1895.

Howells, William Cooper. *Years of My Youth*. New York: Harper and Bros., 1916.

Hurt, R. Douglas. *American Agriculture: A Brief History*. Ames, Iowa: Iowa State University Press, 1996.

Hutchinson, Thomas. *The Diary and Letters of Thomas Hutchinson*. Compiled by Peter Orlando Hutchinson. New York: Houghton Mifflin, 1884.

Hygiene United Methodist Church, 100 Years Serving Our Lord, 1903-2003. Edited and compiled by Theresa (Bork) Goldstrand. Hygiene, Colorado: Hygiene United Methodist Church Trustees, 2003.

Jacoby, George W. *Electricity in Medicine*. Philadelphia: P. Blakiston's Son and Co., 1919.

Jacques, D. H. *The House: A Pocket Manual of Rural Architecture*. New York: Fowler and Wells, 1859.

James, George Wharton. *California Romantic and Beautiful*. Boston: The Page Co., 1914.

_____. *Travelers' Handbook to Southern California*. Pasadena: G. W. James, 1914.

Jefferson, Thomas. *The Life and Selected Writings of Thomas Jefferson*. "Notes on Virginia". 1782. Edited by Adrienne Koch and William Peden. New York: Modern Library, 1972.

Jenkins, Warren. *The Ohio Gazetteer and Traveler's Guide*. Columbus, Ohio: Isaac N. Whiting, 1837.

Jones, Mary Ellen. *Daily Life on The Nineteenth-Century American Frontier*. Daily Life through History Series. Westport, Conn.: Greenwood Press, 1998.

Jones, Robert Leslie. *History of Agriculture in Ohio to 1880*. Kent, Ohio: Kent State Univ. Press, 1983.

Josephy, Alvin M. *The Civil War in the American West*. New York: Alfred A. Knopf, 1991.

Kay, Jane Holtz. *Lost Boston*. Boston: Houghton Mifflin, 1980.

Kelsey, Harry E., Jr. *Frontier Capitalist: The Life of John Evans*. Boulder: Pruett Press, 1969.

Kennedy, Frances, ed. *The Civil War Battlefield Guide*. Boston: Houghton Mifflin, 1998.

Knauer, Kelly. *The Making of America: Life, Liberty and the Pursuit of the Nation*. 2nd ed. New York: Time, Inc., 2005.

Krakel, Dean Fenton. *South Platte Country: A History of Old Weld County, Colorado 1739-1910*. Laramie, Wyo.: Powder River Pub., 1954.

Lamar, Howard R., ed. *The New Encyclopedia of the American West*. New Haven, Conn.: Yale Univ. Press, 1998.

Langguth, A. J. *Patriots: The Men Who Started the Revolution.* New York: Simon and
Schuster, 1988.

Larkin, Jack. *The Shaping of Everyday Life 1790-1840.* The Everyday Life in America Series. New York: Harper and Row, 1988.

Leckie, Robert. *"A Few Acres of Snow": The Saga of the French and Indian War.* New York: John Wiley and Sons, 1999.

Leonard, Stephen J. *Lynching in Colorado, 1858-1919.* Boulder: University Press of Colorado, 2002.

Limerick, Patricia Nelson. *The Legacy of Conquest: The Unbroken Past of the American West.* New York: W. W. Norton, 1987.

Littleton Cemetery, Littleton, Colorado. Mount Rosa Chapter, National Society, Daughters of the American Revolution, 1983.

Lockridge, Kenneth A. *A New England Town: The First Hundred Years Dedham, Massachusetts, 1636-1736.* Expanded edition. The Norton Essays in American History. New York: W. W. Norton, 1985.

Lottich, Kenneth V. *New England Transplanted: A Study of the Development of Educational and Other Cultural Agencies in the Connecticut Western Reserve in Their National and Philosophical Setting.* Dallas, Texas: Royal Publishing Co., 1964.

McCormick, Edgar. *Brimfield and Its People: Life in a Western Reserve Township 1816-1841.* Grantham, New Hampshire: Tompson and Rutter, 1988.

McManis, Douglas R. *Colonial New England: A Historical Geography.* Historical Geography of America Series. New York: Oxford Univ. Press, 1977.

McMechen, Edgar Carlisle. *Life of Governor Evans: Second Territorial Governor of Colorado.* Denver: Wahlgren Pub. Co., 1924.

McTighe, James. *Roadside History of Colorado.* Boulder: Johnson Books, 1984.

Magnusson, Magnus. *Scotland: The Story of a Nation.* New York: Atlantic Monthly Press, 2000.

Maddock, Alfred Beaumont. *Practical Observations on the Efficacy of Medicated Inhalations in the Treatment of Pulmonary Consumption, Bronchitis, Chronic Cough and Other Diseases of the Respiratory Organs, and Also Affections of the Heart.* 2nd ed., London: Simpkin and Marshall, 1857.

Marshall, Josiah T. *The Farmer's and Emigrant's Hand-Book: Being a Full and Complete Guide for the Farmer and the Emigrant.* New York: D. Appleton and Co., 1845.

Marshall, Thomas Maitland, ed. *Early Records of Gilpin County, Colorado 1859-1861.* Boulder: Univ. of Colorado, 1920.

Miller, Edward and Frederic P. Wells. *History of Ryegate, Vermont, from Its Settlement by the Scotch-American Company of Farmers to Present Time.* St. Johnsbury,
Vermont: The Caledonian Co., 1913.

Miller, John C. *Sam Adams: Pioneer in Propaganda.* Stanford, Calif.: Stanford Univ. Press, 1960.

Miller, Lillian B. *In the Minds and Hearts of the People: Prologue to the American Revolution: 1760-1774.* Greenwich, Conn.: New York Graphic Society, 1974.

Milner, Clyde A., II, et al. *The Oxford History of the American West.* New York: Oxford Univ. Press, 1994.

Morgan, Edmund S. and Helen M. Morgan. *The Stamp Act Crisis: Prologue to Revolution*. Chapel Hill, North Carolina: Univ. of North Carolina Press, 1953.

Morison, Samuel Eliot, Henry Steele Commager and William E. Leuchtenberg. *The Growth of the American Republic*. 7th ed. Vol. 1. New York: Oxford Univ. Press, 1980.

Mumey, Nolie. *Bloody Trails along the Rio Grande: The Diary of Alonzo Ferdinand Ickis 1836-1917*. Denver: Old West Publishing, 1958.

_____, comp. *History and Laws of Nevadaville*. Boulder: Johnson Press, 1962.

Ogg, Frederic Austin. *The Old Northwest: A Chronicle of the Ohio Valley and Beyond*. New Haven, Conn.: Yale University Press, 1919.

Parrington, Vernon L. *The Colonial Mind 1620-1800*. New York: Harcourt, Brace, 1954.

Paul, Rodman Wilson. *Mining Frontiers of the Far West 1848-1880*. Histories of the American Frontier. New York: Holt, Rinehart and Winston, 1963.

Pegram, Thomas R. *Battling Demon Rum: The Struggle for a Dry America 1800-1933*. The American Ways Series. Chicago: Ivan R. Dee, 1998.

Pfaff, Elmer. *Rediscovering Mantua (Portage County, Ohio): The First 100 Years of Survival, 1799-1899*. Mage-in Nation, 1985.

Polk, William R. *The Birth of America from before Columbus to the Revolution*. New York, HarperCollins, 2006.

Portrait and Biographical Record of Denver and Vicinity, Colorado. Chicago: Chapman Books, 1898.

Portrait and Biographical Record of Portage and Summit Counties, Ohio. Logansport, Indiana: A. W. Brown and Co., 1898.

Plough, Cyrus T., ed. *1874-1978 Bicentennial Atlas of Portage County, Ohio*. Ravenna, Ohio: Portage County Historical Society, 1978.

Reece, Richard. *The Medical Guide*. 15th ed. London: Rees, Orme, Brown, and Green, 1828.

Reed, George Irving, ed. *Bench and Bar of Ohio*. Vol. 2. Chicago: Century Publishing Co., 1897.

Reid, Whitelaw. *Ohio in the War*. Vol. 1. Cincinnati: Moore, Wilstach and Baldwin, 1868.

Reynolds, David S. *John Brown, Abolitionist: The Man Who Killed Slavery, Sparked the Civil War and Seeded Civil Rights*. New York: Knopf, 2005.

Riddle, Albert Gallatin. *Bart Ridgeley: A Story of Northern Ohio*. Boston: Nichols and Hall, 1873.

_____. *The Portrait: A Romance of the Cuyahoga Valley*. Cleveland: Cobb, Andrews, 1874.

Rowe, John. *Letters and Diary of John Rowe, Boston Merchant 1759-1762, 1764-1779*. Edited by Anne Rowe Cunningham Boston: W. B. Clarke Co., 1903.

Remondino, P. C. *The Mediterranean Shores of America, Southern California: Its Climatic, Physical and Meteorological Conditions*. Philadelphia: F. A. Davis, 1892.

Reynolds, David S. *John Brown, Abolitionist*. New York: Knopf, 2005.

Roseboom, Eugene H. *The Civil War Era: 1850-1873*. A History of the State of Ohio. Vol. 4. Columbus: Ohio State Archaeological and Historical Society, 1944.

Roster of Ohio Soldiers in the War of 1812. Adjutant General of Ohio. Columbus: Press of E. T. Miller Co., 1916.

Ruchames, Louis. *John Brown: The Making of a Revolutionary*. New York: Grosset and Dunlap, 1969.

Rutkow, Ira. *James A. Garfield*. The American Presidents Series. New York: Henry Holt, 2006.

Saint John de Crevecoeur, J. Hector. *Letters from An American Farmer*. 1782. Reprint of 1912 edition. New York: Dutton, 1971.

Schwartz, Seymour I. *The French and Indian War 1754-1763*. Edison, New Jersey: Castle Books, 1994.

Schwayder, Carol Rein, comp., ed. *Weld County Old and New*. Vol. 5. Greeley, Colo.: Unicorn Ventures, 1983.

Scott, Glenn. *Colorado Voters in the 1861 Territorial Election for A Delegate to the 37th Congress: A Supplement*. Denver: 1999.

Scott, Robert. *Glory Glory Glorieta: The Gettysburg of the West*. Boulder: Johnson Books, 1992.

Shikes, Robert H. *Rocky Mountain Medicine: Doctors, Drugs and Disease in Early Colorado*. Boulder: Johnson Books, 1986.

Shoemaker, Robert. *The London Mob: Violence and Disorder in Eighteenth-Century England*. London: Hambledon and London, 2004.

Smith, Duane A. and Ronald Brown. *No One Ailing Except A Physician: Medicine in the Mining West, 1848-1919.* Boulder: University Press of Colorado, 2001.

_____. *Rocky Mountain Mining Camps: The Urban Frontier.* Lincoln, Neb.: Univ. of Nebraska Press, 1967.

_____. *Rocky Mountain West: Colorado, Wyoming, and Montana 1859-1915.* Histories of the American Frontier. Albuquerque: Univ. of New Mexico Press, 1992.

Smith, Abbot Emerson. *Colonists in Bondage: White Servitude and Convict Labor in America, 1607-1776.* Gloucester, Mass.: Peter Smith, 1965.

Smith, Henry Nash. *Virgin Land: The American West As Symbol and Myth.* Cambridge, Mass.: Harvard Univ. Press, 1950.

So Long, Longmont: A Critical Look at Longmont As It Was And as It Is. Longmont, Colorado: CQG Publishing, 1996.

Starr, Kevin. *Americans and the California Dream 1850-1915.* New York: Oxford Univ. Press, 1973.

_____. *Inventing the Dream: California through the Progressive Era.* New York: Oxford Univ. Press, 1985.

Steinel, Alvin. *History of Agriculture in Colorado 1858-1926.* Fort Collins, Colo.: State Agricultural College, 1926.

Stone, Wilbur Fisk. *History of Colorado.* Vol. 1. Chicago: S. J. Clarke Publishing Co., 1918.

Taylor, Alan. *American Colonies.* The Penguin History of the United States. New York: Viking, 2001.

They Came to Stay: Longmont 1858-1920. Longmont: St. Vrain Valley Historical Association, 1971.

Thomas, Peter. *Tea Party to Independence: The Third Phase of the American Revolution, 1773-1776*. Oxford: At the Clarendon Press, 1991.

Tocqueville, Alexis de. *Democracy in America*. 1835. Translated by George Lawrence. NewYork: HarperPerennial, 1969.

Torrey, Clarence Almon, comp. *New England Marriages Prior to 1700*. Baltimore: Genealogical Publishing Co., 1985.

Towner, Lawrence William. *A Good Master Well Served: Masters and Servants in Colonial Massachusetts, 1620-1750*. New York: Garland Publishing, 1998.

Trollope, Frances. *Domestic Manners of the Americans*. Edited by Donald Smalley. 1832. New York: Vintage, 1949.

Troyer, Loris. *Portage Pathways*. Kent, Ohio: Kent State Univ. Press, 1998.

Turner, Frederick Jackson. *The Frontier in American History*. 1920. New York: Holt, Rinehart, Winston, 1962.

United States. War Department. *The War of the Rebellion: A Compilation of the Official Records of the Union and Confederate Armies*. Vol. 9. Washington, D. C., 1883.

Upton, Harriet Taylor. *History of the Western Reserve*. Vol. 1. Chicago: Lewis Publishing, 1910.

Utley, Robert M. *The Story of the West: A History of the American West and Its People*. New York: Hydra, 2003.

Van Tassel, David, with John Vacha. *"Beyond Bayonets": The Civil War in Northern Ohio*. Kent, Ohio: Kent State Univ. Press, 2006.

Walker, Henry Pickering. *The Wagonmasters: High Plains Freighting from the Earliest Days of the Santa Fe Trail to 1880.* Norman: Univ. of Oklahoma Press, 1966.

Weisenburger, Francis P. *The Passing of the Frontier 1825-1850: A History of the State of Ohio.* Vol. 3. Columbus: Ohio State Archaeological and Historical Society, 1941.

West, Elliott. *The Contested Plains: Indians, Goldseekers and the Rush to Colorado.* Lawrence, Kansas: Univ. Press of Kansas, 1998.

Wheeler, Robert, ed. *Visions of the Western Reserve: Public and Private Documents of Northeastern Ohio 1750-1860.* Columbus: Ohio State Univ. Press, 2000.

Whitcher, William F. *History of the Town of Haverhill, New Hampshire.* Concord, New Hampshire: Rumford Press, 1919.

Whitford, William Clarke. *Colorado Volunteers in the Civil War: The New Mexico Campaign in 1862.* 1906. Boulder: Pruett Press, 1963.

Whittlesey, Charles. *Early History of Cleveland, Ohio.* Cleveland: Fairbanks, Benedict and Co., 1867.

Wight, William Ward. *The Wights: A Record of Thomas Wight of Dedham and Medfield and of His Descendants 1635-1890.* Milwaukee: Swain and Tate, 1890.

Woolf, Virginia. *A Room of One's Own.* 1929. New York: Harcourt, Brace, & World, 1957.

Wright, John. *Letters from the West, or A Caution to Immigrants.* Ann Arbor, Mich.: Univ. Microfilms, 1966.

Wyckoff, William. *Creating Colorado: The Making of a Western Landscape, 1860-1940.* New Haven: Yale Univ. Press, 1999.

Wyman, Thomas Bellows. *The New North Church, Boston, 1714.* Transcribed by Robert J. Dunkle. Edited by Ann Lainhart. Baltimore: Clearfield Co., 1995.

Young, Alfred. *The Shoemaker and the Tea Party: Memory and the American Revolution.* Boston: Beacon Press, 1999.

Young, Clinton. "Hiram", in *Portage Heritage.* Edited by James B. Holm, Ravenna, Ohio: Portage County Historical Society, 1957.

Zinn, Howard. *A People's History of the United States 1492 – Present.* New York: HarperCollins, 2003.

Zobel, Hiller B. *The Boston Massacre.* New York: W. W. Norton, 1970.

Articles

Allen, Alonzo. "Pioneer Life in Old Burlington, Forerunner of Longmont." *Colorado Magazine.* 6 (January 1929): 145-157.

Banks, C. E. "Scotch Prisoners Deported to New England by Cromwell, 1651-1652." *Proceedings of the Massachusetts Historical Society,* 61 (1927): 4-29.

Brown, B. Katherine. "Puritan Democracy in Dedham, Massachusetts: Another Case Study." *William and Mary Quarterly,* (1967): 378-396.

Cisnes, Jonah Girard. "Across the Plains and in Nevada City: Journal of Jonah Cisnes". *Colorado Magazine,* 27 (January 1950): 49-57.

Clark, George T. "Across the Plains and in Denver, 1860: A Portion of the Diary of George T. Clark", *Colorado Magazine* 6 (January 1929): 131-140.

Coffin, Morse. "Pioneer Days: Reminiscences No. Four." *Boulder County Miner* January 15, 1914.

Dalton, Len. "The Melrose Fence Viewer." *Melrose Mirror* August 4, 2000, n.p.

Downing, Finis E. "With the Ute Peace Delegation of 1863, Across the Plains and at Conejos." *Colorado Magazine* 22 (September, 1945): 193-205.

Flanders, Lea. "'Shorty' Lohr Has Farming in His Blood." *Longmont Times-Call* July 18, 1981.

Henretta, James A. "Economic Development and Social Structure in Colonial Boston." *The William and Mary Quarterly* 22 (1965): 75-92.

Howard, Betsy. "Pot of Gold Awaits Him at End of Farming Career". *Boulder Daily Camera* May 27, 1984.

Leonard, Stephen J. "John Nicolay in Colorado: A Summer Sojourn and the 1863 Ute Treaty". *Essays and Monographs in Colorado History* 11, (1990).

Moore, Jesse T. "Seeking a New Life: Blacks in Post-Civil War Colorado." *The Journal of Negro History* 78 (1993): 166-187.

New England Historical and Genealogical Register. Entries from Ephraim Clark's family Bible. 90 (1936): 376.

_____. "Elizabeth Maverick." 97 (1943): 56.

_____."John Maccantosh of Dedham, male heir to *John Maccantosh*." 99 (1945): 312.

Penee, Richard A. "The Hidden Clues in Guardianship Bonds." *Missing Links: A Magazine for Genealogists* 7 (June 2, 2002): np.

Sanford, Albert B. "Camp Weld, Colorado." *Colorado Magazine* 11 (January, 1934): 46-50.

Sandsten, E. P. and C. M. Tompkins. "Orchard Survey of the Northeastern District of Colorado." Bulletin 272. Agricultural Experiment Station of the Colorado State University, 1922.

Troyer, Loris. "Benefits Endure from Patriotism of Portage General." *Ravenna-Kent Record-Courier* (1983), n.p.

Westcott, Lois. "Boulder County [Colorado] Naturalization Records." *Boulder Genealogical Society Quarterly* 15 (1983), 13-18.

Oral Histories

Lohr, Neil, interview by Susan Allison-Smith, 1987, Oral History 363, Part I, Maria Rogers Oral History Program Collection, Carnegie Branch Library for Local History, Boulder, Colorado.

————————, interview by Anne Dyni, 1987 (updated 2007), Oral History 363, Part II, Maria Rogers Oral History Program Collection, Carnegie Branch Library for Local History, Boulder, Colorado.

Pamphlets

The Brethren Church. 5th printing. Published by the Hygiene Cemetery Association. Etta Marie Marcy, Publisher, 1996.

Directory of Farmers of Boulder County, 1892.

Ferguson, Thomas E. "Ohio Land Grants." State of Ohio, n.d.

Gates, Paul W. "Free Homesteads for All Americans: The Homestead Act of 1862". Washington, D. C.: Civil War Centennial Commission, 1962.

"Summary of Long Beach History"

Theses and Research Papers

Corson, Dan. "The Black Community in Boulder, Colorado". Research paper. University of Colorado, Boulder, 1996.

Foppes, Ellen K. "Ebenezer Mackintosh and Crowd Action in Boston, Massachusetts". M. A. thesis. University of New Mexico, 1980.

Large, Marjorie E. "Appropriation to Private Use of Land and Water in the St. Vrain Valley before the Founding of the Chicago Colony (1871)". M. A. thesis. University of Colorado, 1932.

CPSIA information can be obtained at www.ICGtesting.com
Printed in the USA
LVOW130848011211

257356LV00002B/17/P

9 781457 503702